The
COLUMBIA

RIVERS OF AMERICA
edited by Carl Carmer

as planned and started by
Constance Lindsay Skinner
associate editor Jean Crawford

The
COLUMBIA

by STEWART H. HOLBROOK

illustrated by ERNEST RICHARDSON

HOLT, RINEHART AND WINSTON

New York Chicago San Francisco

Library of Congress Catalog Card Number: 73-10986
ISBN: 0-03-089388-7
Printed in the United States of America: 054

FOR
Philip H. Parrish

Contents

PREFACE TO THE 1974 EDITION

by Herbert Lundy

Editor of the Editorial Page

The Oregonian, Portland, Oregon

Many things have happened to the Columbia River since the late Stewart Holbrook wrote so vividly of the West's mightiest river nearly two decades ago. Not all that has happened is good for man and his environment. Ever since the fur traders and the fish canners of early days, the river's rich resources have been exploited. Now, the benefits it has provided to mankind must be measured against the river's exhaustion; corrective steps must be taken on a massive scale, before it is too late.

Fortunately, people today are much more aware of their heritage. The agencies of government are under Congressional orders—the Environmental Policy Act of 1969—to justify new projects with statements of their impact on nature and man before starting them. But the mistakes of the past must also be corrected.

The Columbia River has been dredged, dammed, polluted, and depleted. But it still pours 180 million acre-feet of water—enough to cover the entire state of Oregon two feet deep—into the Pacific Ocean at historic Astoria each year.

This great flow, fourth largest of the rivers of North

America, is the envy of the people who live in arid regions of the Southwest. Many schemes have been hatched to divert millions of acre-feet of its flow through giant ditches and reservoirs thousands of miles southward to irrigate the desert lands of southern California, Arizona, Nevada, and Utah, and even eastward to Texas.

Northwesterners are prepared to fight to save their river. They believe its resource values would be greatly depleted by diversion. But the pressures for interbasin transfers of water—the most precious resource—are growing and must be considered fairly.

The Pacific Southwest needs water not only to grow crops in a warm climate, where production under irrigation is much greater than in northern climates, but for the industries and for people to drink and bathe in. The warm climate has been a major lure that has caused the overpopulation of California and is likely to do the same for Arizona. But water shortage is a limiting factor.

Not many years ago, residents of the Pacific Northwest were saying, "Let the people come to the water—to our magnificent Columbia River and its tributaries; why spend billions of dollars to send our water, with great loss by evaporation, to the people in the South?"

But now, many are saying: "We will keep our water, but we do not want to be overwhelmed with population, either."

It was Stewart Holbrook, the New England logger turned editor, author, and historian in the Pacific Northwest, who formed the mythical James G. Blaine Society, even before he wrote of the Columbia for the Rivers of America series. Senator Blaine, an American statesman and presidential candidate of the past century, wanted "America for Americans." Mr. Holbrook never missed an opportunity, in speeches and writing, to discourage migration to Oregon and Washington. The James G. Blaine Society, then a creature of Mr. Holbrook's imagination, was dedicated to convincing Easterners and Southerners that the Northwest's magnificent scenery could not be seen because of continuous and torrential rains, blizzards, and fog.

In later years, Oregon's Governor Tom McCall has urged enchanted tourists, "For heaven's sake, don't come here to live." And the James G. Blaine Society has been formally incorporated by others to discourage immigration. The movement remains only half-serious. But it grows out of people's concern with the harm that has been done to the region's environment and their fervent wish to preserve its resources and scenic beauty for all time.

The thirsty Southwest takes a dim view of the impudence of its northern neighbors. Some of its leaders paint a glowing picture of the dispersal of population throughout the broad plains and deserts between the Rocky Mountains and the Cascade Mountains and Sierra Nevada range, if only Columbia River waters can be moved southward. The Columbia carries ten times the volume of the Colorado River which serves the southland.

Such planners also look to the waters of Canada, which are said to be far more than ever will be needed there, to replenish the Columbia. And many studies point toward the need for a continental water exchange program for domestic uses, irrigation, flood control, and generation of electricity.

Plans to divert Columbia River water southward received a stunning blow in November, 1972, when the National Water Commission proposed restrictive guidelines after a four-year study.

The Congress and the President were urged not to provide federal funds to subsidize interbasin transfers of water, "except where some overriding social purpose is served by a subsidy."

The Commission also recommended that if water should be diverted from one river basin to another, as from the Columbia to the Colorado, the following rules should apply: The beneficiary basin must show that the cost of imported water would be lower than the cost of any other supply, such as taking the salt out of sea water; people in the river basin providing the water should be fully compensated for their loss; future needs of the region where the water originates must be considered; and the people of the region providing the water must agree to the diversion.

Without federal subsidies in the form of grants, such as those which go into irrigation and other projects, it would be extremely costly for the people of one basin to obtain water from another.

So, the ultimate exploitation of the Columbia River was left in doubt.

The Northwest is moving steadily ahead in the use of Columbia River water for multiple purposes in its own basin, despite new problems every year.

As much as thirty-four million acre-feet of water flows out of reservoirs through canals to irrigate the crops on seven million acres of land. Regional planners want another twenty-three million acre-feet of water by the year 2020 to provide agricultural production on six million acres more.

The National Water Commission, however, also recommended that Congress stop paying the major costs of irrigation and reclamation projects, such as those of the half-finished Columbia Basin Project which receives water from Grand Coulee reservoir. Such projects have been, in part, responsible for overproduction of some crops, the Commission charged.

But if Congress stopped subsidization of irrigation, many farmers say they would go broke and the land would return to a desert sustaining only jackrabbits and coyotes. Agriculture, supported by industries based on crops, may be expected to fight in Congress and at the White House for continued federal assistance. In the Northwest, that aid comes chiefly from sale of the electricity produced at federal dams in the Columbia Basin.

Most of the irrigation water returns eventually to the river, but some of it is laden with chemicals that are harmful to fish life, and some darkens the river with silt. Irrigation, which has changed agricultural production in eastern Washington and eastern Oregon areas from dryland grain to row crops in greater demand, also has changed the face of the inland plateau.

In 1950, the railroad town of Othello, Washington, had a population of five hundred. Now it supports more than four thousand in the center of a rich, irrigated area. These people went to the water.

Irrigation from the gigantic Grand Coulee Dam, the major federal project of the Depression 1930s, and other smaller projects has done more than provide a movement of population from the cities to farms. It has created thousands of acres of lakes and fields where once there was desert, providing the habitat for rainbow trout and other fish, millions of ducks and geese, pheasants and quail and partridge. These recreational and wildlife values are newly created and immense.

Now, there are plans on the drawing boards to use the warm cooling water from nuclear power plants, which produce electricity, to irrigate the food crops in nearby fields. Experiments have shown that warm water lengthens the growing season and produces more vegetables and fruit. The Northwest does not have the Southwest's year-round warm climate. But warm water compensates, and it takes a lot of water to cool a nuclear reactor.

The greatest benefits to the people of the Pacific Northwest—numbering more than six million in 1970 and expected to increase to twelve million fifty years later—have come from the many large and small dams in large and small rivers. These create reservoirs from which the water is released to generate electricity, control floods, improve navigation, and irrigate farms. Thus are jobs and profits made. But dams also have caused great harm to resources, particularly the tremendous runs of salmon and steelhead trout the Indians dipped and speared when Lewis and Clark came down the Columbia.

Until the 1970s, the Northwest was almost wholly dependent upon falling water at man-made dams for production of energy—hydroelectricity—to run its factories and light its homes. The federal government plunged into dam building in the Columbia Basin in the 1930s, to help out in the Great Depression. By 1973, the Bonneville Power Administration (the federal agency which sells at wholesale the electricity produced at dams built by the Army Corps of Engineers and the Bureau of Reclamation) was marketing power from twenty-seven federal dams on the Columbia and its major tributaries—the Willamette, Snake, and Kootenai rivers. Six of the giant federal dams are on the main stem of the Columbia, from Bonneville Dam at the head of tidewater to Grand Coulee Dam which backs water into Canada.

Only one damsite on the main Columbia remains undeveloped: the Ben Franklin site near Pasco, Washington. When the Army Engineers pressed for that construction a group of environmentalists—chiefly scientists and engineers working on the nuclear energy projects at Hanford, Washington—got together under the leadership of John Sheppard, a research chemist. They formed the Columbia River Conservation League to save the last fifty-seven miles of free-flowing river from either inundation by a reservoir or dredging for a barge channel. The evidence they gathered made a strong case that neither project would pay its way.

"This is all that's left of the Columbia as a river," John Sheppard told an Oregonian newspaper reporter. "You should save little segments of the river for future generations. People should have something to look at besides a series of impoundments."

These fifty-seven miles of free-flowing river contain nesting habitat for ducks and geese, gravel beds where thousands of steelhead and salmon scoop out their redds and deposit their eggs, and Indian archeological sites. They also contain the last of the rapids, which bargemen would like to drown out for easier navigation to Wenatchee, Washington.

But there are railroads and highway truck routes to carry freight to and from Wenatchee. The riverboats and barges today are rivaled in economic importance by thousands of pleasure boats—from canoes to yachts.

Public concern for the environment and for preservation of remaining undammed sections of big rivers has almost ended dam building. It is not likely that Ben Franklin Dam will be built, or that more dams will be raised in the hundred miles of the Snake River from Lewiston, Idaho, to Hells Canyon Dam.

Power production in the eleven dams from Grand Coulee to Bonneville, including five owned by Washington public utility districts, can be greatly expanded, however. Their generating capacity can be almost doubled because of the Canadian treaty dams, which will provide additional water storage in the upper basin. Bonneville Dam is to be made higher. More turbines and generators will be installed in other dams.

This is bad news for the fish and for the dedicated men and women in the federal and state fishery agencies who have been fighting for years against great odds to maintain the fish runs. The Columbia River is the greatest producer of Chinook and coho salmon in the world, as well as producing more hydroelectricity than any river in the world. But these fish runs remain in great peril.

There have always been losses of adult and immature salmon and steelhead at the dams because the fish ladders, elevators, and bypasses have allowed escapement of only a portion of the fish. Not all of the mature fish swimming out of the Pacific Ocean to the streams or hatcheries in which they were born four or five years before have been able to get over or around the concrete barriers. Millions of tiny fish spawned in the gravel beds or released from hatchery ponds perish each year in the turbines or over the spillways, or become easy prey for the predatory fish which are, themselves, of no value.

But enough have survived the perils of the river and the ocean to return to their birthplaces to spawn and die—thus completing the life cycle of the Pacific salmon—to preserve the runs, year after year.

Royal Chinook salmon no longer can go far into British Columbia to spawn, for Chief Joseph Dam and Grand Coulee Dam are impassable barriers. Nor can they go more than 150 miles up the Snake River into Idaho, because passage devices over some power dams have proved useless. But other tributaries remain open for varying distances. And great progress has been made in artificial production of disease-free hatchery young, especially coho or silver salmon, fall Chinook, and steelhead trout. By the 1970s, about two-thirds of the Columbia River runs of anadromous fish were being born in hatchery incubators.

In fact, nowhere else in the world have migratory fish been maintained above a series of major dams comparable to those in the Columbia River system.

However, the great dams, with their intermittent spillage of the major flow of the Columbia, have brought a new menace to the fish. This is a "bubble disease" which blinds or kills adult and juvenile fish. It is caused by nitrogen supersaturation of the water below spillways. Air is mainly nitrogen. When water flows evenly through the turbines which spin the generators to produce electricity, nitrogen gases are not captured in the water. But when the water, instead, spills over, falling great distances, it picks up additional air, including nitrogen, and forces these tiny bubbles of gas into solution. Because of the large number of dams, nitrogen supersaturation remains in the water throughout the river. Many of the fish passing the water through their gills are injured—or killed. They are not able to reach their birthplaces or to reproduce their kind.

Biologists and engineers are working together to combat the bubble disease. Slotted gates to break up the flow at spillways and idle turbines show some promise. A "ski-jump" addition to the faces of spillways may help. Upstream storage in high-water periods reduces the nitrogen saturation.

Other means are being studied. Among them is the capture of fingerling salmon above the spillways and the transporting of them for hundreds of miles for release below the series of dams. It is, of course, very difficult to capture and haul tiny fish in tank trucks without harm to them. And it is more difficult still to handle adult salmon which weigh from six to sixty pounds.

Fishery management people have some confidence that the nitrogen menace will be greatly reduced. But they look with apprehension on still another problem that may lie in the future of their battle to save the salmon. The danger lies in extreme fluctuation of reservoir levels behind the stair-steps of dams.

Because the end is near for construction of dams in the Columbia Basin, man has turned to the production of electricity from atomic fuel, with some help from coal-fired plants. This means that gradually the hydroelectric system in the Pacific Northwest will be used more for "peaking" purposes—that is, the generators at dams will be operated in periods of greatest power demand—while thermal generation (electricity from nuclear, coal, oil, or gas fuels) will provide the steady supply. This, in turn, means that reservoir levels will rise and fall more drastically than at present.

It is figured that when Bonneville Dam forty miles above Portland is made higher, the fluctuation of the river below the dam will vary from four to seven feet. The changes in reservoir levels above Bonneville may be greater.

Even if the nitrogen supersaturation problem is licked, excessive water-level changes could greatly disrupt fish passage at the dams. Some salmon now are "weekenders." As many as 80 per cent wait below the dams to make their runs up the fish ladders on weekends. Then, the flow of water is cut back because industries are using less power and water is being stored in reservoirs.

What will be done about this danger to the fish is not known. The Columbia Basin hydro projects and other generating units owned by public and private utilities are interconnected with transmission lines. In fact, high voltage "intertie" lines connect the Northwest system with the utilities of California, Arizona, and Rocky Mountain states. But full coordination of the systems has yet to be obtained. Water flows are regulated to some degree, when feasible, to encourage the movement of fish. But the people must have electricity, too.

Complete coordination and master control of all generating plants could be used to give the migrating fish of the Columbia River a break. But it is much more likely that this will be used, if achieved, primarily to strengthen the power systems. The fish, as usual, will have to make out the best they can.

In pioneer days, the Columbia River system was capable of producing a yield of fifty million pounds of salmon a year. By the 1970s, the annual yield was averaging about thirty million pounds—still a tremendous food resource.

Many thousands of salmon are caught in the ocean by both commercial and sport fishermen. After the young fish enter the sea from the rivers they follow the schools of pilchards and herring, feeding their way south to California, and as far north as the Aleutian Islands. Then they return as adults to the rivers, creeks, and hatcheries in which they were born—or into which they were released as juveniles. No one is quite sure how the adult salmon find their way back through the trackless sea to their inland birthplaces. It is a mystery the Pacific salmon reveal to no one.

Uses and misuses of the Columbia system must not be allowed to destroy the remaining runs.

The big summer Chinook, those which once ascended the rivers for hundreds of miles to the spawning beds of the Cascades and Rockies, have been gravely depleted. The high dams have cut them off. The upper river runs of spring Chinook and steelhead trout have suffered also, but not so greatly. The sockeye runs are almost gone.

But the news is not all bad. The fall-run Chinook increased moderately in the decade ending in 1971. The coho or silver salmon, smaller and livelier, have increased tremendously because of improved hatchery techniques. Sportsmen fishing in the ocean and lower Columbia River caught no more than 50,000 salmon in any year before 1960. By the 1970s, four or five times as many sport fishermen went out for the salmon, and their annual catch was averaging 200,000 fish, two-thirds of them coho.

Pollution is being controlled and new spawning areas, such as the upper Willamette River in Oregon, are being opened to natural propagation of salmon. In the low-water periods of summer and fall, the natural barrier of Willamette Falls at Oregon City had always prevented fall Chinook and silver salmon from migrating upstream. Now, the pleas of conservation groups have been answered. Government and private agencies built new and much improved passages over the falls and the paper mills there agreed to shut down their turbines when fish are moving. It is anticipated that within a decade the runs of fall Chinook and coho salmon, and steelhead trout, will be so enlarged that anglers will be catching 100,000 and another 100,000 will escape to reproduce.

The new Willamette River fishery, augmenting the spring Chinook runs which sportsmen have harvested for many years while commercial gill nets were barred from this tributary, also will provide more fish to gill netters in the lower Columbia and the sport and commercial trollers in the ocean.

The commercial gill-net fishery has been sharply curtailed in recent years—from 272 days in 1938 to 82 days in 1970—as the sockeye and summer Chinook runs declined and sportsmen brought political pressure to bear to reduce the netting of that grand fighting fish, the sea-run steelhead. The major gains in hatchery production of coho salmon, particularly, have saved the commercial fishery. These fish have returned from the sea in such numbers that the hatcheries could not handle them. Some were transplanted to

lakes and streams elsewhere. In one small Columbia tributary above Vancouver, Washington, anglers have been permitted to snag the fish from the churning horde so that they
would not go to waste.

With new spawning areas being made accessible to the
salmon in the lower basin, and new techniques being found
to increase production of the hatcheries, a limited commercial season may be sustained in spite of the dams and other
hazards.

Thus, it appears that the several races of anadromous
fish—those that are born in fresh water, grow to maturity in
the ocean, and return to fresh water to deposit their eggs
and die—are not equally endangered by the works and care-
lessness of man. The upper river runs are having a hard
time of it. But the lower river runs of Chinook, coho, and
steelhead trout are holding their own or increasing in
numbers.

One benefit to fish and man alike is that the nuclear
reactors which produced plutonium for atomic bombs developed in great secrecy at the Hanford Project in World
War II are being phased out.

The discharge of radioactive wastes from these early
reactors polluted the waters of the Columbia, the marine
life, and the wildfowl and other wildlife along the river.
The new nuclear reactors producing electricity for peaceful
energy are elaborately shielded against radioactive emis-
sions. The Columbia's cold water, or that of its tributaries,
is needed to cool the reactors. But when it returns to the
river it will be harmless. In fact, it can be used to grow
vegetables without harm to consumers.

The Columbia also will be used to cool a new project,

the "breeder" reactor—so called because it will produce nuclear fuel to replace that consumed in the production of electricity. The breeder reactor will conserve the use of uranium so that the supply of this source of energy will last for thousands of years.

But in the production of atomic weapons for war, the Hanford Project left buried in the earth, in metal containers, large quantities of nuclear wastes. Some of these are being solidified for safety. The newer nuclear-electric reactors and the breeder reactor also leave radioactive wastes, some of which can be recycled into nuclear fuel. Unused wastes can remain radioactive for 10,000 years. Some will be buried in old salt mines. But it is a problem scientists must resolve in the nuclear age.

The future for the Northwest, as for the world, in overcoming the impending shortage of electric energy seems to lie in more advanced fields. Some time after the year 2000, the almost inexhaustible supply of deuterium in the oceans and other elements will be used—if scientists can unlock all the secrets—to produce electricity from fusion, rather than from fission as in the nuclear plants of the 1970s. Fusion power is like that created by the hydrogen bomb, man's most awesome and yet unused weapon, and by the sun itself. If the tremendous heat from fusion can be controlled, mankind will have a virtually limitless source of energy which is environmentally clean.

To supplement the great hydroelectric dams of the Columbia Basin, science also is working toward generation of electricity from the heat stored under the surface of the earth, and from MHD (magnetohydrodynamics), a process of drawing electricity from hot gases.

But for many years to come, the mighty Columbia River will continue to work for man. It will provide energy and light. It will offer a passageway with its reservoirs and shiplocks for the movement of grain, wood products, and other consumer items from the Inland Empire to the Orient, the Soviet Union, Western Europe, Africa, and South America. It will be a sanctuary for the salmon returning from the sea, providing fish and other food for the Indians in reservations along its banks, and for the whites in the cities and on the farms. It will give up its water to make nuclear power projects safe and to grow crops. It will make available vast expanses of its reservoirs and fast-flowing stretches for recreation and will welcome the ships from all over the world, as it has since Captain Gray discovered its entrance into the sea.

The Columbia River changes but remains much the same in that it is a workhorse of a river, giving its benefits freely to mankind, although sometimes harshly treated by man. More and more, the people of the Pacific Northwest are learning to appreciate their great river of the West.

The
COLUMBIA

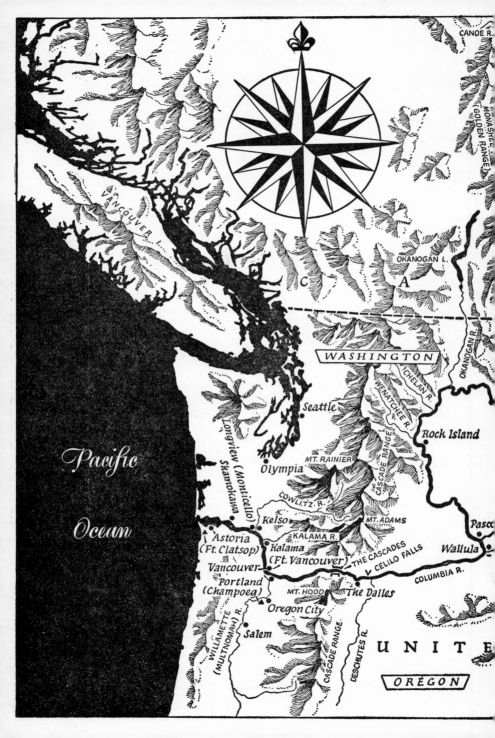

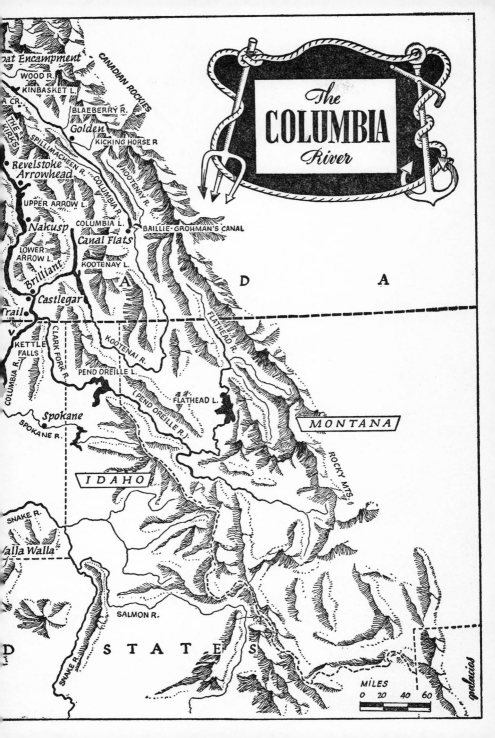

Chapter 1

River Remote and Wild

ABOUT THE headwaters of a river there is something of the mystery of Genesis. I felt it as a boy long ago in Vermont when I heard men who had been there speak of the headwaters of the Connecticut. The word was magic. Though I wanted desperately to know, I did not think it proper to ask what a headwaters was like. I imagined it to be a sort of never-failing geyser, a lonely fountain spouting in one specific spot, and let it go at that.

It seemed to me then that the boldfellows who had seen a headwaters were in the select company of great explorers. They had been to the Source. The source was of necessity in some remote place, wholly inaccessible, even unknown, save to a few God-given men. Beyond the source there was nothing, nothing at all. Here you had arrived at Genesis, and you stood to look in awe upon the First Cause, where Adam drank, Eve bathed, and Deity moved over the face of the waters and commanded this stream to flow and gather together with other waters and be called the seas. And the evening and the morning were the third day. . . .

On the other side of the continent, and forty years later, I discovered again that the magic and mystery of the head-

5

waters were universal and timeless, and they applied to the sources of the Columbia. And at last I stood at the fountain-head which starts the great surging stream on its tortured way a matter of more than twelve hundred miles to the sea. The spell was there. I felt a sense of achievement, not because of any hardships surmounted in getting there, but simply that by being there I was permitted to share in a cosmic secret.

The headwaters of the Columbia are in a small lake of the same name. The lake lies blue and cold and deep in British Columbia, on the high roof of the continent. Its eastern bank rises abruptly as a sheer wall of the Rocky Mountains. On the west are the magnificent Selkirks. It is a most satisfactory place for the giant of Western rivers to begin. Here hemmed by two great mountain ranges is the source of the Columbia. I looked at this complete drama in stone and water and wondered if the slow process of geological architecture had ever fashioned anything more fitting.

By the time I came to see its headwaters, I had already lived thirty years on the lower Columbia. I had also seen long stretches of it over much of a thousand miles, but never seen its source or felt the magic of its headwaters, of standing in a high mountain valley where springs a stream that is to flow in four directions and a thousand miles before it can break through its barrier to be lost in the anonymous sea.

Standing at the source gives a man the sense that he has at last come to understand a river. On him descends the complete assurance of those ancients who composed the books of the Old Testament. *They* had no doubts as to where and how things had their beginnings. Once I had stood here at the headwaters, *I* had no doubts about where and how the Columbia began. Here at the source, too, I found myself looking at the stream from a new viewpoint. It wasn't possessive. The Columbia is not a cosy river, not the kind a man can feel belongs to him. It was rather a satisfying sense of having followed a big stream from its outlet to its source. Only people who have done as much will understand, while those unfortunates who have no feeling about a headwaters will think the whole business inexplicable.

Standing at the headwaters I found it a good spot to reflect on some of the places and people which and who have meant something or other in the life of the river; a good place to follow in imagination its course through wildnerness and desert, to watch while it steadily grows bigger and at last is strong enough to cut through the last mountains that would bar it from the sea. Yet, no guidebook voyage. I like to be leisurely, to pause along the way to relate the river of yesterday to the river of the day before that.

I think I enjoy a dramatic or a soothing piece of scenery as well as the next man; but I happen to enjoy it infinitely more if I know that what I am looking at was once witness to some event in history. Big or small history. I like to know, for instance, that this little lake set between two mountain ranges is little more than six thousand *feet* from the Kootenay River which is here rushing south, while the Columbia starts north; and that once upon a time an ingenious Englishman dug a canal between the two and that a steamboat came up the Kootenay from Montana and crossed over to ply the far upper Columbia. The same geographical oddity may also explain what is otherwise a deep mystery in regard to fish. Not so long ago, huge Pacific salmon fought their way from the sea to these headwaters of the Columbia, twelve hundred miles against current and 2,650 feet against gravity. It was an epic voyage, even for so powerful and determined a species as the seagoing salmon. Then, in some forgotten year of freshet, when the Kootenay overflowed the narrow strip called Canal Flats that separates the two streams, salmon of Columbia Lake went adventuring and became progenitors of the landlocked fish which ever since have stocked the Kootenay. There seems to be no other way to explain the presence of true Pacific salmon in Kootenay Lake whose outlet is wholly proof against the entrance of fish, any fish.

Thus when I look at the headwaters, I see not only a handsome body of water, but can relate it to the heroic event of bringing a steamboat into a river at its source; and can also reflect on the marvel of nature stocking, by a roundabout method, a landlocked stream with fish from the deeps of the Pacific.

But to follow the Columbia. I mean as it was before man started to harness it with dams in the second quarter of this century. For more than two hundred miles after it leaves headwaters it must flow almost straight north, heading for the Arctic, before it can escape around its western barrier of the Selkirks. Then, in an astonishingly sudden bend, it turns to plunge south and to head, after its own fashion, for the Pacific Ocean. This quick turn is at the apex of the stream's northern flow. It is a part of the Big Bend.

Before reaching the Big Bend, the Columbia picks up the waters of Fairmont Hot Springs which, many years ago, good Father De Smet likened in temperature to the fresh milk of a goat. For many miles of the stream's early life it is serene. There is only a minor fall here. It is unhurried, meandering, and all but halts to form what are as much lakes as river. Even the Spillimacheen, tumbling down in its torrent from high in the Selkirks, fails to speed the main river. But at Golden, where the violent Kicking Horse comes in, after dropping fifty feet for every mile from the crest of the Rockies, the Columbia begins to feel its power. A little farther on it also begins to earn its reputation for fearfully sudden change; after flowing gently through a wide silent valley, it dives without warning over the edge of a steep incline to thunder into the fury of Surprise Rapids. This is the place which recalls, seventy years after the event, the carefully measured words of A. P. Coleman, who in 1885 went through this boiling water on a small raft and emerged somewhat shaken to say only that he "did not care to repeat the exploit."

The first known white man to see the Columbia's source missed Surprise Rapids on his first trip. He came in a little above them, by the Blaeberry River. He was David Thompson, "astronomer and geographer for the Northwest Company of Merchants of Canada" whose chief interest was furs. Thompson was to map the river. He was also the first to follow it from source to mouth. He was a thorough Briton, too. When he was first here and comtemplating the headwaters, he looked up to admire the towering mountains on the west. He thought them heroic. By association he thought also of Trafalgar, only two years in the past, and he forthwith named these peaks the Nelson Range. Why the range came to be called the Selkirks is a political matter to be considered later.

Twenty miles below Surprise Rapids the river becomes briefly what must be one of the loveliest lakes on earth, Kinbasket, walled around by peaks that rise above 12,000 feet; yet its cobalt serenity turns immediately at the outlet into miles of roaring water that is still swift when it reaches the apex of the Big Bend at Boat Encampment. This is the extreme northerly point of the Columbia where the river turns in its tracks, so to speak, and heads south, carrying with it the added waters of two more streams. It is a spot that has long stirred men's imaginations. "Amid the universal gloom and midnight silence of the North," wrote one explorer, "and a little above the 52nd Parallel of latitude, seemingly surrounded on all sides by cloud-piercing snowclad mountains, there lies a narrow valley where three streams meet and blend their waters, one coming from the southeast, one from the northwest, and one from the east." The streams which blend their waters are the Columbia, the Canoe, and the Wood.

The first white man here was the same who first saw the Columbia's headwaters, David Thompson. We meet him often in the early annals of the region. He arrived here by coming down the Wood River from the east and thus added Athabasca Pass to the maps by establishing the connecting link between the vast regions lying on the eastern and western sides of the Great Divide. An incredible fall of snow forced Thompson to remain here three months. He named the place Boat Encampment. For decades it was a crossroads and rendezvous of the fur brigades.

At Boat Encampment the river has now turned directly south, around the northern end of the Selkirks which Thompson had christened for Admiral Horatio Nelson. But the river is still hemmed, by the Selkirks that are now on the east, and on the west by the Monashees which a few old-timers still call the Gold Range. It is hemmed here so narrowly that the rush and roar of its dashings make the wilderness traveler believe he is hearing ocean breakers on an open shore. In this stretch is the sinister canyon that well earned the name of the Dalles des Morts applied to it by early voyageurs, several of whose comrades were lost there.

The lower end of the Big Bend is marked by Revelstoke, once called Second Crossing. Revelstoke is on the edge of solitude. Upriver, between Revelstoke and Golden, are two hundred miles of unbroken woods and terrain so appallingly difficult that, when the railroad came, the locating engineers preferred to take the rails over the terrible Selkirks rather than around their northern end. That seventy years later there is a highway of sorts around the Big Bend is eloquent praise for the determined men who made it.

Below Revelstoke, at the dreamy hamlet of Arrowhead, begins the glory of the Arrow Lakes, 130 miles of slowly moving inland sea set amid mountains, the queen of which for more than half a century was *SS Minto,* the Canadian Pacific Railway Company's oldest and perhaps most beloved ship. The *Minto* was a leisurely vessel, and for years it was her custom to tie up for the night at Nakusp on Upper Arrow and to resume her way at daylight, passing through the several miles of narrows which the Scot botanist, David Douglas, a man not given to panegyrics and who was here long before the steamboats, said were of a beauty beyond description.

At the lower end of Lower Arrow Lake, where it becomes a river again, the Columbia is joined by the heaving Kootenay. Since it passed the place so near the Columbia's headwaters at Canal Flats, this stream has been meandering nearly six hundred miles through Montana and Idaho, where it is spelled Kootenai, and returned to British Columbia to tear into the big river at Brilliant below a high cliff, on a shelf of which is the remarkable tomb of Peter the First and Lordly, prophet-king of the Dukhobors, a mighty man, hard to kill, whose death was accomplished only by blowing him into bits along with the railroad coach in which he was riding with one of his several handmaidens. It is still one of the great unsolved mysteries of the Columbia, and of Canada.

When the Kootenay has joined it, the Columbia proceeds swiftly through a mountain valley where a sudden gold rush lured away the gangs of Chinese laborers building the Dewdney Trail, British Columbia's first attempt at a cross-province road, and resulted in a mining and smelting empire whose center stands monolithic in and above the city of Trail. For sixty years this stretch of the Columbia has flowed beneath the billows of smoke of this remote wilderness Birmingham—or Pittsburgh—a drama of spouting flame and fumes and towering stacks set in a grandeur that is all solid rock for a mile above the tallest stack and for half a mile below it.

Ten miles below Trail the Clark Fork (or Pend Oreille) enters the Columbia, and where they meet the tributary is longer than the main stream. Once upon a time this fact was put forward by Americans to claim that the true Columbia was the Clark Fork which has its headwaters not far from Butte, Montana. Nothing came of the claim, save to confuse many Americans as to the actual source of the Columbia. Just below the meeting of the two rivers the International Boundary crosses the Columbia at the 49th parallel.

In former times, the Clark Fork came into the Columbia with a roar over a fall of fifteen feet at low water that sent the main stream hurrying into the United States and soon into the rapids called Little Dalles. When Lieutenant Thomas Symons, Corps of Engineers, United States Army, came along here in a big bateau he saw many Chinese working the bars for their gold. That was in eighty-one. Some of the Orientals had already been around here and elsewhere along the river for two decades, washing the sand which white men said contained too little gold to trouble with. It is still a tradition on the river that many of these Chinese miners made their pile, then went back to China to live and die as wealthy men.

Forty miles below the boundary was Kettle Falls to which for centuries on end the tribes of the upper Columbia migrated, to net or spear their provender for a twelve-month. This was the annual manna sent by the gods of the waters in the form of great Chinook salmon, leaping at the falls by the million. They were taken by the thousands each year, then split and dried, packed in baskets and carried away perhaps as many as four hundred miles, to serve as basic food for tribes living between the Rockies

TABLE OF DISTANCES AND ELEVATIONS
ON THE COLUMBIA RIVER

(Prepared especially for this book by the Corps of
Engineers, U. S. Army, Office of the Division Engineer,
Portland, Oregon, as of February 1, 1955.)

PLACE	ELEVATION MEAN SEA LEVEL	MILES FROM MOUTH
VANCOUVER, WASHINGTON (at bridge)	1.40	106.5
BONNEVILLE DAM, below	8.20	145.3 (west end
BONNEVILLE DAM, above	72.0	of lock)
THE DALLES, OREGON	72.0	189.39
CELILO, OREGON	127.6	201.10 (head of canal)
UMATILLA, OREGON	247.41	289.3
McNARY DAM, below	250.	292.
McNARY DAM, above	340.	
MOUTH OF SNAKE RIVER	340.	324.2
PRIEST RAPIDS, head	467.	406.15
ROCK ISLAND DAM, below	547.	453.35
ROCK ISLAND DAM, above	595.	
WENATCHEE, highway bridge	595.	465.05
CHIEF JOSEPH DAM (Bridgeport)	761.	543.0

Pool when dam completed	946.	
GRAND COULEE DAM, below	946.	596.6
GRAND COULEE DAM, above	1290.	
INTERNATIONAL BOUNDARY	1290.	745.
LOWER ARROW LAKE, middle	1382.	800.
UPPER ARROW LAKE, middle	1386.	870.
REVELSTOKE, B. C.	1400.	910.
BOAT ENCAMPMENT	1925.	1012.
GOLDEN, B. C.	2550.	1115.
COLUMBIA LAKE	2650.	1210.

Mileage: Below International Boundary is from Corps of Engineers Mileage tables and from U. S. Geological Survey's Plan and Profile Sheets. Above Boundary mileage is from "308" Report—Basin Map, (Pl 14) and "308" profiles. Plates 2, 15, 43.
Elevations: From Corps of Engineers profiles, CL-201-15 and CL-106-13-34; U. S. Geological Survey Plan and Profile of Columbia River; "308" Profiles 2, 15, 43, and Canadian map "Kootenay."
Note: Canadian maps do not agree on elevation of Columbia Lake. The Calgary sheet of British Columbia and Alberta Series has it 2650; the B. C. Department of Lands map "Kootenay" has it 2652; while the same Department's map "Windermere" has it 2664.

and the Cascades. Kettle Falls fell a total of twenty-five feet in two descents, then soon went into the wild reaches called the Grand Rapids.

It was at Kettle Falls that David Thompson and his paddlers spent two weeks to find a proper cedar, then to make a canoe, the third on this first voyage of a white man

15

down the Columbia. That was in 1811, and on July 3, Thompson wrote in his journal: "Voyage to the Mouth of the Columbia, by the grace of God, by D. Thompson and seven men." The sea was his goal, God Almighty was his guide, and no matter that fur was his business, his love was to walk up and down and across the Canadian and American West, adding lakes, creeks, rivers, mountains and passes through mountains to the maps.

David Thompson and his men at Kettle Falls.

Sixty miles or so below Kettle Falls the Spokane enters the big stream near where it makes the second of its surprising changes of direction. After its long run almost straight south from Boat Encampment, the Columbia turns west almost at right angles. It proceeds briefly west, then north again, west again, then southeast, forming a wide bow that people who live hereabout call the Big

Bend.* The outstanding geographic feature of this region is the Grand Coulee.

Little wonder that this strange trick of nature on a colossal scale was a fearsome thing to the Indians. No man could see it without feeling a certain mystery. No man could look upon it without a sense of terrible loneliness. There it stood by the Columbia in the middle of seemingly illimitable wastes along this piece of the river—a boulder-strewn nothingness that ran on and on, no matter which way you looked, until lost over the horizon. A coulee by definition is "a steep walled trenchlike valley." It is a description that only technically has anything to do with the Grand Coulee. The widely traveled Alexander Ross stood on its floor, looking up at the black wilderness of walls that rose, in places, a thousand feet, and ran on for more than fifty miles. The sight left him quite numb. The best he could do, in his usually vibrant Journal, was to remark weakly that Grand Coulee was "the wonder of Oregon."

Once upon a time, due to glacial movements, Grand Coulee became a fifty-mile stretch of the river's bed that ended in a waterfall three miles wide and four hundred feet high, perhaps the greatest cataract the world has known. Then, after a few thousand years, when the ice barrier had melted, the stream returned to its former bed. Even its former, and present, bed was enough to give a man pause. When Lieutenant Symons came along here to the Grand Coulee country in his big bateau, he thought the complete silence and lifelessness of the scene made it

* For the sake of clarity this portion of the Columbia will be called, in this book, simply the Grand Coulee country.

"exceedingly wild, almost unearthly," and he welcomed approach to "the dreaded" Kalichen Falls and Whirlpool Rapids. At least they made a noise. His chief boatman, Old Pierre, a Frenchman who had steered bateaux for the Hudson's Bay Company, knew what to expect here at Kalichen. He spoke to his Indians. They removed all superfluous clothing. They tied brightly colored handkerchiefs around their heads. They removed their gloves. The old man gave the word. The paddlers shouted, and away they went, yelling like the Indians they were as the craft heaved and rolled through the chutes and whirlpools. Years before, Thompson had found this going rough. He said they were strong waters, and remarked that "I hope by the mercy of Heaven to take them much better on my return."

Symons camped where Chelan River enters the Columbia, near some Indians, and though the time was 1881 and a railroad had reached and crossed the river below, much of the middle and upper Columbia remained natively primitive. Symons got little sleep that night because of the moanings of an old medicine man "performing his hideous incantations" over a poor girl "nearly dead with the consumption." These Indians were going to have a railroad soon. They already had all of the white man's diseases. Seventy years before Symons, when Thompson came through here, he found savages who wore shells in their noses. By the time Symons was here, no natives were so decorated. The encroaching civilization could remove shells and replace them with fancy combs and derby hats, but none of the white man's notions about medication

and religion could quite obliterate a successful medicine man.

Passing the mouth of the Wenatchee, Symons's men again prepared for wild water ahead and put on their bright headgear to run Rock Island Rapids. Symons looked at the bluffs along here—some of them rising, he estimated, a good twenty-five hundred feet—and was struck by the weird beauty of the black basaltic formations. High in a cleft of rock he noted a single stick of timber, white from the weather, which Old Pierre the boatman told him had been a landmark back in voyageur days. They also passed Victoria Rock, which Symons called one of the most perfect profiles in existence. At one angle, too, it did remind one of the appearance of the durable Queen of England.

Below Rock Island, Symons saw a large number of Chinese working the bars. He found Priest Rapids to be eleven miles of rough water and "about as bad a place as there is on the whole river." He was now approaching the mouth of the Snake and the last of the notable bends of the Columbia. This was the only place east of the Cascade Range where a railroad touched the river. It did so at Ainsworth, where the Northern Pacific crossed the Snake to head north. And Ainsworth, Symons observed, was possibly the most uncomfortable, altogether abominable place in America. This was quite in keeping with the region. Though he looked in every direction, Symons could see nothing but bleak, dreary waste. The land was dry and powdery, virtually a desert. Symons went further. "It is," he wrote, "an almost waterless, lifeless region. . . . It is a desolation where even the most hopeful can find nothing in its future prospects to cheer." Lieutenant Symons was born too soon to see what an Atomic Energy Commission could do in this land of the dead.

But the railroad came here, and Symons paid off his paddlers. Perhaps it was inevitable that in such a hellhole as Ainsworth, Old Pierre promptly made sundry visits to the local "whiskey saloon." Even so, he promised Symons that he would not get drunk in such an ungodly place. He would return to Colville, have two good drinks there on his wages, and call it a day. Symons had nothing but praise for Pierre and the four paddlers, remarking it would be difficult to find five men who would ride four hundred miles of rough river without wanting strong waters.

It is worth remarking that many of the small sectional maps prepared by the Symons party, in referring to lands along the river between the Canadian boundary and the mouth of the Snake, carry notations like Sage Brush Plain, Drifting Sand Hills, Sage Brush, and Sand Drift. Yet Symons saw not only the endless miles of sagebrush, but what was beneath the weed. He wrote that the unusually tall brush was a species of this plant that grew only in the richest soil. If brought under irrigation, he said, it would produce bountiful harvests. This made him a true prophet of an event seventy-odd years in the future.

At the end of his exploration, here where the Snake comes in, Symons paused to reflect that this was where the Lewis and Clark party had first seen the Columbia. They, too, had found this no place to tarry overlong. They noted that all of the natives had sore eyes, doubtless from the torment of the blowing sand; and because the white men wanted horses and provisions, but had few trade goods left, they traded "eye medicine" with these blinking, squinting Indians. "Our prescriptions," drily remarks the *Lewis & Clark Journals*, "though unsanctioned by the faculty, might be useful and we therefore are entitled to some remuneration. . . ."

The next white man after Lewis and Clark to see the mouth of the Snake was, almost inevitably, David Thompson. He was in a hurry, pausing only long enough to erect a small pole on the shore and attach to it a "½ sheet of paper" on which he had inscribed a claim "to this country" for Great Britain, adding that it was the intention of the Northwest Company of Merchants of Canada to "erect at this place a factory for the commerce of the country around." Then he struck out downriver, stopping again three days later to gum his canoe, and while so engaged looked up to see "a snow mountain ahead, say 30 miles, another on the right, behind, say 25 miles." An English Navy man had already named one of these peaks for Admiral Hood, the other had no name, though in good time it became Mount Adams for a president.

When the Snake has added its waters of a thousand miles to the Columbia, there can no longer be any doubt as to where the big river is going. It turns west for the last time and begins its drive on the Cascade Mountains which have barred it from the coast ever since it left the Rockies to meander the deserts of Washington. As it makes this last western turn, too, it becomes the state line, with Oregon on the south bank.

The Walla Walla comes in but adds no appreciable

volume of water. It does not matter. The big river is big enough now. It has begun to surge and boil through its narrowing channel. Gravity, pressure and time took it through the Cascades in the first place; and to get through, the stream had to undermine mountains, crumble them, and dig a channel which men have plumbed and found to reach a depth of three hundred feet below the surface water, and 215 feet below sea level. In a river this is an extraordinary depth. So is the force that made it.

As it reached Celilo, the Columbia plunged into a fall that dropped more than eighty feet in the next few miles of wild churnings. Until recently, its course through the mountains was sporadically furious until it had poured over the last fall called the Cascades, hidden now by dam water, to emerge from the mountains and widen into a calm-looking tidal stream. It was this providential path by which the founders of Oregon came through and not over the great range. It was the last lap of the Oregon Trail.

Crowding both sides of the Columbia's narrow gorge stand mountains that extend for hundreds of miles north and south. Nowhere else in seven hundred miles of the Cascade Range is there a passage like the Columbia. Into and through it went the caravans of the Western migration, and it led them directly to the Willamette Valley which explorers before them had said was incomparably the best place to settle beyond the Rockies.

Once they had passed them, it was obvious to the people of the covered wagons that the Cascade Mountains were the border between two widely contrasting climates. For a thousand miles they had come through a region of light rainfall and sparse vegetation. The winter was cold, the summer blistering. Open pine forests stood on the hills. But as they came floating through these mountains, or followed along the Columbia's south bank, they could see the pines growing smaller by the mile until they were mere scrubs; while the small firs grew larger and taller and at last towered above everything. Meanwhile, they passed beyond the common range of rattlesnakes and magpies, beyond the fields of powdered lava, out of the country of terrible distances. The sky turned leaden, mists crept along the river and swirled in little clouds around the headlands, and the rains began to fall. All these things were notice of the coast climate. They had reached the Promised Land.

When the voyageurs of the fur brigades had come to this stretch of the river, they put plumes in their caps and set up their chants, ready for the cannon salute and the skirling of kilted pipers that would greet them at Fort Vancouver. The place on the north bank that is now the city of Vancouver was for a generation the center of things in the Northwest. Its radiants reached upriver to the headwaters. They reached up the coast into Russian Alaska. They reached overland into Spanish California. The Hudson's Bay Company had no equals in governing an empire of wooded streams and glossy pelts. The Columbia with a hundred of its tributaries was the path to their great headquarters at Fort Vancouver. What finally defeated the hoary old company in Oregon were the swarming settlers represented by the symbol of Portland which grew up on the south bank of the river in sight of the Hudson's Bay

post. This is also where the Willamette joins the Columbia, though its entry is so subtle that even such thorough
men as Lewis and Clark missed it on their way west.

From the Willamette's mouth to the ocean, the course
of the Columbia is marked by islands. No other large
rivers enter it. In places, and in season, it widens and
looks like a lake, though nobody in a small boat would
think of it as lakelike. Not a second time, anyway. Its surface mask of calm suddenly breaks into a swirl that will
suck a huge log down out of sight, then heave it straight
up until twenty feet of it is clear of the water, to stand
there dripping a moment, then fall and go into a fury of
turnings.

The immense deep power of the broad river moving
along here so silently seems destined never to be properly
respected even by those who know the stream well. Failure to judge it has resulted in many personal tragedies
since history began on the river. The roar of a falls, the
thunder of rapids immediately put one on guard. But
the serene quiet of the tidal stream is lulling. It is the only
way to explain many if not most of the lapses of judgment
that have brought disaster to travelers on the lower river.
Either they did not know, or they forgot for the moment,
that they were dealing with the combined waters of (as
yet) uncounted miles of rivers and their tributary creeks
—streams which have their sources in the province of British Columbia and the states of Utah, Wyoming, Nevada,
Montana, Idaho, Washington, and Oregon. These streams
drain more than a quarter of a million square miles. This
is overshadowed by the Mississippi's drainage; but in the

matter of fall and force, which is to say power, the Columbia stands alone in North America. Perhaps it stands alone anywhere. One may read in technical bulletins that there are about 750,000,000 horsepower of potential energy in the rivers of the world. A fifth of this energy is in North America. One third of this one-fifth is in the Columbia. When it has been properly dammed to capacity, it will develop, if engineers are correct, 50,000,000 horsepower. What more could a practical man, a modern man, want?

Well, here and there is an odd soul, doubtless warped by some atavistic urge, who wants both less and more of a river than its measure of horses. For him the Columbia today can offer less than it could twenty, less even than five, years ago. Yet it is happily a long stream, and there are still reaches of it that will fit the River Oregon of which William Cullen Bryant sang so well. A few of his strophes will be quoted so long as men remember that the Columbia was once called the River Oregon. Bryant never stood within two thousand miles of the stream, yet the thought of this great and lonely river moved him powerfully, and lines in his *Thanatopsis* caught its majesty. Never has finer imagery appeared about solitude and "The continuous woods where rolls the Oregon, and hears no sound, save his own dashings."

At Astoria one comes to the end of it, or its beginnings, depending whether you were Captain Robert Gray in a ship, or Trader-Geographer David Thompson on foot. When he crossed the bar, Gray, the first white man to enter the Columbia, saw a stream ten miles wide. Thompson could almost leap the riverlet where it flowed from its headwaters pond. The events were fifteen years apart. The two men had bracketed the River of the West. Today the upper portion of it is British, the lower American. Five hundred miles flow in Canada, seven hundred miles in the United States. The struggle for control of the Columbia was the story of settlement of the Pacific Northwest. In the Columbia's conversion from a wilderness highway into a combination powerhouse and source of irrigating waters appears to lie something of the Northwest's future.

Chapter 2

The Explorers

AT ABOUT eight o'clock on the cloudy morning of May 11, 1792, Captain Robert Gray headed in over the foaming white bar and History began on the River of the West. He was nineteen months out of Boston. His vessel, the *Columbia*, was a full-rigged ship of 212 tons burthen, loaded with trade goods from New England and laden also, as many American historians have liked to remark, with destiny. Spaniards and Russians and British before him had seen what looked to be the bar of a river here, as they cruised up or down the west side of the American continent, but none attempted to enter.

Captain Gray appears to have been the laconic type of Yankee. Three lines in his log serve to bring the ship over the terrible bar, and "we found this to be a large river of fresh water, up which we steered. Vast numbers of natives came alongside." Some six lines are devoted to soundings and bearings, one line to pumping out the casks and filling them from the stream. Then, "So ends," he writes, and is done discussing the actual discovery of a body of water that had existed in men's imaginations for two centuries.

"So ends," he wrote. He might better have written "So begins." The story of the river begins with Gray. His entry also gave the United States a stout claim to the area it drained. A few days later, while moored in the great stream, ten miles wide here near the mouth, he declared it to be Columbia's River. The possessive did not last, yet there was never question but that this river was the Columbia for all time.

Having taken his discovery in stride, Captain Gray sailed up the river some fifteen miles, went ashore to view the land, then proceeded to the business that had brought him to the Pacific, which was trading. Large numbers of Indians came in canoes to the vessel, some with salmon, others with elk and deer meat, and all with furs. Gray's rate for such salmon as he needed was one nail for two fish. He got three hundred beaverskins for two spikes apiece, which must have been satisfactory to the natives, as well as to Gray's sponsors, who were the Messrs. Barrell, Brown, Bullfinch, Darby, Hatch and Pintard, merchant-traders. The Indians kept coming with other furs of different land animals and for these Gray allowed one spike each. Most of all, of course, he wanted furs of the sea otter, which were worth up to $100 each in China. He got 150 of these handsome skins, for which he bartered sheets of copper and bolts of cloth.

Gray was a daring and able mariner in a day when the infant Republic needed such men. He "was loved by his men," it was said, and respected by other captains. He had already taken the first American merchantman around the world; and on this, his second voyage along the Northwest coast, he carried with him a letter from President George

Captain Gray's ship, the *Columbia*, at the entrance of the river.

Washington addressed to "all Emperors, Kings, Sovereign Princes, States and Regents" which requested that they all should receive Captain Gray with kindness and treat him in a becoming manner. This document was also signed by the Secretary of State, who was Thomas Jefferson. Another letter carried by Gray had the bold signature of Governor John Hancock of Massachusetts.

It seems probable that Captain Gray was more pleased with his success at trading with the natives than with the fact that he had discovered and named a river. After all, he had crossed the bar simply to prove to himself that a river did empty into the Pacific at N. Lat. 46° 7′ W. Long. 122° 47′, and doubtless considered it of little importance save to his own satisfaction. He sailed promptly out of the Columbia and virtually out of history also. It is known that he returned to Boston where he lived on Back Street, and he is variously reported to have died in the Atlantic Coast trade in 1803, or maybe 1806, or even 1807, of yellow fever. It seems almost incredible that the man who first took the new American flag around the world, and on his next voyage discovered the Columbia River, should have died so obscurely.

Because he was patently a man who did not seek fame or even care whether or not his name appeared in the public press, it is satisfying that the name of his ship endured and that she also obliterated the apocryphal Northwest Passage, along with the River of the West, or the Oregon. Unhampered imaginations had started to work on these things almost immediately it had become apparent that Columbus had not found a short cut to India. When Gray discovered the Columbia, both the Northwest

Passage and the River of the West were lively subjects for speculation. It was only a few years since a Yankee adventurer named Jonathan Carver had gone so far as to say in a book that the River of the West was really the River Oregon and that it rose "in about the center of this great continent" and "falls into the Pacific ocean." This was in keeping with alleged Indian legend. The river's name had undergone no little change since it first appeared on a map prepared in 1709 by the French explorer Lahontan. It was then the Ouricon-sint, obviously a heroic effort to put the sound of the native word Wisconsin into something a Frenchman could pronounce. The French were an odd people. Their alphabet contained no w.

Jonathan Carver was careless in many ways, but he produced in his *Travels* a narrative that fascinated readers both in England and the United States, among the latter being the young Yankee poet William Cullen Bryant. Bryant was so moved by Carver's prose about the wondrous stream that his own lines on the river, brief as they are, were of such resonance as to immortalize the word which, so an Oregonian was to remark with satisfaction, was already orotund, sonorous, majestic, inimitable. And though Captain Gray's exploration removed the tenuous hold of "Oregon" on an imaginary stream that flowed from Lake Superior to the Pacific, the name was far too good to remain without an object, and the entire northwest corner of the United States became in time the Oregon Country.

When Gray sailed into the Columbia, nobody knew who "owned" the region it drained or knew even its limits. Gray's bold action was the first of a series of explorations by which the United States established its "right" of domain. But before other Americans could take advantage of his discovery, there came the British in Captain George Vancouver's three-vessel fleet. The English and the Spaniards had for centuries fought for domination of world trade, including trading and dominion rights to the northwest coast of North America. Vancouver's party had come to assure Great Britain "a free and undisturbed enjoyment" of commerce and navigation. Captain Gray had met the Vancouver party both before and after he entered the Columbia. On the latter occasion, at Nootka far up the coast, he told them of his discovery and even left a copy of his chart of the river's entrance at Nootka. Gray then sailed for Boston by way of China where he sold his three thousand sea otter skins.

Gray had little more than gone away into the Pacific when Lieutenant William R. Broughton, in command of the *Chatham* of Vancouver's fleet, entered the Columbia. He named Tongue Point and Young's River. Taking small boats, Broughton and men continued upstream perhaps a hundred miles, naming Oak Point, and another point Vancouver. He saw "a remarkable mountain clothed with snow" and named it for Samuel Hood, a remarkable man who among many other duties of empire had been second in command of the English fleet in American waters during the Revolutionary War.

While Lieutenant Broughton was exploring the Columbia, Captain Vancouver, who thought the river's bar too shallow for his flagship, sailed for California. Whether he actually disbelieved Captain Gray's word that he had entered the Columbia, or whether it was strictly for reasons of empire, Captain Vancouver, when he got around to writing a report of Broughton's voyage, remarked pointedly that his lieutenant "formally took possession of the river and the country" in the name of King George, "having reason to believe that the subjects of no other civilized nation or state had ever entered the river before."

Captain Gray had come in May. Lieutenant Broughton had come in October following. In less than a year representatives of two expanding nations laid claim to the legendary River of the West, which now had a name. Gray named it. If Broughton made any effort to name it anew, there seems to be no record. The chief reason for exploration of the northwest coast by both British and Americans was perhaps less with the idea of future dominions than because of the immediate value of the trade in sea otter skins. The big thing was "a free and undisturbed enjoyment" of trading. That the sea otter was very soon to be less an item of trade than a rarity for a museum probably did not occur to anybody.

In any case, the importance to the United States of a foothold on the Pacific Coast seems to have been appreciated by few American statesmen. But Thomas Jefferson was one of these, and to him more than any other is due the decisive action that was to result in American sovereignty of the doubtful Oregon Country. Even before the Louisiana Purchase of 1803, Jefferson was planning an expedition across the continent to take advantage of Gray's discovery. Once the purchase was made, he set almost immediately in motion the overland party headed by Captain William Clark and Lieutenant Merriwether Lewis. Up the

Missouri they went in 1804, and early in November a year later they could hear "the roreing or noise made by the waves brakeing on the rockey shores."

The explorers reached the Columbia by way of the Clearwater to the Snake, and the Snake to the big river near what is now Pasco. It was October 16, 1805, when Lewis and Clark laid eyes on the stream which had been flowing in and out of men's imagination for so many years. If they felt any emotion on seeing for the first time the great objective of their expedition, they did not confide it to their Journals. They were worried at the loss of some of their small stock of trade goods, due to capsizing of a dugout. This was serious enough, for these were the only currency that would be accepted for food or help.

Here by the bank of the main Columbia the astonished natives gathered two hundred strong to see their first white men. They beat drums and danced and chanted to entertain the visitors, who returned the courtesy "by giving them all Smoke." They also presented him described as the principal chief a large medal, a shirt, and a handkerchief; and to the second chief a small medal and a handkerchief.

Everywhere there were salmon. Floating in the river, lying rotting in heaps along the shores, with untold thousands more split and drying on scaffolds—the numbers of fish, Clark wrote, were unbelievable. The drying scaffolds were so many and some of them so extensive that the explorers tried but failed to learn whence they rafted their timbers to this region where there was nothing larger than willow bushes. From here to the river's mouth the party must live in the midst of an age-old salmon economy. They were already and thoroughly bored with fish diet. On their first day on the Columbia, the party traded for seven dogs to vary it. A day or so later it was forty dogs they bought, killed, cooked and ate.

On they went, and soon they had rapids to deal with —not the sort of swift waters they had met on the Clearwater and the Missouri, but a deep churning violence and a power beyond anything these experienced rivermen had dreamed of. They had to portage the worst, and elsewhere often had to line their boats. The local natives apparently knew what to expect at Celilo Falls; sure enough, one of the boats being let down with lines got away and was swept through to be demolished on the rocks below. The Indians were there, on the spot, waiting to collect salvage. Many of these natives were sullen. All of them, the explorers observed, were great and natural thieves. They also swarmed with fleas. But at one lodge they visited, the explorers were cheered by a sign that their journey could not be far from its western goal—two scarlet blankets and a blue one, obviously trade goods from coastwise ships.

There were more bad places on the downriver voyage, including rough water at what the explorers designated as the Great Chute, which were the Falls of the Cascades, since covered by the water of Bonneville Dam; but they made good time and on November 7 were camped where they could see, between the receding banks of the river, the bright expanse of the Pacific. "Ocian in view," wrote Clark. "O! the joy!" This was it. They were looking fair on the Great South Sea. The waves were coming in from China.

It was raining. It continued to rain. It poured and it blew mightily when the party crossed to the south shore

35

and made camp on the bank of a small river, now the Lewis & Clark, which flows into Young's Bay. They built a stockade and seven cabins and called the place Fort Clatsop from the local tribe. It still rained.

During five dreary months the party noted twelve days that were wholly free from rain. If they had previously tired of salmon, they now tired of elk which was their chief provision, a diet broken on one occasion by a dainty three hundred pounds of blubber from a whale washed up on the beach. The party's interpreter, Charboneau and his girl-wife Sacajawea, who had walked halfway across the continent, a papoose strapped to her back, were amazed to see the giant animal that looked like a fish but gave milk.

The two captains kept busy with their Journals, organizing the notes made on the western journey, making route maps, sketches of geographic features. These were conscientious men who meant to carry out in the smallest detail the instructions of their good friend Mr. Jefferson, who wanted to know everything possible concerning the great void beyond the Mississippi. Their botanical and zoological notes described many new species, or notable variations, and their anthropological observations turned out to be permanently important. At least two of the white man's diseases appear to have preceded the Lewis and Clark party. Lewis speaks of treating one of his men for what he calls "Louis Veneri" and remarks that among natives of the lower Columbia he has seen some few males with gonorrhea "and about double that number with the pox." The left arm of one of the Chinook women was tattooed "J. Bowman."

Christmas here beside the Great South Sea was pretty bleak. It rained, it blew, it even thundered. The cabins smoked like the very devil. The blankets were wet and acrawl with fleas so numerous as to call for mention in the Journals. All hands who wanted it got a little tobacco, but there were no ardent spirits. Their dinner "concisted of pore Elk, so much Spoiled that we eate it thro' mear necessity."

On New Year's Day they were still feasting on boiled elk, and Lewis wrote of the repast that it was better than they had at Christmas only because they added to it "anticipation of the 1st day of January" a year hence when "in the bosom of our friends we hope to participate in the mirth and hilarity of the day." For six weeks more the party's diet was mostly of elk, but in late February they got a real treat, when Clark got from the Clatsops half a bushel of small fish which had been taken some forty miles upriver in scoop nets. Clark considered them "superior to any fish I ever tasted." These were the fat silvery little smelt often called candlefish.

One day late in March, the explorers posted notices in Fort Clatsop that their overland journey to the Pacific had been completed. They distributed "certificates of kindness" among the natives. Then they pushed off and started up the Columbia, this time hugging the Oregon shore. Though everybody must have felt a strong urge to get home, the captains were still thorough men; and when encamped near the Sandy River they learned from Indians that they had missed a large stream that entered the Columbia, Clark himself paddled back a good ten miles,

37

threaded his way around islands hiding its mouth, then went up what he named the Multnomah, a river so large, he wrote, that its headwaters must rise in the distant Spanish province of California. The stream is the Willamette which rises high in the Cascade Range of Oregon.

Resuming the return journey, during the Rocky Mountain portion of which Lewis and two companions found it necessary to kill two Indian horse thieves, the explorers continued across the plains without undue incident. They arrived at St. Louis on September 23, 1806, where they were "met by all the village and received a harty welcom from its inhabitants."

For a century and a half historians have been assessing and reassessing the importance of Lewis and Clark. Some have seemed inclined to credit their journey alone for acquisition of the Oregon Country by the United States and to ignore the first man to enter the Columbia who was also an American; and to dismiss or to minimize the aggressive efforts of other Americans who came after Lewis and Clark. But the two land captains need not be cut down in making room for others. They notably bolstered the claim established by Gray. Bernard De Voto remarks that history is not so divisible as to permit us to say exactly how important the Lewis & Clark expedition was in securing the country watered by the River of the West, though he grants its "paramount importance." To De Voto, however, the greatest contribution of this first exploration by land was that it "gave the entire West to the American people as something the mind could deal with." Before, this void had been a region of rumor, guess and fantasy. After Lewis and Clark "the mind could focus on reality."

The minds of both British and Americans began immediately to focus on reality. In the same year Lewis and Clark came down the Columbia from the Snake, men of the Northwest Company of Montreal, fur traders, decided to establish a post west of the Continental Divide. One of their number, Alexander Mackenzie, had already come over the Rockies to explore the river that bears his name and empties into the Arctic Ocean; and also to make his way to the Pacific at Bella Coola. These journeys were of the greatest importance in the field of disinterested exploration, but it was furs that the Northwest Company wanted. Nor was the British government content with Mackenzie's remarkable work. Where lay the boundary between British North America and the self-assertive new republic? No one could be sure under the terms of peace that followed the War of the Revolution. But if no one could know, there were nevertheless men in England who believed that the Great River of the West, the Columbia, might fix the ultimate boundary.

So, now in 1805, while Lewis and Clark were in their soggy camp at the Columbia's mouth, over the Rockies into present British Columbia, came young Simon Fraser who, though born in Vermont of Tory parents, was already a full partner in the Northwest Company. He established Fort McLeod on a tributary of the Peace River in British Columbia, the first trading post west of the Rockies. He and his clerk, John McDougall, also did some exploring, and Fraser made bold to name this region New Caledonia.

Fort McLeod was a well situated post, and New Caledonia doubtless contained furs and native trappers in number, but it was still in the high North, above 55°. This was no way to get control of the Columbia River; and the Northwest Company felt urged to call for help from its chief surveyor, geographer and astronomer, David Thompson, the same, as mentioned earlier, who was the first white man to see the Columbia's headwaters.

Thompson is worth considering. Born in London of Welsh parents, he went out, a lad of fourteen, as an apprentice for the Hudson's Bay Company and was landed on the inhospitable west shore of the Bay itself at Fort Churchill to begin his career. Much of the next decade he served in survey parties mapping the Nelson, Churchill and Saskatchewan rivers. Then he joined the Nor'westers to take charge of exploring and mapping crews in the Upper Mississippi River region. He was made a partner. The Northwest Company never had a greater. If the Columbia River were needed for empire and furs, then Thompson was the man to find its source and to follow the stream wherever it took him.

One must bear in mind that though Gray's ship and Vancouver's party had entered the Columbia by sea, and though Lewis and Clark had followed it down from the Snake, nobody yet knew where or how it coursed above what is now Pasco, Washington, which, though nobody knew *that* either, meant that some nine hundred miles of the main river remained to be explored. Thompson first entered the Rockies by way of Howse Pass, then followed a likely stream which just might be the Columbia but was merely one of the Columbia's larger tributaries, the Kootenay. He probably would have followed it to the parent stream had he not been attacked by a band of Indians.

He was compelled to return to his base at Rocky Mountain House, a trading post on the North Saskatchewan.

In the spring of 1807, Thompson set forth again to find the source of the River of the West. This time he took his wife, a half-breed Cree, and children, a fact indicating he was prepared, if need be, to stay a good while. Late in June the party crossed the height of land and descended the Blaeberry to where it entered a big river. The big river was flowing, incredibly enough, north. It was almost as if the needle of Thompson's compass had suddenly switched its pole to point south. Here on the west side of the Rockies, as the half-dozen men who had been there knew, all rivers flowed south.

Well, here was one that didn't. Thompson was somewhat astonished, but remained calm and pushed on south, or upstream, passing present Lake Windermere. Then, within a few miles, he came to the end, or rather the beginning. He was at the headwaters, the first white man to look upon the source of the Columbia. But, *was* it that river? Thompson thought so, and while taking his bearings and exploring round about, he also established Kootenae House, the first trading post on the Columbia River.

It was an almost unbelievable thing about Kootenae House that among its assortment of trade goods there was not an ounce of alcohol. In that day rum was a customary and highly popular item in the fur trade. Thompson never drank it; and now that he was to establish trading posts in the Far West, he was determined that none of them should deal in it. Although, as he wrote, "I had made it a law to myself that no alcohol should pass the mountains in my

41

company," he was overruled by his partners who insisted that he take two kegs of rum to Kootenae House. On the way west Thompson reflected on "the sad sight of drunkeness and its many evils," and then, when the party came to the Rockies, "I placed the two kegs on a vicious horse and by noon the kegs were empty and in pieces, the horse rubbing his load against the rocks to get rid of it." And lest his partners think that the lost rum was due to accident, Thompson put them right in a letter. "I told them what I had done, and that I would do the same to every keg of alcohol." That made it plain enough. For the next six years during which Thompson had charge of all Northwest trading west of the Rockies, his partners made no further attempt to introduce spirituous liquors.

In the spring of 1808, with Kootenae House settled in the routine of trading, Thompson set out on the kind of work he really enjoyed, which was exploring and mapping new country. Paddling from his post the twenty-odd miles up the Columbia to the headwaters lake, he crossed the brief plain now called Canal Flats and within a mile came to the Kootenay River. This flowed south. The north-flowing Columbia began little more than six thousand feet away. The Kootenay here was already a potent stream. Thompson took it down into Montana and Idaho. He established trading posts he named Kullyspell House and Saleesh House, and by trading goods for 125 pelts probably consummated the first business transactions in present Montana and Idaho. He wintered in Montana. He made an unsuccessful attempt to reach the Columbia by way of the Clark Fork, then returned north to Kootenae

House where his men reported Indians to be harassing Nor'westers who wanted to use Howse Pass through the Rockies.

Taking his wife and family over the Rockies, to leave them at Fort Augustus (Edmonton, Alberta), Thompson went up the Athabasca, stopped briefly at Brule Lake, then came down the Wood River to the Columbia, striking it at the top of the Big Bend. He and his men built a cabin, the first habitation at present Boat Encampment, as Thompson named it. This was the spot where the big river turned so suddenly to flow south. Thompson had felt certain it did, and here was the bend he had expected to find. Possibly because he considered navigation south from here might be more difficult than by the Kootenay, or perhaps because he wanted to visit his trading posts on the way, Thompson decided on the latter route. He knew that he could reach the Columbia again at Kettle Falls. His goal this trip was the very mouth of the Columbia where it came to the ocean. Nothing short of the sea would do.

It would be interesting to know whether this voyage of Thompson's was prompted by matters of empire. During his truly terrible trek through Athabasca Pass to Boat Encampment, he had written in his Journal one bitter January night, that: "Many reflections came to my mind; a new world was, in a manner before us, and my object was to be at the Pacific ocean before the month of August . . . amidst various thoughts I fell asleep on my bed of snow."

Obviously, matters of some import were in the air. For one thing, Thompson's native country and the United

States were bickering again. The British were arrogant. The Americans were cocky. Their Congress was swarming with men who denounced England daily. Doubtless the Northwest Company, alert to all things, kept their chief geographer and astronomer well informed. It is also certain that the Northwesters knew, and must have warned Thompson, of an impending event: An American fur outfit planned to set up a post somewhere on the Lower Columbia River.

So, as spring approached the far upper reaches of the Columbia, Thompson and his men got ready. They built a canoe of split cedar, twenty-five feet long, the boards of which were sewed together with roots. In it on April 17, 1811, Thompson and crew set forth, heading upriver from Boat Encampment. It was 230 miles to the portage over to the Kootenay. They made it in a little less than a month and carried over the flats, then down the Kootenay to Saleesh House. Here they built a new canoe, the second on this trip, and went down the Clark Fork to the site of present Cusick, Washington. They got horses to go overland to the junction of the Spokane and Little Spokane Rivers where the party stopped briefly at Spokane House, a post just established by the Northwest Company. Another three-day ride brought the party to Kettle Falls on the main Columbia. Here they lost some time in finding a suitable tree to make a canoe, their third; and six days after they pushed off arrived at the mouth of the Snake. This, as Thompson knew, was where Lewis and Clark had come to the river.

It was now the ninth of July, 1811. Thompson had long since reminded himself that he must be at the Pacific

Ocean "before the month of August." He could make it now, barring accident. But before taking off again, he took the trouble to write and post a notice on a small pole here in the immense nothingness where the Snake joined the Columbia. In it he claimed the region for Great Britain, and thoughtfully added the significant statement that the N. W. Company of Merchants of Canada planned to "erect a Factory at this Place for the Commerce of the Country around." Then and only then did the chief surveyor, geographer and astronomer for the company in which he was a partner get back into his canoe and push off, still heading downriver.

Chapter 3

The Astorians

WHILE DAVID THOMPSON lay on his bed of snow, somewhere in the wilderness of the Big Bend of the Columbia, telling his Journal that he must reach the Pacific Ocean before August, John Jacob Astor of New York City had just launched the venture he hoped would result in a trading monopoly of North America for his American Fur Company. The venture began with the *Tonquin*, a 290-ton ship mounting ten guns, which sailed out of New York harbor one day in September. The year was 1810.

Astor's plan was as magnificently bold as it was feasible, and just as hazardous: He would plant at the mouth of the Columbia River a central or headquarters establishment, with subordinate posts throughout the interior. The furs would thus be gathered at the point nearest to their sources, and nearest also to the richest market, which was China. Astor's furs would go to China. The Chinese wanted any sort of North American fur—beaver, mink, fox; and for the beautiful sea otter they were ready to pay as high as $100, which was an enormous sum in the early 1800s. Having disposed of the furs, Astor's vessels were to reload with spices for the United States and return to New

York. Here they would take aboard trade goods for the various Astor posts to be established in the Far West and sail for headquarters at the mouth of the Columbia.

Thompson knew about Astor. This emigrant from the Duchy of Baden had been in the fur trade almost since he landed in the United States in 1784. He had done very well. On occasion he and the Northwest Company of Montreal had co-operated to mutual advantage. Many of his best employes had worked for the Canadian concern. Indeed, three of his partners in this new venture, which he had organized as the Pacific Fur Company, were veteran Nor'westers. He had also offered a one-third interest in his new outfit to the Northwest Company itself, but the offer had been politely declined because the company believed it could by itself control the fur-bearing region.

So, away sailed Astor's *Tonquin;* and overland for the mouth of the Columbia went an Astor party, heading up the Missouri from St. Louis. The captain of the one and the leader of the other were appallingly bad choices.

The *Tonquin* arrived at the Columbia's mouth in March of 1811, after touching the Sandwich (Hawaiian) Islands to load a crew of natives, called Kanakas, to work around the post. The voyage to this point had been something of a nightmare, due to a "rigid commander and a restless crew." Captain Thorn was a martinet, which was only to be expected of a skipper in that era, but he was also a thoroughly humorless and disagreeable person. Among his passengers and crew were trappers and traders who were not used to the discipline thought proper for a ship's company or, perhaps, used to much of any discipline at all. They took delight in holding long discussions in Gaelic, which offended and irritated Captain Thorn. Throughout much of the nightmarish voyage the ship's company was not far from mutiny.

Even the *Tonquin's* landfall at the Columbia's mouth was filled with foreboding and evil. Due chiefly to Thorn's incompetence, seven of the crew were lost in crossing the bar, and the *Tonquin* came to anchor in the Columbia to the wailing of the Kanakas, lamenting the loss of one of their number. When his body had been recovered, his comrades buried him in a shallow grave in the Columbia's sands, with a biscuit under one arm, a little lard under the chin, and some tobacco. It was the first grave to be made in what that same day became Astoria.

There was bickering as to where the post should be built. One favored this site, Thorn chose another, but at last the chief partner, Duncan McDougall, ordered that construction should be on an elevation facing north, with the great estuary, its sand bars and foaming breakers spread out before it. All hands set to work, felling trees, clearing the junglelike underbrush, and marking out places for the residence, storehouse and powder magazine.

Everything was green with the freshness of April. The weather was perfect. After long confinement on shipboard, the men worked with a will in these strange yet happy surroundings. The natives came swarming about, already bringing sea otter skins to barter. They also displayed childlike curiosity in what was being done, and considerable facility in stealing anything that workmen left for a moment unguarded. The principal chief appeared to be the Chinook Comcomly who, though one-eyed, seldom missed seeing anything that would benefit himself or his people.

Members of the Astor party came to understand the effect of different modes of life upon the human frame and character. The veteran traders among them had long been familiar with the hunting Indians of the East who were continuously on horseback, getting their food by ranging far, subsisting mostly on flesh, and who were generally tall, thin, and sinewy. The Plains Indians, and even those of the Canadian woods were bold and of "commonly fierce deportment." But these tribes along the lower Columbia, who called themselves Chinooks, Clatsops, Wahkiacums, and Cathlamahs were different. They lived on fish. They spent much of their time squatting in canoes, some of which carried thirty men, and they were generally of low stature, with crooked legs, thick ankles and broad flat feet. They seemed to be less active than members of Eastern tribes, and of markedly less muscular power.

There were other differences. These natives who lived between the Cascades and the sea had no tepees. They lived in houses made from planks split with wedges of stone, horn or hardwood. Several families lived in the same house. Partitions made of mats woven from rushes separated the families. The center of the house was lower than the sides, and here the cooking was done. A roof hole let out some of the smoke, but enough remained to cure the salmon which hung in strips from poles just under the roof.

Other than for the main dish of fish, these Indians made a sort of bread from camas roots; and cooked arrowhead tubers they called *wapato*. They picked and dried huckleberries, salal berries, and fern and flag roots. They had both whale and seal oils, which were stored in bladders and with which they liked to drench their dried berries before eating. Their kitchen equipment was sparse and consisted of bowls and trenchers hollowed out of wood, cups of horn, horn spoons, and baskets woven so tightly as to take the place of jugs and pails.

There was a dismaying linguistic diversity. In the northwestern corner of Oregon, for instance, were half-a-dozen tribes all speaking different languages which appeared to have little in common with the tongues spoken by the several tribes in southwestern Washington. Yet, these tribes were able to communicate one with another through the medium of a trading jargon called Chinook. The Chinooks appear to have been a family of tribes. The Chinooks proper occupied the north bank of the extreme lower Columbia and also the coast for an indeterminate distance northward. On the south shore of the river were the Clatsops who were also of the Chinook family. It is probable that once upon a time the Chinookan family, as anthropologists call it, had full possession of the Columbia River from the Cascades to the sea. By the time white men came, however, the Chinooks had given way in several spots to alien tribes. The Klickitats had established themselves on the Klickitat and Lewis rivers. Salishans were living along the Cowlitz River. And Athapascans had villages on the south bank of the Columbia at two places.

The trading jargon or lingua franca of Chinook was first noted by Captain James Cook, at Nootka Sound on the British Columbia coast as early as 1778. Captain George Vancouver detected it a dozen years later around Grays

Harbor. It doubtless existed long before the white man heard it, and it spread rapidly out of necessity as trading increased. It took on words from the French, Russian and English languages. By the time the Astorians came to found a post, Chinook was the recognized medium for trading. Half-a-dozen years before Fort Astoria was built, an English sailor, John Jewett, escaped from the captivity of Indians at Nootka Sound. Three years among them made him something of an authority on their manners, mode of living and language; and in 1815, at Middletown, Connecticut, his narrative was published under title of *The Captive in Nootka*. In it Jewett listed almost one hundred words of the Jargon, and mentions, significantly, that among the many tribes who came to trade with the Nootkas were people he calls "Keltsups," who doubtless were Clatsops. This would indicate a range of more than three hundred miles for the Chinook Jargon.

During the next few years, missionaries, explorers, and traders added to or revised words in Jewett's vocabulary; and still later the subject interested ethnologists like Dr. Franz Boas. As early as 1852 a Chinook dictionary was published in Portland. Since then, numerous editions have been compiled and published by John Gill of Portland.

Over the years, the Chinooks and all other coast tribes came to be called Siwashes, a corruption of the French *sauvage*, meaning savage. The Jargon itself is often called Siwash. A few of the Siwash or Chinook words are still used in the Northwest, like *hi-yu*, meaning plenty, many, enough, as *hiyu muckamuck*, plenty to eat. *Potlatch* which in original Chinook meant a gift, or to give, has come to denote almost any sort of social doings, picnic, celebration or even a convention; it appears also in corporate titles, on lakes, ponds, rivers and creeks; and there have been at least two Potlatch post offices, one in Washington, the other in Idaho. *Skookum* is almost as popular as an adjective, meaning strong, stout, brave, or great. *Kultus* is bad, worthless. A *tillicum* is a good friend. A *tyee* is a chief, a big shot, perhaps the president of a logging outfit. Indicative of the several non-Indian sources of the Jargon is the Chinook for salt: both *le sel* (French) and just plain salt were used. The sea was *saltchuck*. In later editions of John Gill's dictionary are some three hundred words which he believed were "of the ancient language of the Chinooks." The others were from the Nootka, Chehalis, Klickitat, and Wasco tongues, and of course from French, English and Russian. There is no word for Russian in Gill's dictionary, but the term for Englishman is given as King George; and no matter that the Astor traders came from New York, an American trader, explorer, or sailor was a Boston-Man. This may have stemmed fom Captain Gray's first entry into the Columbia. In any event, these Scotch, Irish, French-Canadian and assorted Americans of Astor's party had arrived at the mouth of the river in a ship flying the American flag. They had erected a pole at their trading post, and it too displayed the American or Boston flag. Hence they were Boston-Men.

While "Boston-Man" McDougall and his men continued their labors at building Fort Astoria, Captain Thorn and twenty-three men sailed out over the bar and northward, to trade along the coast. Evil still rode with the

Tonquin. At Clayoquot harbor on Vancouver Island, she put in to trade with a tribe headed by old Nookamis, a chief long accustomed to the wiles of New England skippers and who prided himself on ability to hold his own with any white man. Nookamis was indignant at Thorn's offer for otterskins, demanding it be doubled. Thorn was deficient in patience. He was wholly wanting in the chicanery of trading. He also held the Indians, here and anywhere else, in contempt. And when the chief began openly to jeer at him and his offers, Thorn snatched an otterskin from his hands, rubbed it brusquely into the Indian's face and ordered him and his gang off the ship.

Next day, early in the morning, some twenty Indians approached the *Tonquin.* They were unarmed and holding aloft otterskins. They were admitted to the *Tonquin.* A little later came other canoeloads of tribesmen, all wearing fur mantles under which were long knives. By the time Captain Thorn took alarm and prepared to sail away, the vessel was surrounded on every side, and still more savages were coming aboard. A long yell gave the signal, and the Indians set about with their knives, tomahawks and clubs. In a little while it was all over. The traders were butchered, though not before one of them set fire to the ship's magazine, blowing the *Tonquin* and the Indian attackers to bits. Such was the melancholy end of Captain Thorn's command, as related by his Indian interpreter who escaped and made his way back to Astoria.

Meanwhile, the Astor overland party under Wilson Price Hunt was having a fearful time. They were long overdue at Fort Astoria, and Factor McDougall watched anxiously, each day expecting a fleet of canoes to arrive from upriver. He could not know that the Price party had started later than planned and that they were also to meander more than thirty-five hundred miles in covering the approximately eighteen hundred miles between St. Louis and Astoria. But at last, on July 5, the Astorians set up a cheer when a craft was sighted coming down the Columbia. The cheer died when a spyglass showed the craft to be a long canoe, manned by eight Indians and one white man, and flying the British flag. The white man was none other than David Thompson, a good two weeks ahead of the time limit he had set for himself six months before.

The long cedar canoe swung toward the shore below the fort, to be made welcome by McDougall and all his company. Thompson came to land. He was, says Bancroft, a tall and fine-looking man of sandy complexion, with large features, deep-set studious eyes, high forehead and broad shoulders. He was also too late. The American flag on the pole at Fort Astoria told him as much.

McDougall, a former Nor'wester himself, was so happy to see his old comrade that he figuratively turned out the guard. Many others of the Astorians were Canadians and ex-Nor'westers, too. Out came the rum, and a fine time was had. Yet, Thompson who did not touch liquor was not working for John Jacob Astor, and between drinks of the others he gave Astor's men to understand they would waste their time if they should attempt to erect posts and trade for furs east of the Cascades. Why, said he, warming to his subject, his own outfit had found the interior to be so bare of furs that they had decided to abandon everything west of the Rockies. This kind of talk fooled nobody. It was the standard method of attempting to discourage competition.

When the genial visit was done, McDougall outfitted Thompson and sent him on his way—followed by a party of Astorians in two big Chinook ocean-going canoes, just to make sure Thompson did not secure all of the good locations upriver. Two of these Astorians, David Stuart and Alexander Ross, went to the junction of the Columbia and the Okanogan and there established the first American trading post on the middle river. Whilst Stuart went on to explore elsewhere, Ross began a brisk trade and to learn the native speech. In six months he took in some fifteen hundred beaver, plus other peltries, for which he gave trade goods amounting, he figured, to about one sixty-fifth of the value of the furs. It was, he calculated, a fine business.

Down at Fort Astoria, McDougall still waited for the Astor overlanders. They were not to arrive as a single party, and it was January before the first of several straggling sections showed up. February was nearly gone when Hunt, the leader, appeared with the last of his men.

Hunt had made errors enough during the early part of the journey, and then he accomplished a misjudgment of some size: He decided, against all advice to the contrary, that it would be easier to float down the Snake to the Columbia than to continue by land. It was not easier. It was disastrous. Having stopped to build fifteen canoes, the party left their horses in care of Indians, then started down the river. Nine days later their first wreck occurred, and one canoe and a man were lost. During the next few days, four more canoes were lost. Deciding that the Snake was not navigable, they attempted to get their horses, but found this impossible. Now they split into two parties. Another man was lost in the river. The two groups trudged on, often having to retrace their steps for many miles, to try again to find a path that would lead down and along the banks of the Snake. Provisions ran short. How short, one may judge from the fact that one man "became so frantic at the sight of meat that he upset a canoe and was drowned."

Trappers coming to Fort Astoria.

The heroine of the Wilson Price Hunt tragedy was a woman, wife of Pierre Dorian, guide and interpreter, who carried a pack every step of the way and also one and sometimes both of her two children. It was an example of strength and determination which more than once put heart into the discouraged white men of the party. Madame Dorian was also pregnant. When at last she had to stop, while crossing Idaho in winter, her husband stayed with her while she retired into a clump of snow-weighted pines and became a mother again. A few hours later, her pack and new child on her back, she resumed the trek.

By the time all of the battered survivors of the overland party had reached Astoria, the United States and Great Britain were moving rapidly toward war, which was declared in June. Yet, heartened that at last they were all together, the Astorians were further cheered when an Astor ship arrived bringing a fresh supply of trade goods and more men.

The bad news that war had begun reached the Astorians by way of John George McTavish, a Nor'wester, who said that a British warship, the *Raccoon*, accompanied by a Northwest Company ship, was on its way to capture Astoria. It might be best all around, suggested McTavish, if Astor Partner McDougall sold the Astor post and business to the Northwest Company, a Canadian outfit, rather than to be blown out of Astoria by the British navy.

McDougall did not need threats. In a deal marked by gross opportunism, if not actual treachery, this partner of Astor's sold the whole business to McTavish of the Nor'-westers for less than a third of its value. What was more, McDougall himself went with the trade. He was promptly made chief factor for the new proprietors of Fort Astoria.

When *HMS Raccoon*, Captain W. Black, arrived to capture the fort, her commander and crew were disgusted to find the place already in British hands. There was no chance of prize money. So Captain Black took possession for His Majesty, ran up the British flag, and declared the place to be henceforth Fort George. To take charge of Fort George and of all the Northwest Company's new domain along the West Coast presently came still another

Scotsman, Donald McTavish, a veteran partner who had served his time in Canada and had retired. When offered the governorship of the Company's coastal empire, however, he accepted, and arrived at Fort George from England.

Governor McTavish had an abiding interest in hard liquor and a liking for female company. With him came a pretty blonde barmaid from Plymouth, England, whose name may have been Jane Barnes. She was the first white woman of record on the Columbia, and her stay at Fort George, though brief, was such as to make her the heroine, or at least the subject, of short stories, longer stories, whole novels, learned essays, and of barroom legends beyond number.

Jane was a handsome strumpet. She dressed to kill in more ways than one. After a riotous few weeks, during which she seems to have dropped McTavish in favor of Alexander Henry, while McTavish had to be content with a flathead Chinook, known as Mrs. Clapp, both McTavish and Henry, while better or worse from drink, were drowned, along with five other men almost in front of Fort George. Whether or not Jane went into mourning isn't known, but she did not lack for attention. Now appeared the son of old Chief Comcomly, painted and decked in all the glory of a prince's vestments, to offer Jane his hand in marriage, suggesting a gift of one hundred otterskins for the privilege. She refused, and presently left for Canton, China, and eventually returned to her hometown, Plymouth, and was heard of no more.

For the next decade, as Philip H. Parrish writes, the Northwesters took their cue from the hard-boiled policy of the late Governor McTavish and "ruled with bullets and whiskey." It would have saddened David Thompson, who by then had retired from the fur trade which, so far as the Northwest Company's posts west of the Rockies were concerned, had carried on their business during Thompson's regime, without recourse to rum.*

It may well have been rum that had something to do with the troubles which beset the cynical crew in charge of affairs at Fort George. Their troubles began immediately when one of their brigades got into a fracas with Indians and killed two. A blacksmith at the fort fomented a mutiny among the Kanakas. Three different expeditions to explore the Willamette for furs were turned back by attacks of hostiles. Seven Nor'westers in another party lost their lives in and gave a name to the Dalles des Morts, or Death Rapids, far up on the Big Bend of the Columbia, when they lost their canoe and provisions, and then, while attempting to get out of the canyon, had died one by one of starvation and been eaten by the survivors. The eighth man had survived the other seven and, wandering around Upper Arrow Lake, was found much later by friendly Indians who took him by canoe to Spokane House.

---

* Not long after leaving the fur trade, Thompson was put in charge of the British commission for establishing and marking the Canadian-United States boundary from its crossing of St. Lawrence River west to the angle of Lake of the Woods. During his active life, so a biographer wrote, Thompson had "placed on the map main routes of travel within 1,200,000 square miles of Canadian territory and 500,000 square miles of the United States." Though he died forgotten and in extreme poverty, British Columbia has honored him in recent years by marking the site of Kootenae House and of Boat Encampment, and late in 1954 a marker and plaque commemorating his exploration of the Columbia was unveiled at Castlegar, at the foot of the Arrow Lakes.

Other troubles of the Northwest Company came from its policy of bringing from the East a number of Iroquois as rivermen. They were perfect on the river, but intractable. One band of them, working out of Fort George, stole some horses from the native Umpquas, then shot them up, killing fourteen. This and other raids made the Nor'westers hated. Then, Factor McDougall—he who had sold Astoria and joined the Nor'westers—announced to the Indians that he was a worker in magic. To keep the natives in their place, he called several of their headmen together at the fort, showed them a small black bottle, telling them it was filled with the dreadful disease of smallpox. Should he pull the cork, said McDougall, the invisible but terrible germs would escape and destroy all Indians in the region.

The tribes feared nothing so much as smallpox, and McDougall's was a potent threat. It was also to act as a potent curse on the white men, for a little later when smallpox did strike tribes over much of the Northwest, the black bottle story, still devoutly believed, helped to madden the Indians to massacres of settlers. The black bottle of McDougall has been specifically cited as a contributing factor to the tragedy of the Whitmans at Walla Walla, a melancholy incident we shall come to a little later.

When the War of 1812 was over, the American negotiators at the Treaty of Ghent held out for a provision which declared that all territory, places and possessions taken by either party from the other during the fighting should be restored. Fort George was thus returned to the United States. But John Jacob Astor decided not to resume operations. The Northwest Company was permitted to continue in business, though under American jurisdiction, until it was taken over in 1821 by its old competitor, the Hudson's Bay Company.

It was a policy of the venerable Bay Company to take a long look at things. Though the Oregon Country had proved to be no field of great profit for the Nor'westers, the governors of the other concern believed it held possibilities for an institution which for a century and a half had seen trading outfits come and go. The Bay was patient with the wisdom of age, changing its practices to fit changing times. It was also as relentless as time. There was also the matter of empire to be considered, the British Empire. Oregon was still of doubtful sovereignty. The Governor and Gentlemen Adventurers of England Trading into Hudson's Bay were not the men to desert the Empire in time of need. True, the Treaty of Ghent stipulated that Englishmen and Americans had equal rights "to trade and make settlements" between the crest of the Rockies and the Pacific, north of the 42nd parallel and south of 54° 40'. This sort of an arrangement might do for a while, but it had been the experience of the Bay people that "joint occupation" of anything was highly unsatisfactory.

So, now to Fort Astoria, in the pleasant autumn of 1824, came George Simpson, officially governor of the Bay's western department but soon to be the company's governor in chief. With him was Dr. John McLoughlin, recently named chief factor of the company. They had made a record trip of eighty-four days after leaving York Factory on Hudson Bay. The two men, who had walked or canoed more than two thousand miles to look at it, made a rather impressive arrival at Astoria. Buglers in an advance canoe gave notice. A piper in full kilt played the party ashore, and all the men of it were seen to be clean-shaven. Each wore a feather in his cap. This was the manner in which Governor Simpson liked to arrive. He and McLoughlin, on their tour of inspection, found the post to be run down. The leading men, as Simpson observed, had been "amusing themselves Boat Sailing." The post had also achieved, over the years, an unholy reputation for debauching the natives.

While the governor in chief and the chief factor were looking over the place, Astoria got a look at the two men who were to change conditions along the Columbia. They were most dissimilar in appearance. Simpson, only thirty-two and a native of Scotland, was short and plump. McLoughlin, forty and born at Rivière du Loup, Quebec, stood six feet four inches tall. Both were extraordinary men. They agreed that Fort Astoria, or Fort George, no matter its name, would not do for their company's headquarters post in the Oregon Country. Then, with their piper and buglers and paddlers, they went away upstream.

At a spot on the north bank of the Columbia, about a hundred miles from Astoria, and nearly opposite the point where the Willamette entered the stream, Simpson and McLoughlin selected a site. Factor McLoughlin set a crew to work. Governor Simpson christened the new post Fort Vancouver, thus honoring the English explorer of the Northwest coast and establishing another honorable British name along the river that had been named for an American ship.

There were both natural and political reasons for the selection of Fort Vancouver's site. For one thing it was a fine open field in the forest that covered the riverbank almost continuously from the sea to the Cascades. For another, it was near the head of navigation so far as deep-sea vessels were concerned. Still again, it was the natural starting point for parties going up the Willamette or overland to Puget Sound. And above all, the site fitted what Governor Simpson had determined should be his company's policy here on the lower Columbia. He believed that nothing now could keep Americans from entering the Oregon Country and instructed Factor McLoughlin, who was to remain in charge, to steer newcomers so far as possible to lands south of the river. If the Yankees could be thus herded and somehow kept there, then when the joint occupancy was over, the Columbia might well turn out to be the boundary between the United States and British Canada. Half of the Oregon Country was better than none.

The governor now bade good-bye to the factor and was away upriver, heading back to the new world-headquarters of his vast empire of furs, which was Norway House on the shore of Lake Winnipeg, more than halfway across North America. The factor proceeded to direct construction of Fort Vancouver, which he planned should be exactly what British orators meant when they referred to a bastion of empire.

Chapter 4

The Bay Company's Capital

FORT VANCOUVER on the north bank of the Columbia was to be a great deal more than a trading post of the Hudson's Bay Company. Its head man or factor, Dr. John McLoughlin, became a legendary figure, not as a trader for furs but as absolutely the most important person in the great region between the Rockies and the Pacific and between the 42nd parallel and the line of 54° 40′. On modern maps this so-called joint occupation country takes in Oregon, Washington, Idaho, parts of Montana and Wyoming, and a good piece of British Columbia. McLoughlin's influence was felt throughout this domain for two decades, or from about 1825 to 1846. In Oregon and Washington, at least, he ushered in what without exaggeration could be termed the McLoughlin Era.

The man was of powerful physique, a hulking figure topped by prematurely white hair. The Coast Indians are said to have called him the White Headed Eagle, and possibly they did. His face, commonly sullen despite his many kindnesses, presented deep-set eyes of an intense blue. The Hudson's Bay Company's Governor, George Simpson, wrote of his first impression of the man that his

John McLoughlin of the Hudson's Bay Company at
Fort Vancouver.

"was such a figure as I should not like to meet in a dark Night in one of the bye lanes in the neighborhood of London." He looked in his antique clothes to the governor like "a highwayman of former days."

Scotch and Irish blood ran in his veins, and to Scotland he was sent from his native Canada to study medicine. On his return he became a partner in the Northwest Company, and at the time this largely Scottish outfit was merged with the Bay Company, McLoughlin was factor of the important post of Fort William on Lake Superior. It was Governor Simpson who selected him to take charge of the company's Columbia Department. Simpson knew the man's shortcomings. He had a violent temper, a "disagreeable man to do business with." He was "wanting in system." He would be a troublesome man for the company "if he had sufficient influence to form and tact to manage a party." Yet he was energetic, he had displayed great ability to get along with and discipline Indians, and he was a man of "strict honor and integrity." Whatever his shortcomings, the memory of Dr. McLoughlin is revered as is almost no other by the sons and daughters of Oregon pioneers a century after his death. This is remarkable in view of his duties as prescribed by the Bay Company's board of governors.

As chief factor of the Columbia department, McLoughlin was to monopolize the fur trade as completely as possible and to produce the maximum annual profits indefinitely. Because it had long been company policy to encourage the taking of furs on the basis of conservation, that is, by restricting the catch to fit the natural increase of animals, he must impose a trapping peace, or an understanding of the necessity of co-operation among the many small tribes of natives. Rival traders must be kept out. And agricultural settlement of the area must be prevented. All of which, so a historian observed, proved a difficult program for McLoughlin to execute "to the satisfaction both of his employers and of his own conscience."

First of all came a headquarters. After a brief start on a site that was soon considered too far from the bank of the river, Fort Vancouver was established where later was to stand Vancouver Barracks of the United States Army. Its wall was twenty feet high, of thick beams set upright and supported by buttresses, and it enclosed an interior divided into two courts around which were set some forty buildings, including offices, apartments for the clerks, warehouses, a bakery, a chemist's shop, a retail store, and the workshops of carpenters, smiths, coopers, wheelwrights, millwrights, tinners, and other artisans. A powder magazine was the sole building of brick and stone. There was also a schoolhouse and a chapel. The factor's house stood at the center of the establishment, hedged with flower beds.

There was a commodious hall where the gentlemen, clerks, chaplain, physician and honored guests dined together. McLoughlin, possibly on order of Governor Simpson, was a strict observer of precedence in seating the company; but in any case the customs of the Bay Company were based on the old feudal ideas that were still largely in force in England. So were the elegances. The gentlemen's table was set with fine china, silver and linen. The fare was excellent and bountiful. Though hard liquor was never served, there were usually several varieties of wine, a beverage the chief factor touched only to open the festivities incident to the return of the fur brigades, when both custom and etiquette were permitted a holiday mood.

A kilted Highlander piped the officers and guests into the dining hall. The fort's pipers also served to impress Indian chiefs and other leading tribesmen whom the factor often invited for the purpose of "overwhelming them with the majesty of the audience he granted them." This began at the very gate where, as the Indians entered, a gigantic Highlander was skirling his pipes and parading in the brilliant magnificence of the Red Menzies, or perhaps the eye-rocking McLeod, tartan. Before this apparition and sound, the red men stood entranced.

Outside of, yet close to, the fort was a village of sixty or more houses, set in rows, where lived the mechanics and servants with their families. Here also the company maintained a hospital. Although a couple of ancient cannon, mounted on sea carriages, were kept at the fort and were viewed with awe by the natives, no defensive measures were ever needed.

Such was the headquarters establishment of the Hudson's Bay Company in its department of the Columbia. In it lived often as many as seven hundred persons, the most populous village in half a continent.

When Fort Vancouver had been properly established, Governor Simpson ordered abandonment of Spokane House and the transfer of its activities to a new post, Fort Colville, to be built at what is now the town of Marcus, Washington. McLoughlin selected the actual site. Fort Okanogan was enlarged and strengthened to care for the brigades that did business in New Caledonia (British Co-lumbia.) And near the junction of the Columbia and the Snake, the former Northwest post called Fort Nez Perces was taken over and renamed Fort Walla Walla. The old trading posts of the Nor'westers in the Kootenay, Pend Oreille and Flathead regions were continued. These were not forts and could be easily moved about to suit changing local conditions.

There were other points that should be kept constantly under watch, for although Astor's and the Northwest companies had been disposed of, Americans had organized the Rocky Mountain Fur Company. This aggressive concern must meet buffers on the fringe of the Bay Company's main empire, so Simpson ordered establishment of a post in southern Oregon, Fort Umpqua, and Fort Boise in present Idaho. A little later the company was also to purchase Fort Hall in the Idaho region of the upper Snake River.

Far to the north, on the coast, the Bay built a post and named it Fort Simpson. Another, Fort Langley, went up on the lower Fraser River. In the interior of New Caledonia were several smaller posts. By deep-sea ships and by river express, furs came from all this region to Fort Vancouver, and from the fort went out trade goods—axes, awls, needles; tobacco, sugar, spices; blankets, ribbons, beads—to the least fork of the farthest stream. The Bay was now ascendant. It dominated the commerce of the region. Its rules and customs were virtually the laws of the region. Occasionally it liked to honor one of its foremost men by geographic nomenclature. It was during this period that the magnificent mountains which David Thompson had named Nelson for the Hero of Trafalgar became the

Selkirks, "in honour," says one account, "of Lord Selkirk, the founder of the Selkirk colony on the Red River, and one of the most enterprising patrons of the Hudson's Bay Company." The account might well have added that no mountains could have been named for a more kindly or greater-hearted man.

Since time began for the Hudson's Bay Company, its first item of peltries had been beaverskins. For at least three centuries, beaver was the preferred material for gentlemen's hats. Then, in 1825, at the fashion capital of Paris, the Florentine silk hat was introduced. Man, no less than his wife, is subject to vogues. The silk topper was a sensation. Only the most casehardened gentlemen were immune. The classic beaver hat started a decline that was soon to leave it an antiquity.

Possibly no man was quicker to note a trend presaging an economic change than Governor Simpson. It was not long before the Bay Company was operating a sawmill at Fort Vancouver and selling boards in the Sandwich Islands and elsewhere. The Company also began trading for salmon which were salted and exported. It organized a subsidiary, the Puget Sound Agricultural Company at Fort Nisqually, which contracted to supply the Russians in Alaska with hay, grain, vegetables, butter and cheese; and shipped wool, hides, horns and tallow to England.

Meanwhile, Dr. McLoughlin disciplined the natives as he thought best, using what appears to have been kindness and fine judgment. He would not trade rum to the Indians save in the high Rockies where his traders had to compete with the Americans. His over-all policy with and discipline of the natives was such that the trails and river

routes, which in the twenties and early thirties were subject to robberies and murders, became comparatively safe
even for unarmed travelers.

Soon or late, all travelers to and in the Oregon Country called for one reason or another at Fort Vancouver.
Here they were customarily met with a kindly if reserved
welcome by Dr. McLoughlin. Botanists, missionaries, promoters, traders, even downright crooks, one and all they
found occasion to stop at Fort Vancouver. One rather difficult guest was the young Scotsman, David Douglas, fanatically interested in flora, who cruised the wilderness
from California into British Columbia, undergoing priva-
tions and dangers as great as those of any voyageur. He
identified many species, some for the first time, and his
name was later given to the noble Douglas fir. He was a
sour man who repaid McLoughlin's hospitality by remarking there was no officer of the Bay Company "with a soul
above that of a beaver skin."

There came, too, to the fort, a strange and consecrated
character from New England, Hall Jackson Kelley, who
considered himself God's own messenger in respect to settlement of the Oregon Country. He is mentioned here
chiefly because he succeeded in touching off a sequence, a
sort of apostolic succession, which was of the greatest
influence in the American colonization of what for all
practical purposes was a province of the Hudson's Bay
Company. In 1831, during what he thought was a visita-
tion, Kelley incorporated under Massachusetts laws the
American Society for Encouraging Settlement of the Oregon Country. Though he had never been nearer the place
than the eastern shore of Lake Champlain, which was

Vermont, he prepared literature and posters showing beyond question where God intended His Yankees to settle. Kelley's statements had all the assurance of the complete fanatic.

Kelley meant that his settlers of Oregon were to be no weak little group of pioneers. His legion was to number five thousand, including a "regular army" of five hundred men, mounted and "armed with light rifles, pistols and sabres." As to the quality of his colonizers, he minced no words: There must be no vicious characters, nor drones, nor even "cunning persons without virtuous principles." And he would not tolerate "idle dreamers." Ironically, that was the term often applied to Kelley himself. Idle dreamer. Dreamer he might be, but never idle; and though most folk called him mad, there was really nothing wrong with his plan except it was premature, and even then by no more than a dozen years.

Up went Kelley's posters all over New England. Recruiting handquarters was at 18 Cornhill, Boston. Agents were appointed in each Yankee state. In all his talk and literature, the place of settlement was referred to specifically as "that portion of the American Republic called Oregon."

Kelley's campaign made a big noise. It did not, however, attract more than a handful of men who set forth, with Kelley himself, by way of New Orleans and Mexico. His few "colonists" deserted in New Orleans. In Mexico his trade goods were confiscated. Kelley kept on. Two years after he left Boston he arrived at Fort Vancouver, a very sick man. McLoughlin refused him the gentlemen's table and had him housed in one of the shacks, which was good enough for him who had spoken of "that portion of the American republic called Oregon." Yet he gave Kelley medicine and sent him away on a company ship to the Sandwich Islands where he took passage for Boston. For a few years more, Kelley continued to write and speak of the wonderful country along the Columbia, and at last he died in poverty.

Kelley's apostolic successor began long before his death, when Nathaniel Jarvis Wyeth of Cambridge, who had been impressed by Kelley's dream, fitted out a ship and cargo and sent it around the Horn for the Columbia. Wyeth himself, heading a small party, set out overland. At Fort Vancouver he was received as a distinguished visitor, though McLoughlin gave him the bad news that Wyeth's ship had been wrecked. Wyeth set out almost immediately to return to Boston. Most of his party elected to remain, one of them, John Ball, to teach the quarter-breed children of McLoughlin, and the youngsters of other officers who had married Indians, and thus become the first school teacher along the Columbia.

Back once more in New England, Wyeth set about organizing the Columbia River Fishing & Trading Company, a stock venture. The West had got thoroughly into his blood, and his enthusiasm plus his known integrity made it fairly simple for him to raise the money. Outfitting a ship with supplies for trading, and gear for taking and salting salmon, he sent her around the Horn, and set out overland with a company that included seventy traders, hunters, and trappers; two scientists, Thomas Nuttall and John K. Townsend; and Methodist missionaries Jason and Daniel Lee. The Columbia River was the goal of both the ship and the party. With the latter went a train of 250 horses carrying more trade goods, these on contract for the Rocky Mountain Fur Company. When Wyeth reached the place of rendezvous on the Green River, however, the Rocky Mountain people refused to accept the goods. This was a sore blow. Wyeth had cited this contract, which involved $3,000, to attract capital to the enterprise. Here he was now, in the wilderness, and nobody to buy the large amount of goods he had bought for another's account. He acted with characteristic promptitude. On the Snake River in present Idaho he started whacking up a trading post. "Having done as much as was requisite for safety of the fort," he wrote in his Journal, "and drank a bale of liquor and named it Fort Hall, in honor of the older partner in our concern, we left it and with it Mr. Evans in charge of 11 men and 14 horses and mules and three cows."

Wyeth and party arrived at Fort Vancouver one day in September (1834) to find that his ship still had not arrived. It came next day, delayed three months because she had been struck by lightning and needed much repair. Wyeth had expected that she would have long since been in the Columbia to get, cure and load spring salmon. But it was now too late for any considerable number of fish. Wyeth dispatched her to the Sandwich Islands on a voyage of trade, while he and his men set about building a trading post on Sauvie Island where the Willamette enters the Columbia, a few miles below Fort Vancouver.

It is probable that Wyeth made some sort of agreement with Dr. McLoughlin not to interfere with the Bay Company's trade and that he, at his new Fort William on Sauvie Island, would be permitted to trade for salmon and cure them for export. In any case, McLoughlin wrote his principals that "Captain Wyeth has most honourably kept his word." So, apparently, did the Company, though it is certain that McLoughlin, who treated Wyeth with every honor and courtesy, managed to undermine the Columbia River Fishing & Trading Company before ever it had started. One observer wrote of the Bay Company and Wyeth that "they preceded him, followed him, surrounded him everywhere and cut the throat of his prosperity with such kindness and politeness" that the Bostonian was induced to sell out to "his generous and too indefatigable, skillful and powerful antagonist." That was what presently happened, and though he and McLoughlin remained fast friends ever after, Wyeth was glad to get out of the fish business. Events during the first season had been too much. While leading a trapping party to the source of the Deschutes River, four of his men were lost by drowning or were killed by Indians. Several more died of illness at Fort William. He himself nearly died. So he abandoned Fort William, and sold Fort Hall on the Snake to the Bay Company, then returned to Boston.

No figure in the early Oregon Country has had greater appeal to those who knew him. Wyeth's great courage and energy were factors in his popularity. So was his honesty. Others felt he was their friend because he sought to break the Bay Company's monopoly. When he left the West for good in 1836, apparently a failure, he was just thirty-four years old. Back in Cambridge, he resumed the position he held at the time of his adventure to the Columbia, that of superintendent of the ice business established by Frederic Tudor. Wyeth went on to help Tudor earn his title of Ice

King of the World. To this end Wyeth invented special saws operated by horsepower. He made a great auger to bore through a field of ice that had water on top, thus to drain it. He adopted the curved slip and endless chain used at sawmills—making a moving belt from pond to warehouse. Under impetus of his mechanical genius and Tudor's salesmanship in domestic and foreign parts, the concern which shipped only twelve thousand tons in 1836, a decade later shipped sixty-five thousand tons. In 1849 the export figure was one hundred fifty thousand tons. At the time of Wyeth's death, in 1856, the Tudor Ice Company dominated the ice business of the world. By then, too, the Hudson's Bay Company had long since retired from the Oregon Country.

Though Nathaniel Wyeth failed to establish an empire in Oregon, or even a successful trading post, he brought with him, and left on the Columbia, an able apostle to carry on the work which Hall J. Kelley, the Oregon Fanatic, had declared to be God's own mission. It will be recalled that it was Kelley who first interested Wyeth in the West. In Wyeth's second overland party to the Columbia, as mentioned, were the Reverend Jason Lee and his nephew, Daniel, Methodist missionaries. Nobody believed more devoutly in God's designs than Jason Lee. His original plan had been to found a mission in the Flathead country of the interior, but his visit to Oregon made it clear that this was the country God had chosen for his efforts. Specifically, the Willamette Valley, that lush, green and damp region extending south from the Columbia for more than a hundred miles. So, in 1834, the Lees settled not far from present-day Salem and soon opened a school for the natives.

Jason Lee believed no more devoutly in God's designs than he believed that God was in favor of majorities, a sound enough American proposition anyway. Within a year or so after his arrival there, Lee had come to think that this Oregon, now in the hands of a British concern, could be taken, exactly as poor old Hall Kelley had declared it could be, by colonization. With the mission school now established, Lee turned his talents to politics. Making the rounds of the few scattered settlers in the Willamette Valley, about half of whom were retired veterans of the Bay Company's trap lines and trading routes, Lee managed to get signatures to a petition he drew up requesting that the United States provide a territorial government for Oregon. This he sent to Washington.

Nothing came of the petition. The energetic Lee was far from discouraged. He himself returned overland to the Atlantic coast and in person presented a second petition to the government. He remained in the east for nearly a year, talking up his mission and the need for American government. Congress failed to act. Then, in May of 1840, Lee arrived at the Columbia in a ship with a party of fifty-one new settlers which his eloquence had shaken from their native homes. This party went into Oregon history, with capitals, as The Great Reinforcement. It was well named. Not before had so large a number of genuine settlers come into the region. Most of them promptly took farms along the Willamette River.

In less than a year all the settlers in the Valley were

called to a meeting to discuss how best to dispose of the property of a pioneer who had died leaving, so far as was known, no heirs. The deceased was Ewing Young, possibly the wealthiest settler south of the Columbia in Oregon. Because the mass meeting to dispose of his estate quickly turned into something of a political affair that got results, the name of Ewing Young occupies a solid place in Oregon history.

Young leads us back to Hall Kelley again. Young was one of Kelley's few converts who had come to Oregon with him. He was a decent, honest and extremely able man, none of which could have been said about most of the others who had attached themselves to Kelley on his way West. Indeed, several of these were horse thieves or worse. The Spanish governor of California called them as much in a letter which came to Dr. McLoughlin at Fort Vancouver ahead of the Kelley party. As a result, McLoughlin gave the lot of them a cold greeting. This included Ewing Young, who staked out a farm in the Valley, but was refused seed for planting by McLoughlin.

Now, Young not only was not a horse thief; he was one of the leading men in the Rocky Mountain fur trade. For many years his headquarters had been in Taos. He had given Kit Carson his first training. Young himself had headed whole brigades of trappers which had followed beaver streams all over the mountain country. His unjust treatment at the hands of McLoughlin was a notable insult. It was worse; it acted as a blight. Other settlers, who well understood the power of the Hudson's Bay Company, feared to have any dealings with Young lest they too fall into disfavor with the Bay Company's autocrat at Fort Vancouver.

Young was not a weakling. Being refused seed and other supplies both at Lee's mission and the Bay's trading post, he announced that he was setting up a whiskey still on his place, that it would soon be in operation, and that he proposed to sell the product to all comers, red man and white man alike. It is believed that the still had been a part of the equipment Wyeth had brought to his trading post on Sauvie Island and then abandoned. Young's announced plan horrified the Rev. Jason Lee, who had already organized a temperance society. McLoughlin was also against rum. Distiller Young soon received a letter asking him to abandon the project and offered to reimburse him for any expenses already incurred.

Being a man of good will, Young replied to the temperance group that he would do as they wished, the still should not go into operation, and that he would not accept any recompense. He also took occasion to air his views on current conditions in Oregon. "The reasons for our first beginning such an enterprise," he wrote in regard to the still, "were the innumerable difficulties and tyrannizing oppression of the Hudson's Bay Company. . . ." This was an astonishing talking-up, and Dr. McLoughlin may have regretted the misinformation that had caused him to class Young among thieves. The factor was doubtless anxious to make up for the slip, and a course to do so was offered by Lieutenant William A. Slacum, U. S. Navy, who just then arrived at Fort Vancouver with orders from Washington to see how the American settlers in Oregon were doing, a mission, incidentally, that was touched off by complaints made on his return to Washington by Hall Kelley, who made it appear that the honest American settlers were being harassed and lorded over by the Hudson's Bay Company, a British outfit of aggressive monopoly.

Lieutenant Slacum was the diplomatic sort. He had no difficulty in clearing Young's reputation. McLoughlin was happy to offer to supply Young with seeds. Slacum had another good idea. Seeing that the settlers needed nothing more than cattle, he organized a company to buy cattle in California and drive them overland to the Willamette Valley. He even induced McLoughlin to take stock in the venture. When Slacum sailed out of the Columbia a month later, he took a party with him, headed by Young, to get and fetch the cattle.

By the time Young's party returned to Oregon, driving more than six hundred head, Young had won the reputation of a fearless leader. The drovers had to fight a running battle with Indians through the Siskiyous. Young knew how to fight Indians. He also kept his own men under discipline with a heavy hand, and they quickly came to see the mountain-man abilities of this competent pioneer. The trip was highly successful. The settlers got their cattle. As for Young, he emerged a hero. He was also a pretty fair businessman. What was more, as one historian put it, Young performed an odd service to the American cause by dying intestate in 1841.

The meeting of settlers to dispose of Young's estate was well attended. They elected a judge "with probate powers." They elected four justices of the peace and four constables, and named a committee to frame a constitution and draft a legal code. It was the first get-together of several out of which came a provisional government that was to last from 1846, when the Oregon boundary dispute was settled, until Oregon Territory was formed in 1848 as a part of the United States. The birthplace of Oregon is generally held to have been Champoeg, on the bank of the Willamette, where many of the meetings were held. The site is now cherished by the State of Oregon as a public park.

Dr. McLoughlin must have known, with the arrival of Jason Lee's Great Reinforcement, that the end of joint occupancy could not be far off. Over the years the Bay Company's factor had prevented more than a trickle of settlers from driving their stakes north of the Columbia; and in 1841, the company itself, in an attempt to have settlers it could control, brought twenty-three families from Red River in Canada and helped them to begin farming around the company posts on the Cowlitz and the Nisqually rivers in present Washington. Yet, at some point in the early 1840s, it became apparent to McLoughlin that the swell of American migration would break the bounds of the Columbia River. This point may have come in forty-three, still known in Oregon as the year of The Great Migration.

In May of 1843, an astonishing concentration of people gathered at Independence, Missouri. Without any general plan they had come from the border settlements and from farther east. They had suddenly been taken with the newest fever of their kind, the Oregon Fever. Either they or their fathers had been through migrating fevers before.

They were professional pioneers almost, and this time they were going to rut the Oregon Trail so deeply it could be seen a century afterward. Almost nine hundred of them were crossing the Missouri border into Kansas on the early morning of May 23rd. By the time they reached the Willamette Valley, the settlers already there had adopted their plans for provisional government. It is worth knowing that many of these Americans, who had set forth with desire not only to get and settle a farm but with belligerency toward Great Britain because of national excitement over the "Oregon Boundary Question," were grateful when they reached the Columbia gorge, with its fearful surge of dangerous water, to find some boats waiting to take their women and children safely through the rapids. They were the boats and men of the Hudson's Bay Company, sent expressly by order of Dr. McLoughlin.

The Great Migration of forty-three was followed a year later by another almost twice as large. In 1845 the wagon trains brought no less than three thousand settlers. The Covered Wagon was joining the *Mayflower* as a symbol of America. The ship of the great plains was on its way into song and folklore. Until the very last of the Covered Wagon people passed, they remembered the biggest sun and the biggest moon in the biggest skies they had ever seen. It was the hottest sun, and the coldest moon; and the sky or something played cruel tricks. Mirages danced ahead of their wagons, or flickered in their wake; and the youngsters cried with joy, then wept bitterly as a handsome blue lake suddenly appeared, shimmering cold and inviting for a few moments, then sank out of sight into the horizon. It came to seem that their goal and the horizon were moving in unison; they weren't getting anywhere. The wind never ceased. It blew out of hell, then from the antipodes. It piled up purple murk that split in thunderous crashes, and out of it came salvos of cast-iron hailstones to stun the imagination and to fell oxen.

Some said the sun was worse than the wind. Here in the great void there was no getting away from the sun. You could not hide from it. Worse was its confusing brightness. A gopher was seen plainly to be a coyote, a clump of sage-brush became a mounted and plumed Indian; a wrecked and abandoned wagon grew and grew until it loomed like a monstrous barn with weather vanes that glinted, then fused with nothingness. But on went the Covered Wagons, and out of the wagons, when desperate men saw that Time was passing them, that they must mend their pace lest they be caught in a mountain winter—out of the great wagons went a massive bureau of carved oak, or a chest, a chair or two, or even an organ. Winter must not find them on the trail; out went the furniture. . . . Parkman the historian saw the furniture along the trail that led to Oregon. He recognized, as did lesser men, that these things were not the mere trumpery of households, but were the last physical evidence of family importance, or at least of family continuity. They were not discarded lightly. Next to food and powder, they were the last things to be left along the way. The family who jettisoned them was a family in desperate straits. . . . These were some of the things talked or thought about in later years, when the Pioneers gathered for reunions and remembered their youth in the circle of campfires blinking like small red eyes in the endless dark.

The Covered Wagons of 1845, with their three thousand immigrants, must have indicated which flag was to fly over the Oregon Country. It mattered little that American immigration in the following year dropped to half that number, for in that year joint occupancy came to an end. The boundary was fixed at the 49th parallel. And the Hudson's Bay Company began to move out of Fort Vancouver and transfer its headquarters to Fort Victoria, on Vancouver Island in Canada.

Dr. McLoughlin, who had been severely criticized by his superiors in the Company for his humane treatment of the American settlers, did not go with the post. He retired to Oregon City, at the falls of the Willamette River, and declared his intention to become an American citizen. There he died in obscurity. By that time Fort Vancouver was a small city of Washington Territory, growing up around a long-established post of the United States Army, soon to be called Vancouver Barracks.

Chapter 5

Oregon Is Born

THE HUDSON'S BAY COMPANY was still in process of moving out of Fort Vancouver when an event of the first importance in establishing Oregon Territory occurred. This was the Whitman Massacre.

Marcus Whitman and his wife Narcissa were Americans and Presbyterian missionaries. Narcissa was one of the first white women who crossed the Rockies. She had lived as a guest at Fort Vancouver while her husband built the mission station about twenty-five miles from the Bay Company's post of Fort Walla Walla, and she was remembered by the Vancouver people as a cheerful and good-looking, blue-eyed blonde woman, wholly devoted to her husband and the work of the Lord among the savages. Dr. McLoughlin had been most kind to the Whitmans and, when the mission house was ready, he gave them a large quantity of clothing and bedding, and also an order on the Bay post at Walla Walla for any flour and grain they might need. This was characteristic of McLoughlin. He himself and many of the Hudson's Bay people were Catholics. A year or so later he made welcome to the first Catholic missionaries, who were the Reverend Francis Norbert Blanchet and his assistant the Reverend Modeste Demers. For the next several years the center of religious work for Catholics throughout the Northwest was the little settlement called St. Paul, which the two priests established on French Prairie beside the Willamette where old veterans of the Bay Company's fur brigades had retired to farms.

The Whitmans had come in 1836. Now, eleven years later, they were still at their mission in the Walla Walla valley. Matters had not gone too well with them, and Whitman himself was contemplating closing the mission when tragedy came. Speculation and controversy have attended the affair; and though there seem to have been several contributing factors, the Whitmans appear to have been marked by fate to be victims of the brutality and cynicism of the early fur traders. Then, there was the fact that Whitman was a physician, a medicine man, a sorcerer. Medicine men were good only so long as their charms, which were pills and bottles, worked beneficially. When they didn't, medicine men might expect trouble. There were a number of examples of Indian medicine men being killed by relatives of patients who responded to charms by dying. Even at a later period, when Lieutenant Phil Sheridan was stationed at Fort Yamhill, Oregon, he often let a native medicine man hide in the fort's cellar when a patient had died.

Dr. Whitman had successfully treated many scores of Indians. Now and then, naturally, one had died. This was not well, and to the record was added the fatal suspicion, dating back to the trick played on the Coast Indians at Fort Astoria by Duncan McDougall, who had threatened to pull the cork of a bottle which he said contained smallpox. No terror could be greater. There were other items:

Whitman and his brother missionaries often used poisoned meat to rid their settlement of wolves. Some of the multitude of dogs around the Indian encampments died from eating the prepared meat. Nor did it help matters that the Indians around the Whitman mission, who thought it less than a venial sin to steal melons from the Whitman garden, got a good stout dose of emetic carefully placed in the fruit as a discouragement to thievery. But worse—worse than all else—was the recent epidemic of deadly measles which had spread throughout the middle Columbia region, taking many native lives. Had Whitman pulled the cork from McDougall's bottle?

Omens of evil had appeared during the summer. There had been more destruction of mission property than usual, and several acts of personal violence. Whitman and his brother missionaries had noted a tendency to "return to gambling, licentiousness and sorcery." Several Hudson's Bay men had warned Whitman that his life might be in danger; and Paul Kane, a Canadian artist visiting at Fort Walla Walla, heard an Indian deliver a speech lasting some three hours which apparently had to do with the necessity for revenge for a war party that had been killed by whites in California. Kane himself was so disturbed that he mounted a horse and rode promptly to the mission to warn Whitman that his charges were getting out of hand.

The blow fell on November 29, 1847. That morning the white people were busy with their customary tasks. An unusually large number of Indians gathered on the premises. Weapons were hidden beneath their blankets. While one of the chiefs engaged Dr. Whitman in conversation, another tomahawked him from behind. The massacre was

87

on. The Whitmans and twelve more were killed. Fifty-odd were taken captive. Of the several who escaped death and capture, Peter Hall made his way to Fort Walla Walla to report the disaster, then set out alone downriver and was never more seen.

Factor William McBean at Fort Walla Walla sent a canoe courier with the news to Chief Factor James Douglas, McLoughlin's successor at Fort Vancouver. Douglas sent the news to George Abernethy who had been elected "governor of Oregon," which did not yet exist, by the American settlers. And without waiting for action by the Oregonians, Douglas sent one of his Company's best men, Peter Skene Ogden, with sixteen paddlers up the Columbia to see what could be done to rescue the mission survivors.

Ogden's bold rescue of the captives has been called "one of the noblest chapters in the history of the Hudson's Bay men." He was just the man for it. Calling all the Cayuse headmen to Fort Walla Walla, this tough veteran of the trails gave them a tongue-lashing in their own language. He began by chiding them for allowing their foolish young men to sway their judgment; he went on to deny that Dr. Whitman had poisoned their people; he warned them that if the Americans should now begin war, they would wipe out the whole Cayuse tribe. He told them that though he could not promise to prevent war, he could give the Indians some sound advice; and wound up by saying that if the Cayuses would deliver the captives safe to him at the fort, he would pay ransom.

It is probable that Ogden was the one man whose advice the Indians could take without loss of pride. He was known to them, and to Indians all over the Northwest, and throughout the mountain country, as Uncle Pete, a white man to be believed, to be trusted, and to be feared as well. The chiefs were quick to accept Ogden's proposal. The captives were delivered. Ogden paid the ransom, which consisted of sixty-two blankets, sixty-three cotton shirts, twelve Company muskets, six hundred loads of ammunition, thirty-seven pounds of tobacco, and twelve flints.

While Uncle Pete was treating with the Indians at Fort Walla Walla, the provisional government of Oregon acted. It had no militia. In its treasury was $43.72. Yet within thirty days a regiment of five hundred men was recruited at Oregon City, in the new village of Portland, and from scattered farms and settlements in the Willamette Valley. The Hudson's Bay Company advanced supplies valued at $1000 on the personal pledges of Governor Abernethy, Jesse Applegate, and Asa L. Lovejoy; and from the Methodist mission on the Willamette these men got an additional loan and supplies amounting to $3,600. This was enough to begin a war, and the home-grown army set off for the Cayuse country. Shooting started near The Dalles. Another battle took place near the Deschutes River. There was more fighting on the Tucannon and Touchet rivers, and chase and skirmishes continued until harvesttime (it was then 1848), when a majority of the Oregon army was released to return to their farms, but the murderers of the Whitmans had given themselves up, and more than fifty Oregonian soldiers volunteered to remain in the troubled region and man the posts that had been established during the war.

To get word of the Whitman massacre to Washington, the provisional government sent a messenger overland. He was Joe Meek who before settling in the Oregon country had walked over much of the West in company with Jim Bridger, Kit Carson and other noted Mountain Men. He arrived at the national capital a huge, buckskinned, ragged, lousy and dirty fellow, to become a sensation for the public of Washington and the entire press of the East Coast. Declaring himself to be "envoy extraordinary and minister plenipotentiary from the Republic of Oregon to the Court of the United States," he painted the massacre in all its horror, prompting President Polk to demand immediate action by Congress to establish Oregon Territory.

A bill to admit Oregon as a territory had been before Congress for a long time, and it had been consistently delayed by Southern members with the idea of incorporating an amendment permitting slavery. Even now, with the country aroused over the Whitman disaster, and the settlers engaged in a full-scale Indian war, the Oregon bill was delayed another two and a half months. It was passed August 13, 1848, and President Polk appointed General Joseph Lane territorial governor and Joe Meek United States Marshal.

While these events were going forward, Oregon's volunteers were fighting or chasing Indians over a region roughly bounded by the Cascade Range and the Rockies. Governor Abernethy had for months been expecting a regiment of United States troops to discipline the Cayuses. What he got, instead, was the U. S. Transport *Anita* which brought no troops, but delivered an Army recruiting officer who had come especially to raise an Oregon battalion for service in the war with Mexico. This was typical of the delays due to its remoteness from Washington which harassed the new territory until the telegraph came.

At last Army troops did come, and eventually they were quartered in the new barracks at Vancouver. By then the Cayuse troubles were virtually over, and five of that tribe had been hanged at Oregon City in connection with the Whitman massacre. The drop was released by United States Marshal Joe Meek, who used a tomahawk for the purpose.

The Whitman massacre and resulting Cayuse war are generally credited as being the urgencies which established Oregon Territory much sooner than otherwise might have been the case. The Oregon Country, which for a quarter of a century had been dominated—and governed well for the most part—by the Hudson's Bay Company, was now free of the British. Chief Factor James Douglas had moved to take up his headquarters at Fort Victoria, named for the young Queen, on Vancouver Island which, in 1849, was declared to be a Crown colony; and Douglas himself was appointed its governor. His Company's posts continued to trade and rule the vast interior from the Arctic to the 49th parallel. This boundary had finally been agreed upon after considerable horse trading and some excited talk of "Fifty-four Forty or Fight" by Americans.

South of Forty-nine, the Columbia flowed to the sea through American territory which was being rapidly if sparsely populated. North of Forty-nine was Canada, and there the river continued to flow through a wilderness silence that was to be little disturbed until the railroad should come, thirty years in the future. A trapper could still trade his beaver or marten for powder and tobacco at Bay Company posts throughout the British Columbia interior. To say that the Queen ruled the empire was a pleasant and harmless fiction. The real ruler of the Queen's wilderness in her British North America dominions was yet, as it had been for a century and a half, the Company of Adventurers Trading into Hudson's Bay.

For twenty-five years past, Fort Vancouver had been the center of commerce and civilization on the lower Columbia. With the Bay Company now departed, Vancouver quickly lost its dominating position. Oregon City at the falls of the Willamette River had taken its place. But soon Oregon City was being left behind by the rising new settlement of Portland. The two places were only twelve miles apart. Both were on the banks of the stream Captain Clark had named Multnomah but which instead had become, by stages, including Wallamt, Wahlmet, Wilarmet, and Wilhamet, to be spelled Willamette and pronounced, surprisingly enough, with accent on the second syllable.

The more one reflects on it, the more does the rise of cities seem to depend often on some slight thing or event having little to do with the site selected. Sometimes, it would appear, the difference stems from a single person. The case of Portland, which was to become the largest city on both the Willamette and Columbia rivers, comes to mind.

Even with the hindsight of a century, many an Oregonian believes he would have chosen Oregon City in 1850 rather than Portland. Those great white tumbling falls, pouring over a rock ledge, dropping full forty feet, must have looked to the early settlers, as they look today, to be the best place along the Willamette to found an industrial city. Portland's site could offer nothing, save for a fair stretch of level ground on both sides of the river. Oregon City had a steep hill to contend with. Yet hilly ground, as Seattle and Tacoma were soon to demonstrate, will not prevent the rise of a metropolis.

No, it was something other than level ground that made Portland. A weatherbeaten deep-sea skipper, who wore on occasion one thumping big gold ring in an ear, had something to do with it. "To this very point," declared Captain John H. Couch, late of Newburyport, Massachusetts, "to this very point I can bring any ship that can get into the mouth of the Columbia. And not, sir, a rod further."

This was not quite true, but near enough. Captain Couch had taken ships to Oregon City, though the shallows where the Clackamas entered the Willamette were most troublesome at low water. But the captain was a man of no halfhearted opinions. He had also decided to sail the seas no more, but to settle in Portland, a site on the west bank in which for the sum of twenty-five cents, Asa Lawrence Lovejoy, from Groton, Massachusetts, had just bought a one-half interest. His partner in the enterprise, who was Francis Pettygrove from Maine, had to pay "$50 in store goods for his half." Captain Couch staked out a donation claim adjacent to the property of Lovejoy and Pettygrove. "He was instrumental," wrote a local historian, "in getting many of his seafaring friends to bring their ships to Portland, in place of landing at some rival community."

The two proprietors of the new settlement put a small crew to work felling some of the gigantic Douglas firs that covered most of the site. In spite of which, Lovejoy was elected major of Oregon City. But this did not deter his ambitions. He and Pettygrove went ahead to plat a few streets among the stumps, and to consider a name for their town. Pettygrove won the toss of a coin and called the place Portland for the principal city of his native state, thus contriving the most notable opportunity in the United States for the misdirection of mail. Still, it could have been a little worse. Lovejoy, who possessed no more soaring imagination than his partner, wanted to call it Boston. Neither seems to have given thought to the unique Multnomah, which was later attached to the county that contains Portland.

Captain Couch's forthright statement traveled far. He enjoyed a fine reputation for reliability, and back in New England, where Yankee merchants and speculators were already leaving for the West Coast, looking not for a placer mine but for a place where they might exercise their native talents, he was heard and believed. The Yankees came, starting a tradition that seems still, a century later, to have some influence on foot-loose New Englanders.

In 1849 a leisurely Post Office Department got around to approving Portland with an office and a big round postmark. (Astoria already had a post office.) A year later the village boasted, and may well have had, eight hundred inhabitants, a log-cabin hotel, a *Weekly Oregonian*, and a steam sawmill with a whistle that could be heard on a still day in Oregon City. There was a fine civic spirit from the first. Municipal improvements included the whitewashing of the many monstrous stumps standing in the un-lighted streets to prevent collisions with teams and pedes-trians.

Across the Columbia, Fort Vancouver, as related, was becoming an Army post in spite of desertions. In the spring of 1850, 120 soldiers took off without leave for the gold diggings in California. On the way up the Willamette Val-ley they pretended to be a government expedition, getting food and other supplies on credit from the settlers. Things went fine until they got to the Rogue River where they were attacked by Indians. Less than half of the crew man-aged to cross the river. Hard on their trail came Territorial Governor Lane and Army Colonel Loring, with a few squads of volunteer Mountain Men. Several groups of the desert-ers were found in the Umpqua Valley, half starved, and were quite willing to return with Lane and their colonel to Vancouver. A school was opened in Vancouver, and a ferry started to carry passengers and goods between the two cit-ies. Vancouver was soon made the seat of the newly organ-ized Clark County.

There were other cities downriver competing with Portland. Captain H. M. Knighton had laid out a town on the south side in 1847, calling it Plymouth, then changing it to St. Helens because of the white-crested peak a few miles to the north which Captain Vancouver named in honor of a fellow countryman, Alleyne Fitzherbert, Baron of St. Helens. Not far from Knighton's new town, boosters platted the city of Milton and opened an aggressive land-shark office in Portland. The Columbia River presently un-did their labors by washing Milton down the river and out to sea.

Most boosters of the time believed that what their town needed to put it on top was a steamboat. Dr. McLoughlin had believed no such thing. Although he didn't want it, and had told his directors it would be of no help in doing Company business on the Columbia, the directors went ahead, anyway, built a paddle steamer in England and sent her across the Atlantic and around the Horn. She was the *Beaver*, copper-sheathed all over, powered by two thirteen-foot paddles, and needing a good nine feet under her keel. She was as ugly as sin, and she was the first steam

The *Beaver*, first steamer on the Columbia.

vessel in the Columbia and on the Pacific Coast. She reached Vancouver in 1836, and at least one who saw her there was amazed. Wrote the American missionary, the Rev. Samuel Parker, of the *Beaver*: "It was wholly an unthought-of thing that I should find this forerunner of commerce and business." A steamboat on this remote river set

him to reflecting on the speed with which the "improvements of life" were being introduced in the new world, and
he saw "cities and villages springing up in the West" and
a new empire being added to the kingdoms of the earth.

But Dr. McLoughlin greeted the vessel coldly. He
could find little for her to do on the Columbia, and shortly
he sent her off to Fort Nisqually on Puget Sound. Both there
and at Fort Victoria she was to perform great services for
another fifty years or until 1888, when she was wrecked in
the harbor of the other Vancouver, which was growing into
the metropolis of British Columbia.

The *Beaver's* departure left the Columbia and the Willamette without a steamer. A few locally built sailing craft
and keelboats did all the river work. But steam was very
much in style, and the men of Oregon City, no less than
those of Portland, St. Helens and Astoria cried for steam.
An inhabitant of Oregon City heard the call. History has
not done him justice, for he is remembered in print only
as Mr. Truesdale, yet he put together the most wondrous
vessel ever to ply the Willamette. She was a craft eighty-two
feet long operated, not by steam, nor yet by sail or oars,
but by six strong horses on a treadmill. She worked, too.
Truesdale took her down to Portland, twelve miles, then
back up to Oregon City in three hours, even crossing the
swift water where the Clackamas comes in with little trouble. But something or other must have been lacking. Mr.
Truesdale and his six-horsepower rig do not seem to have
got into print again.

It was left to a reviving Astoria to launch the first
locally built steamboat on the Columbia. The oldest settlement on the river had faded almost to extinction as soon

97

as the Hudson's Bay Company dismantled Fort George-Astoria and transferred its activities to new Fort Vancouver. As late as 1841 a visitor had described Astoria as "a miserable squatter's place." Nothing remained except one disreputable cabin and an old shed. Yet, the river was still there at its door, and so was the sea. There were men coming who liked a big salty river.

So, in the year of the Great Migration, which was forty-three, a covered wagon immigrant decided not to stop in the promised land of the Willamette Valley. He was J. M. Shively. He pushed on down the river and staked his claim in what for several years was to be called Shively's Astoria. Two more adventurous settlers came to stake claims adjacent to Shively's, and these were known as McClure's Astoria and Adair's Astoria. The energetic Shively made a trip to the Atlantic Coast, and when he returned in 1847 he brought with him his commission as postmaster and promptly opened the first post office anywhere west of the Rocky Mountains. For the next six years Astoria was the post office for distributing mail to Oregon, Washington, Idaho and Montana.

The California gold strike, news of which hit Oregon in 1848, drew a number of Astorians to the diggings, but the town continued to flourish from sawmills that had opened just in time to meet the almost incredible demand for lumber on the Mother Lode. A year later the United States eatablished a customs house at the rejuvenated Astoria. Almost simultaneously, Captains Hustler and White "arrived and brought with them the first pilot boat to operate on the Columbia River, the Mary Taylor." From this time onward, the growing numbers of river pilots were to make their headquarters at Astoria. Then, on the glorious morning of July 3, 1850, citizens John Adair and James Frost launched the vessel on which they had been working for many months. She was christened the *Columbia*, even though, as some non-Astorian took pains to observe, she was no gem of the ocean, or even of a river. But she was the first Columbia-built ship and that is fame enough. She was a double-ender, much like a ferryboat, a side-wheeler ninety feet long, and she was all functional. She was none too well built, either, but when steam got into her cylinders she would go.

On this memorable day in Columbia River history, Captain Frost headed his primeval steamer against the current on her maiden trip. He didn't know just where the channel lay, but he probably worried more about his engine than the channel, for the *Columbia's* speed was nothing to beach her hard in any event. She plodded along until dark, which came late in early July, then Captain Frost brought her in to the bank and moored her to a convenient tree. She had done a good fifty miles. Frost felt pretty good. Next morning, both ship and crew refreshed, the *Columbia* cast off and continued upstream. By three o'clock, when she came abreast Portland, she was coughing loudly. Frost let go her whistle, and the new city's water front was soon lined with a good share of its eight hundred citizens who, it being the Fourth of July, were in a suitable condition to welcome the biggest and only steamship in all Oregon Territory. The Portlanders cut loose with enthusiasm. An hour later the *Columbia* docked at Oregon City.

The *Columbia* was a success. She began regular service between Astoria and the upriver towns. Passengers had to bring their own food and blankets. Between trips from Astoria to Oregon City and return, she did general towing work, and went to the Cascades to bring down immigrant parties. Captain Frost charged high rates and for six months he had no competition and reputedly made a lot of money. When a new steamer, which we shall come to presently, proved too fast for the *Columbia,* the latter's engines were removed and put into the *James F. Flint,* a middle-river vessel that had been wrecked when she ventured below the Cascades. Now the *Columbia-Flint* became the *Fashion* and as such did a good business for ten years or so, running from Portland to the Cowlitz, then up to the Cascades. She was junked in 1861, and her engines may have gone to work in some sawmill, which was the fate of many other marine engines on the river.

The vessel that took the palm from the *Columbia* was the *Lot Whitcomb,* built in the new city of Milwaukie rising beside the Willamette between Portland and Oregon City. She was no jerry-built scow like the *Columbia,* but first-class in every department. From her keel that was a solid stick of Douglas fir to her pilothouse, the *Lot Whitcomb* was a fine ship, a side-wheeler 160 feet long, with fourteen-horsepower engines that could drive her twelve miles an hour. Christening her called for all of the pageantry that Oregon Territory could muster. Governor Gaines came to make a speech, on this Christmas day of 1850. Many other dignitaries were present. Between speeches the Army's brass band from Vancouver Barracks played stirring marches. Cannon were fired, one of which blew up and killed a celebrant. Otherwise, all came off in fine shape, and the affair closed with a grand ball.

The *Lot Whitcomb* went immediately into service, undercutting the *Columbia's* extortionate rate to Astoria from $25 to $20, then to $15. Within a year she defeated the ocean vessel *Goliah* in a race from Astoria to Portland. Her usual schedule was two round trips a week between Oregon City and Astoria. Though Milwaukie was her home port, the town did not grow as had been expected by the *Whitcomb's* builders and owners; and the vessel was sold in 1854 and went into service on California's Sacramento River. Of infinitely more importance to the Columbia than the *Whitcomb* were her two officers, Captain John C. Ainsworth and Chief Engineer Jacob Kamm. They did not go away with their vessel, but moved to Portland. Theirs was to be the story of the Steamboat Era on the Columbia.

Chapter 6

The Steamboat Era

STEAM-PROPELLED VESSELS were seen to be in-comparably better than sail, yet it took a war and a couple of gold rushes to bring a genuine steamboat era to the Columbia. The war began brewing soon after the Whit-man murderers were hanged, as we have seen, at Oregon City. The Cayuse tribesmen had been tamed, but not so the other tribes of the Columbia basin and Puget Sound regions. The Klickitats and the Yakimas especially did not like the way things were going; settlers were arriving now in such numbers as to make an Indian fear for his fishing grounds, his hunting grounds, and to wonder if these white people would leave him room even for his village. Added to the settlers were the wild men who called themselves miners and who had come up from California and were even now ranging up every creek, looking for gold.

The Federal government was slow in making up its mind what to do with the tribes already driven from their hunting grounds. But the settlers would not wait. Men who had walked two thousand miles or more to take up land wanted surveys, courts, protection; and wanted them now. Late in 1852, some of these importunate men acted. Fifty delegates representing settlers north of the Columbia and west of the Cascade Mountains, gathered at the home of Harry Darby Huntington, a leading figure who named his settlement on the north bank of the river for his hometown back in Indiana, which was Monticello. This new Monticello was near the point where the Cowlitz River entered the Columbia and where seventy years later the city of Longview was to rise.

The fifty delegates were feeling their oats. They thought the time had come to break away from Oregon Territory with its "remote capital" of Salem far up the Willamette Valley; and to this end they drew up and signed a memorial to Congress, asking that "all of that portion of Oregon Territory lying north of the Columbia River and west of the great northern branch thereof, should be organized . . . under the name and style of the Territory of Columbia."

During committee work on a bill in Congress, the proposed name of the territory was changed to Washington, and its boundary lines designated to run along the Columbia to its intersection of the 46th parallel, near the mouth of the Walla Walla River, then due east to the summit of the Rockies. This virtually doubled the area suggested in the original petition. To govern the new division President Franklin Pierce appointed Major Isaac Ingalls Stevens, a West Pointer with a fine Mexican War record. Late in 1853 he arrived to enter this capital alone, tired and hungry, unnoticed by the few citizens of Olympia.

The wagon trains continued to roll into both Oregon and Washington territories. Occasionally they were attacked by Indians. As delegate from Oregon in the national capital, Joseph Lane had been raising his voice to demand protection for the immigrants; and in the fall of 1852 the Fourth Infantry took up quarters at Vancouver on the Columbia. The regimental quartermaster was First Lieutenant U. S. Grant. The Indian attacks continued sporadically, but during the year Grant was to be at Vancouver the fighting was too remote to involve the Fourth Regiment. Something of an explosion of violence was, however, in the making. Over in the Yakima valley, on a tributary of the Columbia, a Yakima chief named Kamiakin had started to lay plans for war on a scale that was far too great for the average savage mind to contemplate. Meanwhile, all was quiet at Vancouver. The officers drank considerably more than was good for them. Army morale was at a low ebb, anyway. Many of young Grant's old friends of West Point and Mexican War days already had resigned their commissions and entered civilian life; but what troubled Grant most of all, as he contemplated what he expected was to be a long tour of duty in this remote spot, was how to earn extra money to bring his wife and babies here to Vancouver. Perhaps the experience here on the Columbia of the future commander of the Northern Army is worth a brief interlude.

Intent to bring his family to the Northwest, Grant looked around for some method to make an extra dollar. Other young officers at the post had a similar urge. Hearing that ice was bringing fantastically high prices at San Francisco, Grant and two others bought a hundred tons of it and shipped it to the California city in a Pacific Mail schooner. The wind turned, the trip occupied six weeks, and meanwhile the ice market went to pieces. The scheme was an expensive failure. Potatoes might be the way to wealth. Borrowing money at 2 per cent per month from Lieutenant Colonel Benjamin Louis Eulalie de Bonneville, who commanded the Fourth, Grant and a partner ordered seed potatoes from California, bought a pair of worn-out horses from a covered wagon immigrant, and rented a fine piece of black-soiled land on the Columbia's bank. The two men plowed and planted, then sat back to await harvest and a big cash return. Their hopes rose with the tiny green clusters shooting up and which by June were great plants promising a prodigious crop. Just then the river suddenly came over its banks and destroyed most of the nearly ripe crop. This was bad enough, and it was common talk in the officers' mess that Bonneville held the debt onerously over his subordinates and that for his part Grant had to borrow the amount from a sergeant to pay his commander.

Other troubles came thick. Most of a flock of chickens which Grant and his partner bought and shipped on a chartered vessel died before they reached San Francisco. Then came the strain of fitting out a surveying party headed by a perfectionist, Captain George B. McClellan. Little Mac was a hard man to please. For almost a month he harassed Lieutenant Grant night and day; and one day the lieutenant grew tired beyond bearing. He drank himself into a quiet but obvious spree. Captain McClellan was greatly annoyed. Grant resolved to resign from the Army. And this he did a little later despite the fact that, after a decade as a first lieutenant, he was promoted to captain and transferred to Fort Humboldt, California. While at this post Grant "respectfully tendered" his resignation. It was approved on June 2, 1854, by the Secretary of War, who was the Honorable Jefferson Davis.

By the time Grant was out of the Army, the plans of Yakima chief Kamiakin were well along. This able and highly intelligent man had done his best to get along with the whites, even adopting several of their ways, urging his tribesmen to plant gardens and to maintain a herd of cattle. But it would not do, and he watched with increasing alarm while Indians who had contact with whites quickly degenerated from liquor and disease. Discouragement came over him, even as it had Lieutenant Grant, and he concluded that the only salvation for his people was to kill or drive every white person out of the Northwest. Not just out of the Yakima country, but everywhere that they cursed the land with their presence.

Kamiakin's plans were not the windy talk of chiefs bragging to their people. He moved quietly up and down the region, conferring with the headmen of all the tribes, explaining a campaign which he believed would wipe out white civilization in one great attack. First, the sawmill settlement of Seattle would be taken and sacked. The victors would then raid the Puget Sound forts at Nisqually and Steilacoom and burn the white man's capital at Olympia. At the same time other raiding parties were to attack isolated farms all the way from the Sound to the Columbia. Simultaneously, the Yakimas and Klickitats would sweep down the Columbia and take Fort Cascades, the key position to the invasion of Oregon. This fort Kamiakin knew to be ill equipped and manned. It must fall at once, then the braves would push on to take Fort Vancouver.

On the same day, so the great chief planned it, the Oregon coast tribes were to wipe out the small settlements, mining camps, and farms on the Umpqua and the Rogue rivers, then swarm into the comparatively populous Willamette Valley. They would meet their brothers of the Yakimas and Klickitats at the ruins of the white man's military headquarters of Vancouver. To prevent aid from newly arriving immigrants, the Snake tribes would stand across the Oregon Trail and massacre the wagon trains before they had reached the Columbia.

Such was the general plan of Kamiakin. The details were to be worked out as the day approached. It was a magnificent plan of strategy, conceived on a monumental scale compared to anything the Northwest tribes had known. To put it into effect, Kamiakin in person continued with quiet eloquence to rouse the many tribes involved.

Some two thousand warriors took the field. They were defeated at Seattle by the presence of Navy men-of-war and no little cannonading. They failed to take the Puget Sound forts at Nisqually and Steilacoom. They were frustrated elsewhere because the settlers had hastened into forty-odd blockhouses that were hurriedly erected when rumors of war came to the whites from friendly Indians. But all over the Northwest the families on isolated farms were butchered and their homes burned.

And finally Kamiakin sent a band of his best men to lead the Cascades Indians in an attack on the blockhouse erected by soldiers at the Cascades in the Columbia's gorge. This fort, as related, was the key to the campaign in western Oregon. It must be destroyed before the braves could attack the many farms and settlements in the Willamette Valley. The attack was made. Sixteen whites died in the fighting. But the attack was repulsed. The over-all plan had failed in every instance. There were simply too many whites to be exterminated by two thousand red men, no matter how well they fought. Led by Colonel George Wright, Lieutenant Phil Sheridan and others, Army troops chased and harassed the defeated warriors over much of eastern Washington, and at last, in 1859, Congress ratified peace through ten or more separate treaties with the tribes involved.

That the blockhouse at the Cascades was built so quickly and manned, and that other posts were ready for the Indian attacks, was due in no small part to the new steamboats on the Columbia, among them notably the *Jennie Clark*, different from all other boats on the river. She was a stern-wheeler, designed by Jacob Kamm and Captain John Ainsworth, the latter her master, who had decided that neither side-wheelers nor screw propellors were the best type for the Columbia and Willamette. The *Jennie Clark* took the water just in time to help move troops, ammunition and supplies from Fort Vancouver and Portland to the Lower Cascades. Captain Ainsworth found her wonderfully responsive to the helm. Her stern wheel was just the thing for maneuvering in swift currents and narrow channels. She was comfortable to ride in. And she could outrun any boat on the river.

The Indian uprising also stimulated the building of

two steamers at The Dalles. These were the side-wheelers *Mary* and *Wasco,* which ran downriver to the Upper Cascades from their home port. Between the Upper and Lower Cascades, the owners of the *Mary* laid a portage railroad, six miles of wooden tramway with mules for power. This facilitated movement of freight. It was much faster than packing everything.

The blockhouse at the Cascades.

During the years of Indian wars, stray prospectors found gold in the Walla Walla valley of the Columbia basin. The news got around, and with the end of the fighting, a small rush of would-be miners headed for the diggings. It didn't amount to much, but it touched off another stampede, this time to the Clearwater River country in Idaho. In a little time the seekers were spreading all over the eastern portions of Oregon and Washington, and were combing Idaho's streams and gulleys from Boise City north. The quickest way to get to these places from the west was by the Columbia. The few boats on the river were loading at Portland with all the miners and provisions they could hold.

It was the kind of emergency that has always prompted a few men to rise equal to the emergency. In this instance one of this kind of man was the same Captain Ainsworth, master of the *Jennie Clark* who, it appears, had already seen the advantage of making a monopoly of a good thing. He had proposed to the several individual owners of steamers a series of agreements in regard to rates, routes, and schedules. But after a brief trial the agreements were seen to be too loose. There were no disciplinary methods. And the steamboat men, so it turned out, were still at the mercy of the operators of the portage railroad at the barrier of the Cascades. The attempt at monopoly broke down.

Captain Ainsworth was only thirty-eight years old in 1860, yet he had seen a good deal of steamboats as a master on the Mississippi, again on the Sacramento; and he was thoroughly convinced that the proper way to run a river line was as a monopoly. So, with a few friends and associates like Jacob Kamm and Simeon Reed, the latter a Portland businessman who happened to own a few boats, and R. R. Thompson, who operated a stern-wheeler above The Dalles, Ainsworth incorporated an outfit that was to dominate the Columbia almost to the virtual end of the steamboat era. This was the Oregon Steam Navigation Company. Into it went the six major boats below the Cascades; four others that operated from the Cascades to The Dalles; and Thompson's stern-wheeler which operated above Celilo Falls just east, or upriver, from The Dalles. And, shortly after its organization in 1862, the company got control of the portage road, then supplanted the wagons and mules with a steam railroad.

The monopoly was now complete. From Portland to Astoria, and from Portland to the far inland points on the Columbia and the Snake, the OSN was in control. The time was propitious. Few concerns have started business with such prosperity from the beginning. The wild gold seekers, still hoping for another Mother Lode, continued to demand river passage as far as a boat would take them. In its first year of operations the OSN was running boats up the Snake to Lewiston, every trip a heavy payload. During 1864 when the Idaho rush was at its height, the company made a clear profit of $783,339, a figure that doubtless would have seemed astonishingly high to almost anybody other than shippers who had occasion to use the monopoly's boats.

Rates were high enough. Freight from Portland to Lewiston was $120 a ton. A ton, according to the OSN's way of thinking, was not two thousand pounds. It wasn't as simple as that. It was a ton of cubic feet. The method for assessing the cubic content of a farm wagon, for instance, was to measure its extreme breadth, its extreme length with the tongue extended and its extreme height with the tongue turned straight up. Only then was it rolled aboard and the tongue tucked beneath the wagon box. Or so the legend has it. In any case, the company was not formed to carry freight for a penny less than the traffic would bear; and many stories were told to illustrate the "unconscionable greed" of this outfit that charged about ten times as much a ton-mile as was common on Missouri River steamers. When a merchant at The Dalles was asked why he charged twenty-five cents for a single darning needle he said: "Madam, you forget the OSN freight charge."

The company was in many ways a hard-boiled concern. Captain Ainsworth watched out for the interests of his stockholders, and the whole lot of them made a great deal of money quickly. Yet the company had many of the virtues associated with pioneering. No passenger was denied a ride if he had no money but really needed to go somewhere. No shipper, especially no settler, was refused his freight simply because he could not pay on delivery. The company would wait, and wait it did, often for many years before the bill was paid. Ainsworth took a long view of matters. He planned that the OSN should grow up with the country.

And grow it did. Though Ainsworth and his associates differed from one another in personality, and often in character, they shared, as Fred Lockley who knew many of them wrote, one trait in common. They were magnificent fighters and when they joined forces in the OSN and "requested a competitor to sign on the dotted line, he usually signed or lived to regret his refusal." When a new group, the Merchants Line, entered the trade, OSN promptly cut its own freight and passenger rates. The Merchants joined. When the Peoples Transportation Line built the fine *John H. Couch* and put her on the Astoria run, the OSN placed their *Julia* on the route, announced a ridiculously low fare, and soon took the *Couch* and two other Peoples' steamers into camp. Another effort, which was organized as the Washington Territory Transportation Company, and headed by Donohue, Kohl and the well-known Captain Ankeny, brought the big stern-wheeler *Cascades* from Puget Sound and put her on the lower Columbia. After a single trial run, she became just another boat of the OSN's fleet.

There was no beating the Monopoly. The Columbia River Transportation Line, whose president was the able Levi Farnsworth, lasted less than a year, then its *Celilo* and *Pioneer* started to fly the OSN's house flag. There were to be other boats, many of them quickly shoddy-built and placed in service on the river with no idea other than to sell them at fancy prices to the OSN. The Monopoly did not pay fancy prices, and it did not want shoddy boats in its fleet. But it would and often did pay an owner so much money a month just to keep his craft off the river.

Captain Ainsworth meant also that any boats on the more profitable runs of the Columbia's tributaries should be operated by the OSN. He organized a subsidiary, the Oregon & Montana Transportation Company, and on Lake Pend Oreille in Idaho had the *Mary Moody* built to run on the Clark Fork. Her timbers and lumber had to be hewed and whipsawed by hand on the spot. Packing in the machinery was done at enormous cost. And the *Mary Moody* never returned a dollar of profit to the company. But she accomplished her main purpose, which was to hold the Clark Fork inviolate for the OSN. Nor did another far-inland boat make any money. She was the *Shoshone*. The OSN had her built at Fort Boise, Idaho, near the head of navigation on the Snake. No matter that she failed to repay her cost, she made history on the river.

The *Shoshone* is one of the great stories. She was built out back of beyond, on the very edge of nowhere, with the idea that she would make a fortune carrying men and goods in the gold rush. She was little more than finished when the rush petered out, so she was tied up more than six hundred miles from where she might be of some use, which was Portland. Worse, there lay between her and the Columbia's main stream some three hundred miles of water which had never known a steamboat. The Snake above its junction with the Clearwater was held to be unnavigable, a supposition that was not far from the truth.

Now, Captain Ainsworth, over in Portland, was no man to enjoy the thought of an OSN boat idling and drying out at a dock. He sent an order that the *Shoshone* be brought down to the main river. On her first try, her skipper gave up at Lime Point. He tied her up and reported that Copper Ledge Falls of the Snake could not be run by man or devil. For another season the *Shoshone* remained idle where she lay, with two watchmen aboard. Then Ainsworth sent two of his best men to bring her down—Captain Sebastian Miller and Engineer Dan Buchanan. If these two couldn't do it, said the head of the OSN, then she might as well be burned where she stood.

Captain Miller was already a noted river character. As pilot on the *Elk*, a small stern-wheeler on the Willamette run, he was present when her boiler blew up, taking the cabin, the stack, much of her deck, and Miller himself high into the air to be scattered around on water and land. Miller was somewhat shaken, but basically undamaged. Now he and Buchanan were on their way to see what could be done with the *Shoshone*.

Getting to the *Shoshone* was something of a trip in itself. The two men traveled by boat as far as Umatilla, then started in a buckboard over the Blue Mountains. The road gave out. Snow came on. They discarded the wagon, made a sled, and went on until the snow gave out. They rode horseback for fifty miles or so. The horses gave out. The men walked the rest of the way, and came to the *Shoshone* in her wilderness berth, in mid-April.

Captain Miller immediately signed on her crew, who were the two watchmen on the boat and one other man who seems to have come out of the earth or down from the sky. They set to work overhauling the engines. Miller and Buchanan found them serviceable, but did not like the look of the vessel's seams, which had opened wide from the weathering of more than a year. Miller didn't want to spend valuable time calking them; and Buchanan allowed they would tighten sufficiently by pumping water over the boat for a while. This was done. The planks swelled somewhat. Enough to keep her afloat, Miller thought. While they worked, the river began to rise. It was time to start if they wanted plenty of water under the keel. Fuel was piled aboard, a fire put under the boiler, and when steam rose to the popping-off point, Miller and Buchanan, with the crew of three men, cast off and headed into the boiling Copper Ledge Falls.

It was going to be quite a voyage, and it did not even begin well. Miller misjudged the power of an eddy at the falls and the *Shoshone* was swept around three or four times as though on a turntable, wracking her terribly, before Miller could get her straightened out for the run through the worst water. At the first drop of the falls, the boat tilted forward and let the paddlewheel go spinning furiously out of water. At the second drop, the wheel spun again, then dipped, and a sizable piece of her paddle which had become brittle from long weathering, broke off, letting the boat run wild and crash into rocks that took eight feet off her bow in a second. The vessel not only shivered; the impact sprang the safety valve free and steam shrieked until Buchanan, down in the engine room and by then pretty well shaken himself, could get the weight back on the rod and close the valve. Miller brought her to shore below the falls, and they tied up to repair damages.

After two days of furious work, Miller cast off again, and they proceeded through rapids and eddies, and such brief calm stretches as the Snake offered, shipping enough water to drive the fireman out of the hold, but otherwise getting along pretty well, even in the swirling treacherous miles of the canyon where the walls rose seven thousand feet above the river. They had to tie up again for minor repairs and to replenish with fuel. Captain Miller was felling trees when a log knocked him down, and out. When he had got his wind and senses back, off they went again. On April 27 they came through the Wild Goose Rapids, rocking like a long box on the white water, and were soon at Lewiston, only 140 miles from the Columbia. Here they tied up and all hands went ashore, looking for the OSN agent, to show him that the *Shoshone* had come through battered but safe, if not quite all in one piece. She had been given up for lost when her jackstaff had been found floating downriver near Umatilla four or five days before

Bringing the *Shoshone* down the Snake to the Columbia.

Miller and boat arrived at Lewiston. The jackstaff had snapped off somewhere in the upper Snake. Captain Miller and his crew were greeted as men who had miraculously returned from the land of the dead.

The *Shoshone* worked briefly on the middle river as a cattle boat; then went on down the Columbia to shoot the Cascades, with Captain Ainsworth himself at the helm, and was put in service on the Willamette after being hauled on skids around the Oregon City Falls. Within a year this hardy vessel which had run waters that were never run before struck a rock in the quiet river near Salem, and sank. A freshet removed and sent her hulk careening down the Willamette and deposited it on the bank near Lincoln. Here a farmer hacked off her cabin and made it into a snug chicken house. In the eight years of her career, two of which she had spent idle, the *Shoshone* had seen as much of rough life and times as any boat on the river. Perhaps any river.

Keeping their monopoly of the main river in a tight grip, the OSN continued to run things as its shrewd officials thought best. Yet the quality of their boats and the service given never let down. They improved steadily with the years. This was due in some part to John Gates, chief engineer, a State-of-Mainer under whose supervision was built such beautiful and efficient craft as the *R. R. Thompson,* the *Harvest Queen,* and the *Wide West,* of which more presently. Gates invented a hydraulic steering gear, an automatic oiler and many other improvements. He built a total of twenty-four big boats for OSN and was highly regarded not only for his talents but because of his staunch character. While still employed as chief engineer for the river concern, he was elected mayor of Portland.

There was one thing you could be sure about in regard to the Oregon Steam Navigation Company. Even its worst critics, of which there were many, agreed that the company's boats left Portland at the times advertised. They might be late elsewhere, late even in arriving at Portland, but they left their home port on the dot. If you were going upriver from Portland, you had better be early at the dock. By half-past four the passengers started to arrive. Twenty minutes later the last freight had been stowed. The pilot climbed to his little house. The big stern-wheel turned lazily a few times, bells rang, the lines were cast off, and a pillar of steam shot up from the tall escape pipe. The stacks were already belching smoke and cinders. The wheel started to churn, and the long white vessel backed out into the Willamette's current. You could set your watch by her. It was five o'clock.

As she entered the Columbia and turned east, the passengers went in for a bountiful breakfast. After touching briefly at Vancouver, the boat started upriver in earnest. In a short time she was in the gorge, and by eleven o'clock she docked at Lower Cascades. There was a wait here while freight was transferred to the little cars of the portage railroad. Passengers got aboard to sit in the small and rather elegant coaches. Six miles brought them to Upper Cascades where everybody and everything had to be moved to one of the middle-river boats of the OSN fleet. It might be time for dinner when she pulled away, and it surely was evening when she arrived at The Dalles. Meanwhile those passengers in need of refreshment could find it in the boat's barroom. Captain Ainsworth had at first been against bars on his vessels, but he broke down in time. The OSN leased its bar concessions at what reputedly was a stiff price. The concessionaire, who was usually also the bartender, says Randall Mills, ranked high enough to be addressed by the honorary title of captain.

At The Dalles the traveler likely put up at the Umatilla House, probably as fine as anything in much larger Portland. It was known to harbor fleas and bedbugs —as what pioneer hotel didn't—but its fittings and furnishings were quite gorgeous, even to the rococo desk and "the most elegant key-rack in the state of Oregon." There were 123 rooms and two baths, an imposing ratio for the time and place, plus a toilet in the basement. The dining room was enormous. So were the amounts of good food put before the guest. No hotel on the whole river appears to have been recalled with more pleasant nostalgia than the Umatilla House.

If he were going still farther, the traveler spent the night at The Dalles, then rose at dawn to catch the train on the portage railroad for Celilo. There he could board another OSN boat that would get him to Umatilla city by midafternoon, and still on to Walulla in time for supper. Next morning he might take another steamer for the run up the Snake to Lewiston, or get a stage for Boise, or Salt Lake City.

The several gold excitements played out, but by then the OSN had a new and more stable business to care for.

Early settlers in the Walla Walla valley were raising enormous crops of fine wheat. Downriver shipments of it started in the mid-sixties. In 1867 a cargo of it was delivered in San Francisco at a good profit. Within the next year a British ship sailed from Portland with a hold filled with wheat for Liverpool. Sawmills at Portland and other lower river places were cutting lumber for export, but this product was commonly loaded from dock direct to deep-sea vessel and hence meant little to the OSN. Wheat was what for many years permitted the OSN to pay fat dividends.

The nearest port to the wheat growing country of the Walla Walla valley was Walulla on the Columbia. To it lumbered big six- and eight-horse wagons, operated by freighting outfits which, so claimed the farmers, charged rates well beyond exorbitance. For a decade the farmers complained. They even threatened, idly enough, it turned out, to build a railroad. It was no farmer but a practicing physician, Dr. Dorsey Syng Baker, who did something about it. Dr. Baker was a pioneer who had crossed the plains from Illinois. He was as bearded as Moses. He was also the most energetic and purposeful figure in the Walla Walla country; and when, on his rounds, he became tired of the grumbling on every hand about the lack of a railroad, he swore he would remedy the condition.

As good as his word, he collected a crew of wheat hands, cowhands and Indians, and set them to making grade over the thirty-two miles between Walla Walla City and Walulla. He got a charter. He sent to Pittsburgh for a locomotive and several sets of car wheels, and put a gang of carpenters to making freight cars and a couple of passenger coaches. In the matter of rails, however, he refused to pay the cost of iron. "Preposterous!" he called it. His trains, said he, were to run on wooden rails on which he would lay a thin strip of metal.

That is exactly what happened; and on a wondrous October day in 1875, the first train of Dr. Baker's home-grown Walla Walla & Columbia River Railroad ran the entire distance from Walla Walla City to Wallula on the Columbia. It was successful from the beginning, and the cost of moving a ton of wheat, which in freighting days had been $6, dropped to $1.50. Good Dr. Baker was more than ever a hero.*

Baker's line took care of the Walla Walla valley's wheat crop, but there were other grainfields coming into production along the Snake and the middle Columbia, and there were no railroads to serve them. The product had to be toted by wagon to what was called a wheat landing. Getting to a wheat landing, especially on the Snake between Lewiston and the Columbia, was something of a task. Mile after mile the Snake flowed in a deep and narrow gorge. Team and wagon had to descend a steep pitch to get down to the water. A dragging log was used for a brake; or the load might be snubbed down. In either case it was a slow and dangerous operation.

His name is lost, but somebody suggested letting gravity do the work. In 1879, at a Snake wheat landing, shippers built a wooden pipe, four inches square, and laid

* Baker's pioneer railroad eventually became a part of the Union Pacific. It also went into folklore as The Rawhide Railroad, one of the most popular myths in the region and which I treated in some detail in a previous book, *Far Corner*, published in 1952 by Macmillan.

it from the canyon rim to the river. At the first trial the wheat went down with such speed that it was ground into coarse flour. It also cut holes in the pipe. The chute was rebuilt with a series of upturns, or baffles, and this time it worked. The wheat came out at the bottom in perfect condition. This was the answer to getting grain down to the stern-wheelers. Similar chutes were built at Ilia, Kelley's Bar, Moxwai, and other wheat landings, some few of which continued in use after railroads had supplanted most of the river fleet.

The ingenious chutes at the wheat landings, plus the steady increase in grain production, often inspired local writers to describe the Columbia as "a majestic, broad highway to the mighty Pacific." This was all well enough. The Columbia was indeed majestic. It was broad, in most but not all places; and it was a sort of highway to the mighty Pacific. But for shippers in the seventies and eighties it was no easy path to market. At least one clear-eyed reporter looked at it, then described exactly what happened to a sack of Walla Walla wheat before ever it reached salt water. It was first hauled, he said, to the railroad warehouse in Walla Walla City and there stored. Then it went by Doc Baker's line to Walulla where it was transferred to a boat and taken to Umatilla; at Umatilla Rapids it was transferred to another boat for Celilo; at Celilo it went through a warehouse and to a car of the portage railroad and was wheeled to The Dalles, and stored again even if briefly; then it was put aboard a boat and taken to Upper Cascades, and there transferred by portage railroad to Lower Cascades. Here it was put into the hold or on the deck of another boat for Portland. At Portland it was stored again, and at last was loaded into an ocean-going vessel, and so away to the deep. The complicated process was gradually simplified by the coming of canals and locks, and by that time railroads were moving much of the wheat.

For all the rapidly increasing freight traffic, the OSN found it profitable to attract and hold passengers, and in 1877 real elegance came to the river in the company's new boat, the pride of Chief Engineer John Gates. This was the *Wide West*, 236 feet over-all from stem to the waterfall of her stern wheel. With a virtually unsinkable hull, her cargo deck was planned to take 550 tons, and her two engines could drive her anywhere on the Columbia that a boat of her size could go. But it was her "appointments" where grandeur came in. The *Wide West's* main cabin and staterooms were tasteful "in a delicate tint of lilac," and the floors were covered with "handsome mosaic oil cloth. The dining room was filled with tables for four. Twenty-two cabins were fitted not with bunks but with gorgeous bedsteads, and were in most favorable contrast," wrote a Portland editor, to "the cramped-up little dens called state-rooms on eastern steamboats." The Ladies Saloon was done in pale lemon with gold beading on the doors. It was carpeted with Brussels.

Over the long main saloon was a clerestory ceiling of glass panes, some plain, others tinted so that the sun made bars of colors on woodwork and carpets. At night the room glowed from scores of nickel-plated lamps. All the decks were railed and scrolled with gingerbread. The *Wide West* was a real beauty. For a decade she was a continuous wonder to travelers, even those who had ridden the steamers on the Hudson, the Ohio, and the Mississippi.

After the *Wide West* came a host of fine vessels, some stern-, others side-wheelers, still others propellors. Among the best remembered appear to have been the *Telephone,* and the *T. J. Potter.* Into the latter's hull went the same dependable engines that had moved the *Wide West,* and the side-wheeler *Potter* continued to make records for another twenty years. As late as 1899, when the OSN had long since been reorganized as the Oregon Steam Railway & Navigation Company, it built the swift *Hassalo,* third of the name which, using the new locks at the Cascades, swept over the Portland-The Dalles run "like a scared greyhound of the river."

For a while the OR&N got some competition from the Regulator Line which operated two fast boats. But the old company, with "Railway" now added to its title, was more interested in transportation on rails than on the river. Traffic on the middle and upper rivers was steadily if slowly decreasing, anyway. After the turn of the century came agitation for an "Open River"; and hard-shelled river-boat men organized an Open River Navigation Company which, despite the times, brought about an astonishing revival of activity for a brief period on the upper river and the Snake. The activity, of which more later, soon subsided. Few people could have doubted but that the heyday of river transportation was in the past.

Chapter 7

Coming of the Steamcars

THE STEAMBOAT era on the river did not end with the coming of railroads. It persisted for another three decades even while orators at picnics of pioneers were bemoaning its passing. Almost nobody wanted it to pass. The people who lived along the river had come to love the stern-wheelers as old friends—even to love the side-wheelers and the propellor boats. The great long vessels, white as snow and pouring black smoke from tall stacks, moved swiftly against the backgrounds of town and forest, making a picture none ever forgot. They were a picture at night, too, a long row of lighted windows gliding through the dark, into and out of the mists, their voices giving notice to isolated towns that all was well on the big river; or again, muted by fog and distance, sounding melancholy notes that haunted one's memory long after the grunts of diesel engines had become common if not particularly pleasant sounds on both land and river.

A few of the great names of river steamers persisted in memory and remained while young boys grew to manhood, and aged in an era when transportation had generally discarded boats and trains for automobiles and planes.

The names persisted because boys along the river knew all the boats and liked to catalogue their knowledge by listing to each other, as a sort of catechism game, the magic identifications—the *Joseph Kellogg*, the *Shaver*, the *Telephone*, the *Baily Gatzert*. They also could recognize most of the whistles and tell you it was the *Undine* blowing for the wharf, or the *Ione* fleeing past with a mere salute.

The name of a stern-wheeler appeared on elaborately lettered boards on three sides of the pilothouse, again on the prow, and still again on the fancy box that covered the paddles. The names might indicate a little bragging, like the *Active, Alert, Rescue, Relief,* and *Monarch;* or hopefully allude to speed as in *Fleetwood, Gazelle,* and *Otter.* Telephone was a popular name from the eighties until the last of the line in 1909. A *Telegraph* rode the river for nearly four decades. There were *Gamecocks* and *Beavers.* There was an *Eva,* an *Ellen,* a *Hattie Belle,* a *Julia,* a *Naomi,* four *Ruths,* and a *Three Sisters.* For forty-one years there was a *Georgie Burton.* And for forty-three years, the durable Shavers had a fine big *Sarah Dixon* on the lower river, honoring the matriarch of this pioneer family which, in mid-twentieth century, carries on as the oldest steamboat concern on the Columbia.

The fact that an era of river life was passing away even as I watched did not enter my consciousness all at once. It came slowly, but it did come; and one day twenty-odd years ago it occurred to me that if I wanted one more ride on a *regular* freight and passenger boat on the river, then I had best be at it. I had made several trips during the twenties, always with the greatest satisfaction. Even though passengers had never equaled the number of life preservers carried, and though the modest amounts of freight went mostly to places that still could be easily reached only by water, I had come to think comfortably that, like the railroads, there would always be a river line operating on schedules. Yet, one after the other, the boats on schedules disappeared. By the time I got around to my last ride on the lower river, only three such boats were left.

So, one July evening I went down to the East Oak Street dock in Portland and got aboard the little *America,* a propellor steamboat that was built and launched in 1912. At nine o'clock Captain John W. Smith let go a fine blast on the whistle, one of whose three components had once been a part of the *Iralda's* famous voice; and we headed down the Willamette, set for a voyage to Astoria and return which would also include many way points. Those way points were important to me. They were the towns which for one reason or another still had some use for a steamboat on regular call. Here and there we would touch at a town on a railroad, even on a highway; but mostly they were places without rails or modern roads.

It was twilight as we moved down the harbor, and I was struck once again by the fact that a citizen had never really seen Portland unless he had seen it from the river. The lights were coming on, and the old business blocks along the water front, many dating from the seventies, presented a façade of dated elegance such as one might have seen in old prints but nowhere else. It reminded me that Portland, and the lesser places we were to touch on this voyage, had begun life as a single street of buildings close to the river. In that day the river dominated everything. Settlements were laid out to accommodate the river. The river was the town's life line. Now, half a century and more later, I was to see the towns, and the stretches between them, much as they had appeared to travelers who had worn full beards and carried flowered carpetbags. The battered and weathered little *America,* still seaworthy and responsive to the helm, was taking me into what remained of the lower Columbia's past.

The past presently loomed up on our port as we came abreast of the battleship *Oregon,* moored in the harbor as a famous and cherished relic of the Spanish-American War, during which she had made a celebrated run from Puget Sound around the Horn in time to arrive at Santiago, Cuba, her guns blazing in the action that destroyed much of the Spanish navy. She looked graceful and still formidably sinister as we passed her in the twilight. (Her end came a decade later as a barge in World War II.) From the river I could also see the cast-iron Ionic columns of the long obsolescent Newmarket theater, which had become a garage; and the typical 1875 architecture of the block built and named for Jacob Kamm, once a noted man on the river. I even got a fleeting glance at the Boss saloon, a two-story frame flatiron structure which had been a favorite port for steamboat men on shore. This was the Portland that new arrivals saw in the gaslit days of the Oregon Steam Navigation Company.

As we passed the tip of the Peninsula, the *America* swayed gently to the swell of the main Columbia. First stop was at lonely Morgan's Wharf on Sauvie Island where Nat Wyeth's dream of a trading empire had died with

Fort William. It was dark now. We left no passenger or freight at Morgan's, but picked up one box of shad for a packing house at Kalama. At St. Helens, the old Island sawmill, long idle, loomed up blacker than the dark; but the main mill night shift was at work. The lights blinked. A low hum came over the water. We did not stop or even blow at Columbia City. Ten years before it had burned to the ground, removing its big lumber plant. Captain Smith told me that four families still lived at Columbia City and, once a week or so, they used the *America* to go shopping in Portland.

When the *America's* floodlight played on the wharf at Kalama, it revealed an old man waiting to receive the box of shad, and a short blonde young woman smoking a cigarette. She must have been an old customer, for she did not wait for any gangplank formality. With an easy leap she landed upright on the lower forward deck, waved at the wheelhouse and gave voice to the universal "Okay." The old man picked up the box of fish and moved slowly up the slip as we backed away. Off went our floodlight, and Kalama, "Where Rail Meets Sail," disappeared into the quiet night.

Now we headed across to Rainier, on the Oregon shore. Captain Smith told me that most of the people who traveled by boat those days did so because it was the cheapest transportation left. A few, he said, took the boat because they liked it, or because of long habit. Mostly, though, it was a matter of money. Captain Smith could see no future for river passenger boats. The *America* lived from day to day, and not very well. She was making no money for her owners. Some trips did not move sufficient freight and passengers to pay the crew's wages.

We had no fog on this trip, but fogs were common in fall and winter. Rotting hulks here and there were evidence of what could happen in soupy weather even to leisurely boats. In fog, you could do one of two things: tie up somewhere, or steer blind. So many minutes NNW, then so many minutes NW, and so forth. In the *America's* pilothouse was a special fog clock, really a large stop watch. You set it, say, for seven minutes. When the time is up, it rings. Then you shift your course and set the clock again for whatever your steering chart calls for.

We got one passenger at Rainier, then turned toward the Washington shore again. It was 1:50 A.M. when we stopped at Eagle Cliff where a load of fish was put aboard for Astoria. We had neither freight nor passengers for the next place, which was Puget Island, and no stop light was showing, so the *America* kept head on for Cathlamet. Once Captain Smith threw his floodlight toward shore and a hulk was framed in the beam. It was the remains of the old *Joseph Kellogg,* the captain said, which had come to grief here in a fog. Stripped of machinery by the owners and towed to the mouth of the Alocoman River, the natives hereabout had continued the stripping. Scarcely a chicken house or pigpen had gone up in the neighborhood in years, Smith said, but that some piece of the wrecked *Kellogg* did duty.

It was close to three o'clock when we docked at silent Cathlamet, one of the older towns on the river and where for decades all commerce had been by boat. A lone male carrying two suitcases walked down the gangplank and disappeared into the sleeping hamlet on the hillside. No one was at the dock to meet him or us. No freight was taken or left. At about half-past three we entered Steamboat Slough. Here the channel was so narrow that a few feet off the course either way would result in grounding. I could imagine it was no place to be in fog. We took it slowly enough in clear weather.

It was beginning to light up on the hills. Vague black things turned into shadows, then became recognizable objects. Captain Wiley was now in charge. He blew a short blast to let Skamokawa know, if it mattered, that the *America* was passing. Here we also passed Pillar Rock, a neolith rising abruptly out of the Columbia, on the top of which was a beacon light. Right off this light, Captain Wiley related, was where the *Welch Prince*, a deep-sea vessel, was rammed, and sank on the spot with the loss of several lives.

There was nothing aboard for the Altoona cannery, and nothing for Megler, so the *America* turned her nose for Astoria. I was sorry not to see Megler again, though I knew the little trains of the Ilwaco Railway & Navigation Company no longer came there to meet the Astoria ferry or the Portland boats. Even its tracks had been pulled up during the twenties. But from 1889 on, this railroad took passengers and freight from river boats to Ilwaco, then up to the end of a slim peninsula at Oysterville. Many Portland people used to spend a summer somewhere on the peninsula, and the Ilwaco company's trains, whose timetable was predicated on the tides, were kept busy during the vacation periods.

Steaming across the Columbia to Tongue Point I saw forty, maybe fifty small boats in the river, gill-netters already on the fishing grounds. When we tied up at the old Hammond dock, Captain Wiley pointed out the *R. V. Kruse*, a truly leviathan sailing vessel with five masts. It was built by Kruse & Banks on Coos Bay, Oregon, one of the last and finest of her kind. In crossing over the bar some years before, she had "broke her back," to use Captain Wiley's term, and was no longer seaworthy. In any case, she looked a beautiful ship and aboard her, I was told, was her old skipper who remained as a sort of watchman until her future was determined.

Just before we pulled away from Astoria, I was astonished and happy to see no less than nineteen passengers troop aboard the *America*. I began to think in ignorance that there might be a future for river boats after all. Captain John Shelley, the relief skipper, did not think so. It was the one-dollar-to-Portland fare that fetched them; and there was no profit whatever in hauling a passenger a hundred miles for a dollar.

The passage upriver in daylight was pleasant enough even to one who had been up all night. There were horses at work, water to their bellies, hauling the enormously long seines on a sand bar. There was the broad water stretching miles from shore to shore, and back of the shores rose the hills and mountains. Wherever you looked there was scenery; and it did not look from the river as it did from the railroad or the highway. There were the little towns to see—Svenson, Knappa, Kerry, Clatskanie, Mayger; and from the waterside they looked much different from the highway view, and twice as interesting.

At a few of these small places we picked up a passenger or two, and by the time we reached Portland in the afternoon we had thrity-six aboard. But we had taken on little or no freight. Thirty-six dollars could scarcely have paid the wages of the *America's* crew, to say nothing of the oil she burned, or insurance, and other fixed charges incident to operating a boat. Even so, thirty-six was an unusually large list I was told. On our way up the river, probably four or five hundred automobiles passed us. We were also passed by a passenger train of the Spokane, Portland & Seattle Railway. How many people it carried I do not know. But its haul, like the *America's*, was doubtless light. The very last run on this rail line, though I couldn't know it then, was less than twenty years in the future. By then the *America* was long since laid up and dismantled; and Astoria, the oldest town on the Columbia still stood on the riverbank, but it was no longer a river town, or even a railroad town. So far as travelers were concerned, you went to or left Astoria by plane, bus or motor car.

Though my voyage on the *America* was not the last day of passenger service on the lower river, it was late enough. The highway blight had removed all of the splendid boats and was about to remove the few small survivors. Like "last trains" of late years, there were innumerable "last runs" on the Columbia. No man in his right mind would care to say that this or that particular trip ended regularly scheduled passenger-boat service on the river. There have been too many claims made. But on March 20, 1947, and with full treatment by the press, the *Georgie Burton* made *her* last run anyway. It will do for a "Last Boat."

The run was made with no little ceremony, for this was a conscious effort to mark the end of something that in reality no longer existed. The *Burton* had been launched on the day of the San Francisco Quake—and fire —in 1906, and for forty years had served faithfully, hauling passengers and freight, towing some four hundred million feet of logs, pushing hog-fuel barges, and helping to dock and to move deep-sea craft in Portland's harbor. So, on this cloudy March day in 1947, she loaded at Portland and Vancouver with a host of veterans of the river, and away she went upriver, heading for The Dalles. Several old captains took turns at her wheel. Judge Fred Wilson acted as purser. She was locked through the lift at Bonneville Dam, and made good time in the slack water that had quieted for good the roaring Cascades. As she passed The Dalles, it seemed as if the whole town was out to watch her, and she continued on to the foot of Celilo Canal, then steamed back and docked at The Dalles. This was voyage's end for her. She was towed up onto land to become a marine museum, a fitting relic of the glorious era that had passed away in the smoke of locomotives and the fumes of internal combustion engines.

The railroad era was of course as inevitable as was the era which supplanted the trains and the rails. On the Columbia the railroads began as an aid to navigation, by moving people and goods around the troublesome portages. Next, in order of time, came Dr. Baker's little inland road to bring wheat to the riverbank where boats could take it, even while other men were projecting railroads leading out from the metropolis of Portland. The big thing was to make a connection with the new transcontinental from Chicago to San Francisco. With a land grant as a prize, two Portland groups started laying rails simultaneously on each side of the Willamette River, building south toward California. Into this battle came Ben Holladay, a jovial and devotedly vulgar character who had made his pile in stage lines and now proposed to put Portland on the map of the world.

Taking hold of the so-called East Side Line, Holladay financed his construction by selling bonds in Europe; took over the West Side Line, started laying track, and every few miles, for the sake of publicity, staged a celebration complete with brass band and hard liquor. He put together a coastwise and deep-sea ship concern. He laid Portland's first horsecar line. He bought a local newspaper. He installed ferryboats to cross the harbor and swore that East Portland, not Portland, was to be the mecca of population, commerce, and industry of the Northwest. He liked his nickname: the Duke of Oregon.

Holladay's empire suddenly collapsed. To salvage as much of it as possible, the (mostly) German bondholders sent Henry Villard, already a growing figure in American railroading, to Oregon. He surveyed the wreck of Holladay's hodgepodge and moved shrewdly and well to make of it a system of transportation. Into it he put the OSN, reorganizing it as the Oregon Railway & Navigation Company. He completed construction of the railroad to California. He started laying track up the south bank of the Columbia, got control of the Northern Pacific, and pushed

his own local road from Walulla on the Columbia across
the Inland Empire to connect with the Northern Pacific at
Spokane, thus giving Portland its first transcontinental
line. At about the same time he began a branch from
Umatilla, Oregon, to meet the Union Pacific's Oregon
Short Line at Huntington. This gave Portland a second
transcontinental.

To anticipate a bit, Villard overreached himself. The
Union Pacific took over his line across Oregon. The Southern Pacific acquired his line to California. And the Northern Pacific, of which he lost control, built across the
Cascade Range at Stampede Pass, far north of the place
where it crossed the Columbia, to reach Puget Sound.

The railroads at first did not have any appreciable
effect on the river business between Portland and the sea.
(There was to be no railroad to Astoria until 1898.) Passenger and express business dropped off at towns served
by the rails, but freight on the river boats actually increased. The wheat crop was growing steadily and it moved
almost wholly by water. The canning of salmon had grown
into an important industry, which called for no little river-
boat help. And topping all was the movement of logs and
lumber. The lumber moved in ship or barge. The logs
were gathered and held in a floating corral called a boom,
and towed.

The elegant passenger boats were of course doomed.
They were retired, or sold, as business declined; but other
new craft took over the growing demand for tugs and
towboats. From the early nineties to the present day, the
Columbia from the Cascades to Astoria has probably never

known an hour when there was not somewhere a tow of logs moving from booming grounds to sawmill. Both timber and salmon must be considered in more detail in later chapters.

The first effect of a railroad was usually on real estate. It was a capricious thing. A railroad could assure almost overnight the building of a town. It could demolish another town by ignoring it. The railroad took you wherever you wanted to go. It carried away whole communities that did not want to go anywhere at all. Steam locomotion, indeed, was filled with wayward fancies. It carried wealth and importance past one place to lay them down in another. In the Pacific Northwest, it whistled past old and important places like Fort Vancouver and Port Gamble to turn secondary hamlets such as Portland and Seattle into major cities. The seeming magic of the railroad also built up in most Americans such a belief in miracles that many of them fell easy prey to town boomers.

Town boomers came in several styles. It was difficult to tell for certain which was a true prophet, which was honest but mistaken, which was an out-and-out faker. On the Columbia the first town boomers, as mentioned, had made a fetish of the steamboat: This or that settlement was to grow into a big city simply because it was the home port of a steamer, or was sure to be a port of call, or maybe merely because it was a place where cordwood for fuel could be easily loaded. But a little later, when it was seen what sudden changes the new steamcars could bring, the public was ready to believe almost anything that enthusiastic—or merely clever and dishonest—men wanted to claim for a projected railroad. For quite a while, *projected* was a word to conjure with. Projected railroads cluttered the maps of Oregon and Washington from border to border.

It was so on the Columbia. Here and there, along both its banks for some seven hundred miles, town boomers raised their voices to announce the opportunity of a lifetime. You were told to move immediately to, or at least to buy a corner lot, in Metropolis, which came under several names. Thus it came to pass that the mists hanging over Gray's Bay near the river's mouth were wafted aside momentarily to reveal what a promoter was pleased to call Mighty Frankfort-on-the-Columbia. In press and pamphlet the Frankfort illusionists declared their city was to be the terminus of three railroads, not just railroads but transcontinental railroads. Many a lot was sold. Then the mists again enfolded Gray's Bay, and when the sun had cleared them Frankfort had evaporated into the keen salt-washed air.

But there was no fake about Kalama. It had steamboats. Then it "got the railroad." With the railroad it grew astonishingly until many believed it was to outstrip Portland. But it stopped growing and began slowly to fade. It seemed that nothing could stop the gradual decline, though almost everything was tried. "I have never," said Hite Imus, who ran a paper there for years, "I have never known a town whose citizens were so hopeful, so optimistic and so cheerful in the face of one defeat after another as those of Kalama."

The first settler was none other than Ezra Meeker, a covered wagon pioneer, who lived long enough past his era to crawl into an airplane at the age of ninety-four and fly back to his native Ohio, covering in a little more than forty-eight hours (it was 1924) the course he had followed for three months over the Oregon Trail. Back in 1853, he put up a cabin on the narrow flat where the Kalama River enters the Columbia, and staked his claim. Luck was with him from the first. A spring freshet brought down a large number of whole trunks of big Douglas fir. Meeker caught and brought them to shore, sawed them into proper logs, made them into a raft, got aboard and started floating them downriver.

Ezra Meeker and his log raft.

One perhaps can find no more typical incident to show the Pioneer at his characteristic best. Meeker was heading his raft of logs for the nearest sawmill, which was a few miles down the Columbia at Oak Point, Washington. The mill was offering $6 a thousand feet for logs. But the currents of the big stream, then as now, were not only powerful but wayward. When almost to Oak Point, Meeker lost control of his raft. It swept on, with Meeker still aboard. Well, Astoria had a sawmill, too. It was only a matter of forty-odd miles farther to Astoria, but he'd have to get the raft over on the Oregon side to land it. This he managed to do, and the sawmill man at Astoria was happy to pay Meeker $8 a thousand feet, instead of the $6 offered at Oak Point. With this fortune in hand, Meeker returned to his cabin on the Kalama. He didn't stay long. Possibly the fortune burned in his pocket. He left Kalama for Puget Sound, where Olympia was said to be booming.

Kalama grew very slowly until 1870 when, suddenly enough, the Northern Pacific Railway, which had started with government subsidy to build from Lake Superior to Puget Sound, unloaded a mountain of supplies at the modest Kalama dock, while other boats came to leave some thirteen hundred laborers there. It was announced that the railroad's terminal was to be here, in Kalama; and that work was to begin at once on a line from Kalama to Puget Sound.

It is probable that no town on the Columbia in the nineteenth century knew a greater boom than that which suddenly hit Kalama. The railroad gangs had money to spend, and you may be sure that arrangements were speedily made for them to spend it in Kalama. All sorts of boom characters came to town. Real estate was subdivided until all the narrow flat by the river was staked out into streets and lots. Then streets started climbing the steep hill. Somewhere among the boomers was the inevitable genius at slogan-making. A blinding light struck him, and Welcome signs went up at the expanding Kalama dock—

KALAMA, WHERE RAIL MEETS SAIL. Nothing could stop it now. Nothing at all. Within a year after construction work began on the railroad there were more than four thousand people in the town, and the seat of Cowlitz County was moved to the new metropolis.

By 1873, and only after heroic work in that year of panic, the railroad was completed from Kalama to Tacoma on Puget Sound. Without more than casual notice, the Northern Pacific promptly moved its Western headquarters, together with its machine shops, to the Puget Sound city. It was a terrible blow to Kalama. Hard on its heels came a disastrous fire that wiped out 90 per cent of Kalama. The stouthearted people rebuilt, better than before. Trains were coming and going, anyway. Here at Kalama, the trains steamed aboard the new big iron-hulled *Tacoma,* 334 feet long, with double tracks on her deck, and were ferried across the Columbia to Goble, Oregon, where they steamed again on Northern Pacific tracks to Portland.

Promotion for Kalama was still going strong, and a new crowd of boomers came to sell lots in a new site adjacent to the established town. These lots were sold, but never used. High water in June put them ten feet under, and nobody wanted to build. And nobody got his money back. Other towns on the river were delighted, and their newspapers played up "Kalama's black eye" in stories relating the horrors, or at least the dangers incident to living in such a place as that where "Rail Meets Sail."

People began moving out of Kalama. More of them moved after the Northern Pacific completed its line over the Cascade Mountains to Tacoma, cutting drastically the amount of freight and passenger traffic which theretofore had gone through Kalama. Yet Kalama citizens girded their loins again and convinced a big fish-packing house that their town was the right place to pack salmon and sturgeon. The concern agreed and leased a generous space on the waterfront. Just as construction was about to begin, the company's president and boss man went insane. Everything stopped. It never resumed. Citizens, however, were cheered when the Mountain Timber Company came to erect a sawmill employing more than three hundred men. It started tearing into the logs at a great rate. Kalama's days and nights were happily filled with the scream of the headsaw and the clatter of planers. It was music to their hard-tried souls, until the mill presently burned down. It was not rebuilt.

Then, the Northern Pacific and other lines got together and bridged the Columbia at Vancouver-Portland. Tracks were laid accordingly. The train ferry from Kalama to Goble was removed. The thousands, who had stopped at Kalama at least long enough to buy coffee and a sandwich, now rolled through Kalama at thirty-five miles an hour. Rail still met sail at Kalama, but the fact had ceased to mean anything. It meant even less when Kalama lost the county seat to Kelso, and became eventually a flag stop for the trains that ran sneeringly, or so it seemed, through town on their way to Seattle or Portland. By then motor cars were doing much of the passenger business, and trucks had cut heavily into railroad freight; and the state highway department lined a fine straightaway past the old terminus of the first transcontinental railroad to reach the Pacific Northwest. Like so many other towns in mid-century, the tourist will see little of Kalama save for a sign that points "To City Center."

It was true that railroads could make 'em and break 'em. Upriver from Kalama, at about where North Bonneville stands, there was a noisy tumult about a city to be called Lower Cascades, seat of Skamania County, Washington. It was platted in three directions and at least four miles each way. A railroad was coming. It did not come, and nothing happened except that quick disintegration set in. Not far off was another mirage, this one Garrison City, with street signs set up until you were dizzy. But the boomers did not trouble to dike it, and the same sort of flood that brought the welcome logs to Ezra Meeker at Kalama washed Garrison City down the river.

There was Pasco, Washington, which managed to jell. "Keep Your Eye on Pasco" was the word here. The promotion grew into true Barnum size on the strength that the town, nay the city, was destined to become the greatest center in all the Columbia's twelve hundred miles. Railroads were to accomplish this. They "got the railroad" all right at Pasco, though the town never reached anything like the proportions envisioned by its promoters.

So potent was the railroad in its heyday that occasionally when a long-settled town was by-passed, it picked up and moved within cinder shot. That was the case with Yakima a few miles up the river of the same name that enters the Columbia near Pasco. When the Northern Pacific started building through the Yakima valley, Yakima City was already an established village with several saloons, a hotel and a newspaper. Townsmen were jubilant.

No railroad would think of ignoring a place with four hundred population. But the townsmen were grasping; they wanted too much, said the Northern Pacific men, for a right of way. The NP management, which had had similar experiences all along the route from Duluth, simply switched the surveyed route to leave Yakima City four miles to one side.

Four miles was no jog for hauling freight and passengers by mule team. Several of the town's leading citizens could see no escape from isolation and consequent decay except to pick up and move to the rails. The editor of *The Oregonian* in Portland gave them encouragement and pointed the way to do it. "If the Yakima City saloons," he wrote, "can only be persuaded to move, the remainder of the town will rise up as one man and gird its loins and get itself hence." But there were other leading citizens who were united in wrath against the Northern Pacific. Let the damnable outfit run where it would, said a spokesman; we shall remain where we are and the road will come to us.

The Northern Pacific's fixers went to Publican David Guilland, offering a free trip to the new site selected by the railroad for his big frame hotel. Guilland accepted. The die-hards threatened to dynamite his place of business. Guilland bought a revolver. The railroad crew put jackscrews and timbers under his rambling big house, and away it rolled north toward the site of the new city, called North Yakima.

The next hard-shell to give in was A. J. Pratt, furniture dealer. He started on his own to move to North Yakima. "Then," as James Stevens told it in his account, "then it was a parade of store and service buildings for weeks through the sagebrush. Houses were swung into the procession, but business continued more or less as usual." Ladders and steps were hung from doors for the convenience of customers. Wines, liquors and cigars were dispensed from the gently heaving structures. Because drunks disliked sleeping in the hot sun and preferred to crawl under the slowly moving buildings, some thoughtful city official provided guards to patrol the parade and haul the inebriates out from under before the rollers flattened them. Meanwhile the Indians gathered in numbers to watch all day and into the night, considering the whole inexplicable business to be the most engaging show since the white men came.

When the first train rolled in, just before Christmas of 1884. North Yakima was ready to celebrate the event. Much later it dropped the "North" (while the original Yakima City became Union Gap) and continued to flourish until it was one of the largest cities on any tributary of the Columbia.

The largest such city, of course, is Spokane which grew up around the falls of the Spokane River after two adventurers from Montana filed homestead claims, platted a town and erected a sawmill. The Northern Pacific, building west, found it to be "a city of 1,500 people and two newspapers" and was glad to build its tracks right through the middle of it. Less than two years later, Spokane Falls, as it was still known, became the supply center of the gold rush into the adjacent Idaho country of the Coeur d'Alenes and was well on its way as Capital of the Inland Empire.

Spokane also began to hatch railroads of its own, and one of these, the Spokane Falls & Northern, had much to

do with the birth of Northport on the Columbia. Now
faded and forgotten, Northport once had good reason to
believe its own siren song, namely that it was fated to be
"the future mining and smelting center of the entire Northwest." No town on the Columbia has known a more startling rise, nor a more sudden fall. In the spring of 1892,
when town boomers started to lay out a site and name it,
Northport had a total population of three homesteaders,
one of whom was in poor health. Two months later an ox
team lumbered onto the wooded flat beside the river, hauling a printing press and a stock of paper. On July 4, the
Northport News appeared and reported the place to contain the three cabins of the homesteaders, a few tents, and
a population of twelve. The editor took a jocular view of
things, remarking that although no map yet showed
Northport, and the latest gazetteer ignored it, it was already a town and tomorrow it would be a city.

Before July was out, the settlement was threatened
by forest fire and was saved only by the fast work of "our
entire fire brigade." In September came the grading and
track-laying crews of the brand new Spokane Falls & Northern Railroad, in charge of which was Chief Engineer
E. J. Roberts, a man clothed with destiny and a long
linen duster who, "walking with slow and majestic tread,
gave orders in a clear and forcible voice." Down went the
tracks, and advancing upon them as quickly as they had
been spiked was the construction train, "a pleasing and
astonishing sight that will never be forgotten by the pioneers of Northport."

The nearest post office was six miles away, at Little
Dalles, and its accommodating postmaster, who was Cy

Townsend, put his saloon and office on a flatcar and it was hauled to Northport and began distribution of mail. So far as Washington, D. C., knew, the post office of Little Dalles was at Little Dalles. But word got around, and a little later a post office inspector came to straighten out matters. He was a little shocked to find the Little Dalles cancellation stamp being used in a place called Northport; and shocked again to see Postmaster Townsend dump the mailsack's contents on top of his bar, then go to the saloon door and shout to come and get the mail. The inspector protested. Townsend was hurt and also appalled. He retorted that he hadn't asked for the job. It had been wished on him in the first place. He had taken it only to accommodate the boys, and if the Post Office Department wanted to, they could find somebody else to take care of their trumpery.

Boom times were ahead, and so were more fires. The town burned twice during 1893 and was promptly rebuilt each time. Prospectors were finding silver deposits in the surrounding hills and at least "indications" of gold. No more than fifteen miles north in British Columbia, some really notable strikes were being made at Rossland. Miners were passing through Northport in all directions. Its new International Hotel was overtaxed to find beds, so straw ticks were laid out nightly in the corridors. Every saloon in town ran with two shifts of bartenders. The new Music Hall was crowded.

Destiny held fast with Northport. The town stood safely above the high-water mark of the Columbia's 1894 flood, the worst in thirty years. All was well. Business boomed. And now came a syndicate to erect a big smelter to reduce the rich ore from the Rossland and other mines.

Doubtless advance knowledge of the smelter project, leaking to a few promoters, was what prompted the townsite of Northport in the beginning. In any case, the largely British syndicate decided on Northport because of the immense quantities of lime rock around the town. This could be used to flux the gold and silver and other ores that were to come chiefly from Rossland. Crews were set to work laying a wagon road over which to tote the ores to Northport.

Up went the smelter, and she was blown in, heralded by clouds of black and yellow smoke that billowed above Northport, the Pittsburgh of the West. Five hundred men were required to operate the plant. Still more were coming. Builders worked madly to provide bunkhouses and homes for the swarming population. The smelter payroll ran to more than $30,000 a month. The editor of the News was wildly happy, and proud too. "Notwithstanding the roar and rush and bubble and life in Northport," he observed, "there hasn't been a shooting scrape nor a highway robbery so far."

Troubles, however, were imminent. A railroad could build a town, build it almost overnight as was the case with Northport. But a railroad could not always preserve a town, even a town which it had helped to build. Such was the case with Northport. Even while the roar and rush and smoke of this new Pittsburgh were filling the air, another new town was coming into being. This was Trail, also on the Columbia River. Its sudden rise was even more spectacular than Northport's had been.

When F. Augustus Heinze of Butte, Montana, first saw Trail, it was an empty townsite where Trail Creek entered the Columbia seven miles from the Rossland diggings. It was one of the many dreams of "Colonel" Eugene Sayre Topping, a typical adventurer who sported a sweeping mustache. He had prospected all over the Rockies. In 1890, when he found himself in British Columbia, and broke again, he was glad to accept a post as mining recorder and constable. Ready as ever to take still another chance, he was easily induced by two Rossland miners to record their claim and accept in payment an extension of one claim which he named Leroi and which, to be done with it, turned out to be one of the richest mines in Canada.

Topping now sought to interest young Heinze, an engineer who was already demonstrating at Butte that he could smelt copper cheaper than anyone else, and also knew a likely mine when he saw one. Topping believed that the Rossland ores could best be shipped down Trail Creek to the Columbia, a short seven miles, and just in case this should happen, he thoughtfully staked a townsite and said it was the city of Trail.

Meanwhile, though hundreds of teamloads of Rossland ore were going overland to the Northport smelter, Topping started a road up Trail Creek from his empty city on the Columbia. He even got help from the provincial government, and some of the Rossland ore started coming over the new road to the Columbia where it was put aboard a stern-wheeler for the Northport smelter. Now came Heinze, Montana's rising copper magnate, to inspect Colonel Topping's project, and things began to happen. The twenty-six-year-old Heinze looked at the Rossland mines. He looked at Trail. He told Topping that this was indeed the proper place for a smelter and that he, Heinze, would build it. He bought one-third of Topping's empty townsite for cash, and won the remainder of it playing poker with Topping and his partner Hanna. He had the Trail-Rossland route surveyed for an ore tramway. He let contracts for bricks and lumber and started work on a smelter. In less than two years the plant was in operation, and Trail had hotels, saloons, stores, and a newspaper.

While this was going forward, the Spokane Falls & Northern, the railroad serving Northport, laid an extension to Rossland. Heinze changed his tramway up the creek to a railroad. Then he organized the Columbia & Western Railway Company and started laying track from Trail to Robson at the foot of the Arrow Lakes. Large deposits of lime rock had been uncovered at Nakusp, on the Arrows, and this would do the Trail fluxing just as well as the stuff imported from Northport. Then, to the dismay of the Canadian Pacific Railway, Heinze applied to the provincial government for a land grant to continue his Columbia & Western through to the Pacific Coast. Whether this was a sort of blackmail threat, or whether Heinze really planned to build such a railroad, doesn't matter. The Canadian Pacific paid Heinze two million dollars for his "rail interests" and smelter, and the fast-moving young man went away and used the cash to finance his rise as one of the Copper Kings of the United States.

Trail grew steadily as a smelter city, while Northport started to fade. It faded not only because of lack of Rossland ores, for other ores for reduction came in from the Coeur d'Alene mines; but because of labor troubles. These began when the Western Federation of Miners called a strike of the Northport local of the Mill & Smeltermen's Union. The union set up a free eating house to feed the strikers. The company brought in strikebreakers. Delegations of strikers met them at the depot. Fights occurred. The sheriff arrived with a posse of armed deputies. Most of the would-be strikebreakers were "Persuaded by one means or another" to leave town. After nearly a year, the desperate strikers voted to surrender their union charter, and work at the smelter was resumed.

Northport's great days, however, were over. The smelter resumed briefly, then shut down. It was closed for almost a year. It reopened, and closed again. The Guggenheims tried it for a while, then they closed it. At last it was dismantled, and there it stands half a century later, the big stack hulking above ruins half lost in the brush and young forest that seeks to cover the glory that was Northport's.

Northport survives, after a fashion, because of a few small sawmills in and near the town, one street of which presents several fine examples of typical frontier architecture—two-storied, false-fronted, empty, and echoing, everything drenched with the special melancholy of Western ghost towns. It is still on a railroad, now the Great Northern, but the branch carries no passengers on its somewhat irregular freight service. The town is still on the Columbia River, though here at Northport it is now the dead water behind a dam 140 miles downstream at Grand Coulee.

As for Trail, the Canadian Pacific Railway Company never had reason to regret its original cost in the Heinze deal. With the inspired management which has often marked the great Canadian line, it consolidated its smelter

Trail, British Columbia.

interests with the several mines in the Rossland district and with the Rossland Power Company, and organized the Consolidated Mining & Smelting Company of Canada, Limited, one of the colossi not only of the Dominion but of the British Empire. A decade later, Consolidated took over the rich but difficult Sullivan mine at Kimberley, two mountain ranges distant, solved the problem of treating its complex massive sulphide ore, and made of it what an authoritative mining engineer has called "the greatest single lead-zinc-silver mine in the world." The Sullivan ores, naturally, come to Trail for treating.

Trail which today calls itself The Silver City is the fourth largest industrial center on the main Columbia. With a population exceeding twenty thousand, only Portland, Vancouver and Longview have more people. Trail climbs the steep hills which are dominated by the enormous Consolidated plant. The great stacks smoke day and night. It is a busy town, and a dramatic one, especially at night, when the lights seem to be climbing the canyon, moving along the heights, twinkling in the mountain night like stars.

The smoke from Trail's great smelters rode the winds south along the Columbia, and in time Americans sued Consolidated for damages to plant life. Extended litigation won the plaintiffs $300,000; and the action also encouraged the company to efforts to recover and use the sulphur in the smoke, to the end that Consolidated has developed chemical and fertilizer plants which are now the industrial backbone of suburban Warfield.

Trail smokes on in its canyon of the Columbia as it has for the past sixty years, even if there is less or even no sulphur now in its fumes; and citizens sometimes complain of the soot. "If they don't like it," so a visiting reporter was told, "let them move down to Northport. They've got a smelter down there that doesn't smoke at all—ever."

Chapter 8

CPR—A Spearhead of Empire

MEANWHILE THE great Canadian wilderness of the far upper Columbia waited, remote and silent. Or so it seemed. Writing of this region in his age, an old pioneer settler there remarked that for more than five decades after David Thompson had come to the headwaters, nothing much happened. "Spring and autumn and winter," he wrote, "followed one another, year in and out, but devoid of events worth recording."

This was not quite exact. In 1865 several hard-bitten prospectors, who had failed to strike it rich in a gold rush to the Cariboo country of the Thompson River, moved eastward, looking for the only stuff that could attract many men to this godforsaken region, chipping a ledge here, panning gravel there. And at last they came to the raging creeks that poured foaming down both sides of the Selkirks into the Columbia. In several streams entering the river on the Big Bend they found gold. A rush was on.

Down at Colville Landing, in Washington Territory, Captain Leonard White was ready. He had just finished building a stern-wheeler. He had seen gold rushes before, and had been the very first man to pilot a steamer above

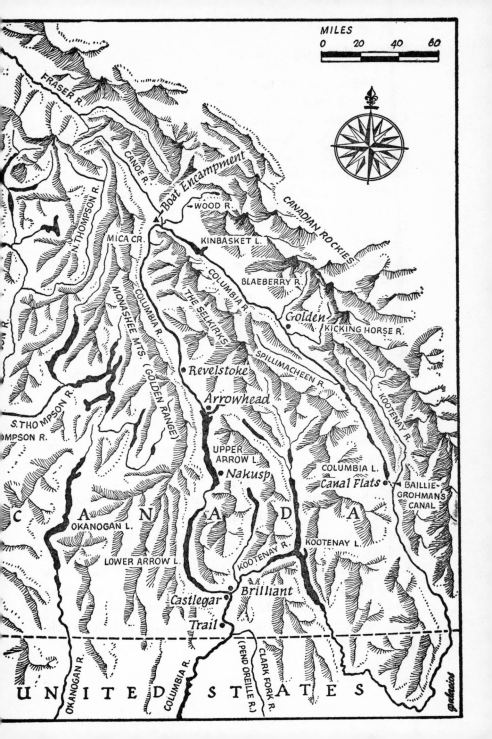

The Dalles, the first to take one up the Snake during the Idaho excitements. The boilers in his new hull had served the old *Jennie Clark*, the Oregon Steam Navigation Company's first stern-wheeler back in the fifties. So, with a fine sense of the fitness of things, Captain White named his new craft the *Forty-Nine* and steamed out of Colville Landing loaded with mad men and their picks, shovels, pans and provisions, heading for the Big Bend and gold. It was December.

This was to be a historic voyage. The *Forty-Nine* was the first steamer to cross the 49th parallel. Few men would have cared, in the first place, to tackle the rapids of the Little Dalles and the Little Rock; fewer still could have got through. Captain White got her past the first white water with her paddle. He made it through the Little Rock with a line, and so on to the mouth of the Kootenay. But the next day, when he pushed on into Lower Arrow Lake, he ran into thick ice. It was useless to attempt going farther. Unloading his freight and passengers, he turned back.

Next April, as soon as the ice was out, Captain White, this time with fewer passengers, headed upstream again. He passed the bad stretches without much trouble, went through the Arrow Lakes at full throttle, and continued on to the very mouth of Downie Creek at the foot of Death Rapids, a voyage of 270 miles from his home port of Colville Landing. It was a voyage one might term epic without abuse of the word. At Downie Creek the *Forty-Nine* discharged eighty-nine wildly optimistic prospectors and took aboard more than one hundred bewhiskered and bedraggled ones who declared bitterly that the whole affair was a complete fake; there was, they said, no gold on the Big Bend.

The upstream run had occupied ten days, almost all of which Captain White spent in the wheel house, awake. The downstream run took five days. The fare was $25 a head one way. Freight was $200 a ton. The *Forty-nine* paid her cost and more in her first season. But her first was also her last profitable season. On her third trip she carried only three passengers north, and came back with miners sleeping all over her decks, most of them dead broke. Captain White took their IOUs. He still had them when he died, only a little later, worn out, said one who knew him, with the tricky currents and large boulders which appeared to move about in the Columbia at will. There were few Captain Whites. Rarely, wrote Randall Mills, had a more adventurous and determined man been seen on the river, any river. "He deserves a monument, at least for his daring." But with an unfamiliar hand at the wheel, the *Forty-Nine* presently hit a rock and sank in shallow water.

The *Forty-Nine* was almost the only steamer on the far upper river for a long time. Curiously enough, the upper river had to wait for a railroad before it had a steamboat era. On the lower stream it was the other way around; when the railroads came, the steamers started to disappear.

The redoubtable advance guard of the Canadian Pacific Railway first saw the Columbia on May 15, 1881. He was Major A. B. Rogers, something of a storybook character in the field of engineering, who had served before the mast, studied at Brown, was graduated from Yale, fought Indians in Minnesota, then laid routes for railroads up and down and across the Sioux country with a rifle in one hand. Here he was now in British Columbia, sent by James J. Hill of St. Paul on the toughest assignment the Canadian Pacific, or for that matter, any other railroad could offer: His orders were to find a route over the Selkirk Range and to survey and choose the best of several possible routes through the Rockies. In that order, for Rogers had come into the British Columbia interior from the Coast.

One of the young men in his party described Rogers as the rough-and-ready sort, a true pathfinder, a short, sharp, snappy man with long, wild-flying Dundreary whiskers. At fifty-two he was a complete master of profanity—not just swearing, but an art form and a sort of reservoir of extra power from which he drew strength to perform prodigies on the trail. His scientific apparatus consisted of a compass and an aneroid slung around his neck. His idea of a day's provisions for an engineer was a plug of chewing tobacco in one pocket, a couple of slabs of hardtack in the other.

Rogers came first to the Columbia at a point near present Revelstoke where a swift stream, the Illecillewaet, entered it. With him were two nephews and ten strapping young Indians. It is indicative of Major Rogers's Spartan methods that the Indian packers, whom he had engaged by contract at the Oblate mission at Kamloops, were "to serve without grumbling until discharged" and if any came back "without a letter of good report, his wages were to go to the Church, and the chief was to lay one hundred lashes on his bare back." The path of British empire must be assured so far as possible; and, anyway, Rogers was no man to stand harassment by temperamental men, red or white. What was more, he had already ordered five complete engineering outfits and 125 men to meet him, on July 1, at Bow River Gap—on the *east* side of the Rockies. His way thence was across an unknown mountain region.

Felling a cedar for a raft, Rogers's party loaded grub and equipment, then all hands got into the Columbia, swimming, pushing the raft across to land just above the mouth of the Illecillewaet. Up that stream they went. They were five days making the first sixteen miles to the forks, the farthest point white men had ever reached. Taking the southerly fork they passed through what became famous as Albert Canyon, and climbed on. Rogers found the packers to be stout trenchermen. To conserve bacon and flour, of which Rogers considered them to be inordinately fond, he had them shoot a caribou or mountain goat on occasion. Snow was still deep in the high reaches. The going was hard even by Rogers's standards. There was no wood for fire, no boughs to lie on. Eating snow was their only water. They reached the summit at last, to look down on a landscape of snow-clad desolation.

But this was the proper pass, the only pass by which the railroad could cross the Selkirks. From there the line would follow the waters of Beaver Creek down to meet the Columbia on the east side of the range. Rogers took his party back over the Selkirks to their starting point. He sent all save two of his Indians home (all with "letters of good report"), then built a raft and set off down the Columbia, using dog tents for sails on the Arrow Lakes, and crossing the line into the United States on June 11. He was still a long way from Bow River Gap where he was to meet his engineering crew. He made it by saddle horse from Fort Colville, Washington, to Bonners Ferry, Idaho; over an old trail up the Moyie River to Wild Horse, then shifted to canoe and up the Kootenay. He crossed over Canal Flats to the Columbia's headwaters, went down that river a few miles, then parked his canoe, and struck out on foot and over the Rockies to where his party waited at the Gap. He was fourteen days late. One may imagine he felt pretty mean about it.

Rogers spent the rest of the year exploring passes in the Rockies, picking the Kicking Horse for the route; and again he reached the summit of the Selkirks by way of the Beaver on the east slope. Those were the mountain routes by which the Canadian Pacific was to reach and pass the Columbia—pass it once where it was flowing north, and again where it hurried south after its course around the Big Bend. An old surveyor for the province, Walter Moberley, had had much to do with suggesting the passes which Rogers actually found and explored. Rogers was quick to give Moberley credit, too, and the names of both men are solidly placed in British Columbia history.

The rails, as said, followed Major Rogers's path through the Rockies, coming down the Kicking Horse River to cross a new bridge over the Columbia where a construction camp grew into the town of Golden; then to head up over the Selkirks. It was here at Beavermouth that the railroad ran into trouble, not from terrain but from lack of cash to meet the payroll. Politics at Ottawa, the Canadian capital, was the reason. Anti-administration forces were blocking a Dominion loan to the Canadian

Pacific Railway Company. Month after month, the poor working stiffs at Beavermouth were told to be patient, that their wages would be paid soon. But after thirteen months of waiting, three hundred laborers went on strike.

Hotheads egged on the trouble. Many of the strikers were armed with guns. The mob attacked an even larger number of tracklayers who were still working, driving them back into camp. The strikers then prepared to raid the camp and destroy it. They were held off, says an old report, "by eight fearless men of the Northwest Mounted Police." There was no shooting. An officer read the Riot Act, and promised the rioters they would be mowed down if they attempted to move upon the camp. An uneasy peace prevailed for several days, with armed sentinels patrolling. But then the paycar arrived, the crew got their long-delayed wages, and the work continued.*

The official Last Spike of the Canadian Pacific was driven at Craigellachie, not far from Revelstoke, on November 7, 1885. The Dominion had been spanned. Old Montreal and new Vancouver were connected by rails. The rails of the main line touched and crossed the Columbia, as related, at two places; at Revelstoke, where Pathfinder Rogers had started up the Selkirks, and at Golden to which he had followed the swift Kicking Horse from the top of the Rockies. Now that the railroad had come to the far upper river, the Columbia here was about to have a

* The Beavermouth trouble occurred at the same time Louis Riel was staging his "Northwest Rebellion" in the prairie provinces. This was put down, with no little shooting, by troops from Winnipeg and Eastern Canada who were moved to the scene with such dispatch by the CPR that the railroad became overnight something of a heroic and patriotic enterprise. Politicians no longer dared to block the government loan to the Canadian Pacific.

steamboat era, while down below the 49th parallel, the elegant passenger steamers were already beginning to feel the deadly competition of the rail carriers.

The far upper river's steamboat era lasted only twenty-eight years, from 1886 to 1914, and it was at best a rough-and-tumble affair. It concerned not one but two streams, for it ranged from Golden on the Columbia up to Columbia Lake, across Canal Flats and down the Kootenay to Jennings, Montana, an over-all distance of some three hundred miles. That either of these waters ever had anything that could be termed a steamboat era is a marvel. The vessels were of necessity almost amphibian. Their captains had to be as ingenious as they were fearless of rocks and white water. Even then, the record is a succession of stove-in hulls, wrecks, sinkings, groundings and beachings.

The outstanding figures of this high-spirited period were Captain Frank Armstrong and William Adolph Baillie-Grohman. Both arrived in 1882 at the headwaters of the Columbia. Both were ambitious and imaginative men, but their careers had nothing in common except they had to do with the Columbia and Kootenay rivers.

Baillie-Grohman was a half Scot, half Austrian whose mother was a Tyrolean countess. He was a big-game hunter and world traveler whose hobby had brought him to the Rockies to have a go at mountain goats and grizzlies. He appears also to have had the instincts of a promoter. He was much taken with the region around Creston where the Kootenay, after having passed the Columbia's headwaters to flow into Montana, then Idaho, re-enters British Columbia and expands into Kootenay Lake before it joins the Columbia at Castlegar. The bottom lands at Creston were wonderfully rich. The trouble was periodic flooding. If the Kootenay's flow could only be regulated at some place above the lake, then these lands could be reclaimed and turned into orchards and wheat fields.

This idea was in Baillie-Grohman's mind while on a hunting expedition to the Columbia's headwaters, during which he noted the narrow portage between the two rivers. Here was the place to divert the Kootenay's freshets into the Columbia. No dam was needed. The Columbia's surface was eight feet lower than the Kootenay. A simple ditch would do the work.

Baillie-Grohman went to Victoria and proposed to the provincial government that he be granted land in return for constructing a diversion ditch that would reclaim the Creston lands and attract settlers. An agreement was made, and away he went to England to raise money, reflecting meanwhile that his project would make the whole three-hundred-mile-long Selkirk Range into "an island as completely water-girt on every side as any little islet in the Thames." So it would, and in his written accounts he alluded again and again to the fact that "the hand of man, in the shape of sundry Chinamen and navvies" could make an island of "a political division of British Columbia very nearly as large as England." Somehow or other this gave him much satisfaction.

Even before the promoter could get construction started, however, trouble was brewing. The Canadian Pacific Railway objected to the project, claiming that diversion of the Kootenay into the Columbia would flood its main line north of Golden. In those days, the CPR seldom protested in vain. Its legal lights pointed out that both streams were navigable waters, hence in the jurisdiction of the Dominion (federal) not the provincial government. A compromise was agreed upon; Baillie-Grohman's syndicate would construct a ship's canal and lock, and guarantee that the Kootenay's surface should never be lowered below the ordinary low-water level, and that the gates of the canal should be closed except to permit passage of steamers or other craft. The canal syndicate was to have its land grant.

Baillie-Grohman himself moved to the spot, built a store and a sawmill, assembled several hundred Chinese coolies, another gang of white workers, and work began. It must have been a sight to startle the Indians and the few surviving ancients of the Hudson's Bay and the Northwest companies, to see the gravelly flat of their old portage acrawl with Canton-hatted Chinese, while the bedlam of teamsters' cries, of donkey engines and a sawmill rose up between the sheer cliffs of the Rockies and the towering Selkirks. The canal was finished in 1889, a ditch sixty-seven-hundred feet long by forty-five feet wide. It was equipped with one lock one hundred feet long and thirty feet wide.

During six years while the canal project was being argued and at last completed, Captain Frank Armstrong had been busy. Only twenty years old in 1882, when he first saw Columbia Lake, this native of Quebec Province was much taken with the headwaters country. He recorded a claim to 320 acres on the east shore of the lake where the Columbia begins. He brought in seed potatoes overland from Montana, and sold his first crop for $140 a ton at Golden, delivering them in bateaux he made from whipsawed lumber. But he wanted a steamboat. Ordering a secondhand engine from Montreal, which arrived at Golden on the CPR's first through train to the coast, the young man, without troubling to draw plans, whacked up a hull, installed the engine, and on May 8, 1886, launched the first steamboat on the far upper Columbia. A surviving photograph shows her to have been made of every conceivable length and thickness of scrap lumber, with projecting decks and bulging super-structure. The picture also indicates her builder's liking for irony: He named her the *Duchess.*

Young Armstrong headed his *Duchess* upstream. Word of her coming kept well in advance. By the time he came to Lake Windermere, some five hundred Indians were waiting to welcome the first steam-canoe any of them had seen. They helped to haul her over the salmon flats on which she had stranded. Her first season's business, however, was disappointing. She moved only a hundred tons of freight and carried 220 passengers.

But things were booming in 1887. A gold strike at Wild Horse on the Kootenay provided a sudden camp that required food and whiskey in vast quantities. Both this unruly settlement and a threatened Indian outbreak called for the Royal Northwest Mounted Police, so at Golden the *Duchess* loaded Mounties and oats for their horses and struck out for the headwaters. She got badly snagged and near the head of Canyon Creek rapids she sank. The passengers escaped. The cargo was a total loss.

The Mounties had no better luck when they tried the *Duchess*'s first competitor, a fearsome craft named the *Cline,* made from a scow and the broken-down engine from a Manitoba steam-plow. She sank near Spillimacheen, while a consignment of scarlet tunics and a deckload of bright yellow oats made a colorful assortment of driftage as they floated away downriver.

The *Cline* was never raised. But the machinery of the *Duchess* was soon recovered and went into a new steamer of the same name. Captain Armstrong also built another, the light-draft *Marion*, for use in low-water periods. Financial help in building his fleet came from Lady Adela Cochrane who with her husband, a kinsman of the Earl of Dundonald, had a placer mine near Canal Flats. Armstrong had ambitions. He added another vessel to his fleet and began a sort of scheduled service between Golden and Lake Windermere, and as far as Columbia Lake when water permitted and, when it didn't, by a five-mile portage. The young captain decided that a system of tramways was needed if he was to build up an effective transportation system.

At this time there appears to have been a striking concentration of money and influence around the Columbia's headwaters. In 1891 Armstrong incorporated the Upper Columbia Navigation & Tramway Company, whose stockholders included the Cochranes, already mentioned; the Honorable Frank Lascelles, son of the Earl of Harewood, who lived at Columbia Lake; and Lord Norbury, who lived on the Kootenay. Provided with a government land subsidy, the new concern laid a tramway from the Golden railroad depot to the steamboat landing on the Columbia; another tramway from what had been Mud Lake, but now became Lake Adela, to the north end of Columbia Lake; and still another stretch of rails across

Canal Flats to the Kootenay. Horses were the motive power.

The company added another steamer. Then Captain Armstrong went down the Kootenay, where the Fort Steele boom was still growing, and built the sixty-three-foot *Gwendoline*, named for still another entry in *Burke's Peerage*, a daughter of the Earl of Stradbroke and a resident of the Columbia Lake community of titled gentry. When the *Gwendoline* was about three quarters finished, Armstrong decided he could best complete her at his Golden shipyard. He got her up to Canal Flats, but found he could not use the canal and lock because the gates had been dynamited to save the Village from being washed away in one of the Kootenay's sudden freshets.

Captain Armstrong was no man to wait. "He bumped a lot of scenery on the Columbia," so a contemporary said of him, "but he always got through." A mile of land did not stop him now. He dismantled the vessel, set the hull on rollers and hauled her across the Flats. At Golden he made her into a stanch ship. She had to be stanch for the career ahead of her. Armstrong took her up the Columbia and put her through the locks, which had been repaired. She was to be the only vessel to make the passage from north to south. Five thousand tons of ore from the North Star mine were awaiting her arrival.

American steamboat lines had already begun operating out of Libby and Jennings, Montana towns on the Kootenai. Armstrong organized an American subsidiary of Upper Columbia N & T, and sent to Portland, Oregon, for Louis Paquet, one of the best-known shipbuilders of the time, who at Libby built a fine stern-wheeler that was christened *Ruth* for Armstrong's daughter. The *Gwen-*

doline was enlarged. If Armstrong's American rivals meant to carry North Star ore, they would find competition aplenty.

The Upper Columbia Navigation & Tramway Company now offered a continuous route three hundred miles long from Golden on the Columbia to Jennings on the American Kootenai. It was also virtually a monopoly, for Armstrong bought out *SS Rustler*, his chief competitor, after she hit a rock in Jennings Canyon and went to pieces. These Kootenai waters did not, however, play favorites. Both the *Ruth* and the *Gwendoline* suffered wreck in the same canyon, though they were patched up and went to hauling ore again. Adding to the fleet was the finest sternwheeler on the river, the *North Star*, built by the same Louis Paquet of the *Ruth*. This was to become famous above all other vessels not only on the Kootenay but on the far upper Columbia.

In 1897 the Upper Columbia N & T lost its mail subsidy, but discovered that settlers persisted in their habit of flagging down a boat to hand over a letter for posting at Golden. To discourage this nuisance the company printed stamps marked "U.C.Co. 5¢" in a wreath of red leaves, to be affixed to letters in addition to the Dominion postage. Only a few had been sold however, when the government notified the company to cease and desist.*

The Fort Steele boom faded to almost nothing in 1898, and several thousand prospectors went away to the Klondike Rush. The North Star mine was still producing

---

* According to BNA *Topics,* publication of the British North America Philatelic Society, these covers are among the most prized items of collectors.

in volume, but the ore was being moved by a new branch railroad. The Upper Columbia Company suffered another disaster when its *North Star*, carrying $3,000 in whiskey and other necessities, struck the rocks in Jennings Canyon. In the following year the *Gwendoline* was wrecked again. Captain Armstrong himself left for the Yukon to command a steamer on Tagish Lake. When he returned in 1900, he found mining on the upper Columbia reviving and took a contract to rawhide and sled ore from the new Silver Giant on the Spillimacheen. The Paradise mine on Toby Creek also began to produce.

Though it was obvious that steamboat days on the Kootenay had faded, Armstrong believed he could still make good use of a boat on the Columbia. The *North Star* had meanwhile been wrecked again, and sold. Armstrong bought her, then set about the feat that was to make him and the battered old stern-wheeler legendary subjects on the upper Columbia.

On an early June day in 1902, Armstrong brought the *North Star* to the Kootenay side of Canal Flats, then he and his crew set to preparing the canal that had been abandoned for eight years. The lock was 100 feet long, the North Star 130 feet stem to stern. She was also nine inches too wide for the gates. Armstrong cut off her guard-rails. Still too wide. He attempted to hack down the gates, failed, and burned them off. Then, with a mountain of ore sacks filled with sand, he constructed two dams, providing a lock long enough to float the vessel and strong enough to keep the Kootenay from "breaking the law" and running wild into the Columbia.

Armstrong now placed and packed carefully a stout

charge of dynamite beneath the forward dam. He took his place in the wheelhouse. And when the ship's boiler began popping off from excess steam, he gave the word. "Let her go, boys," he cried. The fuse spluttered a moment, then the forward dam went up with a roar that shook the settlement. Bells rang in the engine room. The *North Star* churned ahead through the rain of falling debris and so on into the waters of Columbia Lake, when the captain set "her deep bass whistle echoing over hill and dale and re-echoing from peak to peak of the Rocky and Selkirk mountains."

With many a new scar added to her hull, the *North Star* proceeded down the rapids and bends below the lake, in the course of which a big tree came crashing down through the cabin, barely missing Ruth, the small daughter of the Columbia's Jason. Just ahead was a low bridge, the first or uppermost span across the Columbia. Though he may well have felt like ramming it head on, Armstrong brought his ship to shore. He built a "sheer-legs" on the bank, ran out his cable, and lifted the span bodily with power from the ship's capstan. Then he drove ahead, passing under the bridge, and replaced it as sound as ever. At Adela Lake he paused to pick up the abandoned rails of the long disused tramway for delivery to the Paradise mine. The *North Star* got through to Golden on July 2.

The hardy settlers and the by now well-weathered members of the English gentry recognized in Captain Armstrong the size and shape of a classic argonaut. They threw him a party. It was complete to printed programs which declared this was a "Complimentary dinner tendered to Capt. F. P. Armstrong by a Few of His Friends in

The *North Star* going from the Kootenay to Columbia Lake.

token of their appreciation of his indomitable energy in bringing the steamer *North Star* to the Columbia River. Hotel Delphine, Wilmer, B. C., July 19th, 1902." Course followed course, wrote Norman Hacking, the upper river's incomparable historian of steamboat days, "and wines and spirits flowed almost as freely as the Columbia River."

It was fitting recognition of a master mariner. It turned out also to be virtually an epitaph for the *North Star*. After one season hauling ore and settlers, she was seized by the Canadian Customs at Golden and impounded as an American vessel on which duty had not been paid. She lay fallow at Golden for the next decade, when her hull was cut in half and the pieces used as freight barges. The old Upper Columbia N & T had long since sold its assets. Most of the titled shareholdrs had left or were about to leave the region. The wildwood had lost its appeal. Lord Norbury returned to live in England. T. B. H. Cochrane went away to become deputy governor of the Isle of Wight. The Honorable Frank Lascelles had climaxed an eccentric career by shooting and killing a Chinese servant at his home on Columbia Lake. Almost alone now, among the commoners, was Captain Northcote Cantlie, nephew of Lord Mount Stephen, who carried on ably the region's reputation for notable characters. "He preferred champagne for breakfast," wrote Historian Hacking, "and always kept with him as a personal attendant a piper in full Highland regalia."

The steamboat era was about done. A few vessels came and as quickly went. Construction work on the Kootenay Central (CPR) south from Golden through Canal Flats brought a minor and only temporary revival of river freighting. Completion of the railroad put an end to that. It was fitting that the last commercial voyage of a steamboat in this part of the river found Captain Armstrong at the wheel. It was May of 1920. The vessel was the stern-wheeler *Nowitka,* destined for the disgrace of being part of a pile-driving outfit engaged in building a bridge over the Columbia at Briscoe that was to end commercial navigation forever. On the way, Captain Armstrong paused to load a tow-barge with ore he had left on the bank back in 1896. On the way, too, the *North Star* tore loose a telephone line, illegally spanning the river, which put the entire local system out of order. It was a melancholy voyage all around. "Having been in charge of the first boat, as well as the last," wrote Captain Armstrong in the Nelson *Daily News,* "memories crowded on me as I stood at the wheel." He died three years later in Vancouver General Hospital. Though barely sixty-one years old, he had come out of a past that harked back to "before the railroad" and which, so far as the upper Columbia was concerned, was also "before the steamboats." Looking back from mid-century, it seems a remote past indeed.

As for Baillie-Grohman, neither his Canal Flats project nor the Creston promotion returned him or the syndicate a farthing. He returned to Europe a bitter man. The thirty thousand acres of granted land reverted to the Crown for taxes. Only two vessels ever used his canal and locks.* Perhaps Captain Armstrong was the only skipper equal to surmounting the difficulties they presented. In

---

* One cynical oldster of the Canal Flats area was of the opinion that no steamer ever went through the canal, but told me *he* knew what sort of craft it was. "She was a Peterborough canoe."

any case the canal seems to have had no influence in promoting or prolonging the upper river's steamboat days. They came because of the Canadian Pacific Railway; and were brought to an end when that road's northern and southern main lines were connected by the branch from Golden to Colvalli.

On the American side of the Columbia River, as previously indicated, the steamboats started to disappear immediately the railroads began to crawl along the main stream and many of its tributaries. An instance was the once great fleet of the Wenatchee & Okanogan Steamboat Company, based on Wenatchee and serving that stream and the Okanogan which rises in British Columbia. In the nineties the fleet numbered fifteen fine ships. A marked decline in traffic came in 1910, or just as soon as the Great Northern Railway laid its Oroville branch. By 1915 only four boats remained, and of these two were in such bad shape as to be of little use. Then, on a hot morning in July, all four were burned to the water in one grand fire that lasted less than twenty minutes. The company's fire insurance policies had lapsed only a short time before. It was the virtual end of the Wenatchee and the (American) Okanogan steamboat era. But steamers flourished on the Canadian Okanogan for another three decades. This was also true of the two Arrow Lakes and Kootenay Lake.

It was terrain mostly that prolonged the life of steamboats in the British Columbia interior. The Canadian Pacific Railway faced a vast mountainous country marked, so far as the Columbia River was concerned, by three major lake-river regions. From east to west these were the

Kootenay, the Arrow and the Okanogan. To complicate matters, the Canadian Kootenay and its erratic course came in two parts—East Kootenay where it was flowing south into Montana; West Kootenay where it returned from Idaho, flowing north to join the main Columbia. And between West Kootenay and the Arrow Lakes was another large body of water and a river, the Slocan, whose outlet joined the Kootenay not far from where that stream entered the Columbia.

To anyone who contemplates this portion of British Columbia must come an admiration for the high command of the railroad which, once the east-west main line was finished, had to select the places where its branches should be built. The great names of the Canadian Pacific are legendary —Van Horne, Shaughnessy, Mount Stephen, Strathcona, Angus, Holt, Beatty, and a few more. They were empire builders in the grand style, and among them and their associates and subordinates were men who took the hundreds of maps and profiles made by CPR engineers, assembled them into a gigantic whole, then traced through the mazes of interlocking rivers, creeks, and lakes, or mountains and valleys. Where to build next?

Even while they debated the possibilities of this valley or that, news of gold strikes, of silver, lead and coal assailed their ears. So did quieter news to the effect that fruits and berries grew enormously here, that fine wheat was to be grown there. So did rumors that Jim Hill's Great Northern, an American line, was planning to tap British Columbia; and still later, that Canadians were to build opposition lines, like the Canadian Northern, the Grand Trunk Pacific, and the Pacific Great Eastern.

Where to build next? The CPR had a Napoleon in Sir William Cornelius Van Horne, a dominating man, brilliant, short of temper, one of the great railroad builders of the world. But it was others who actually ranged the valleys and the rivers, to estimate probable future traffic, then to decide where the branches and connecting lines were to be built, and in what order. They are nameless, these men, so far as the public is concerned, but they must have been field marshals of genuine stature, worthy their chief.

Here in the mountains, they worked in a country almost without population. It was true that railroads usually attracted population, yet here in the British Columbia interior which was one mountain range after another, it was obvious that some effort must be made to provide traffic, both passenger and freight. Even while the main line was still building through the Rockies and the Selkirks, the CPR was planning resorts for tourists, with special attention to mountain climbers. Here were peaks beyond number, few of which had been climbed. If there is anything a mountaineer likes, it is to be the first man up.

As early as 1886, accordingly, the railroad opened the Banff Springs Hotel on the east slope of the Rockies. Then came Chateau Lake Louise near the summit; and Glacier House high in the Selkirks. The company was instrumental in bringing accredited Swiss guides to British Columbia. One sees them in old photographs—Herr Christian Hasler, Herr Feuz, Herr Sulzer, Herr Huber, resolute-appearing men, bearded, moustached, invariably smoking pipes, posing for pictures taken by members of parties they guided. Herr Huber wrote that though these mountains did not "come nigh those of Wallis and of the Berner

Highlands, they nevertheless surpass them in labyrinthine organization, in the production of thickets, and the vast number of glaciers."

These professional guides, and the fact that a railroad now crossed the Canadian mountains, were doubtless factors in the sudden interest shown by members of what in those days were generically known as Alpine clubs. They came in numbers to the new CPR resorts—from clubs in England, Montreal, Boston and Philadelphia, anxious to make the "first climb" to the top of this or that peak. There came, too, a professional mountain man, the Reverend William Spotswood Green, who proceeded to map the peaks and glaciers of the Selkirks and to write about them for the Royal Geographical Society, to the end that "many of the names in use long afterward were bestowed by him."

Mountain climbing was catching on. More professional guides came from Switzerland, and near Golden on the Columbia, the CPR built a colony of homes for their families, all in the style of their native country. With this for their base, the guides were readily available for parties, either in the Rockies, at their back, or in the Selkirks, which their homes faced. The late eighties and the nineties appear to have been a Golden Age for mountaineering in the Selkirks and Canadian Rockies. One of the noted peaks of the former was Sir Donald, a popular challenge. It was first climbed in 1890. Then the women, or lady-mountaineers as they were known, had a go at it. In 1901 a lady climber made it, too, and got her name in the elaborately kept records of mountain climbing. She was Mrs. E. Evelyn Berens, of St. Mary's Crag, Kent, England.

The CPR resorts at Banff Springs and Lake Louise

quickly became internationally known. They had to be enlarged again and again over the years, and now in mid-century are more effective than ever in "providing a magnet for tourist travel," which was the railroad's declared purpose in building them. Just outside Golden still stands the Swiss village, looking very Swiss indeed with its deep roofs and gingerbread trim. Many of the imported guides never went back to their homeland, and in the region around Golden are many of their children and grandchildren. In the local district telephone book are a number of names that were common for centuries at Interlaken in the Alps. Almost everywhere on Columbia waters in Canada the influence of the Canadian Pacific Railway has been immense.

Chapter 9

The Last Stern-Wheeler

IT WAS left to that delightful portion of the Columbia called the Arrow Lakes to preserve the steamboat era long after it had faded elsewhere on the main river. This 130-mile stretch of water begins at the hamlet of Arrowhead on the north and ends at Robson and Castlegar on the south. Its east shore is the Selkirk Range, rising in many places right out of the water. Its west shore is the Monashee Range. The isolation is such that no settler made his pitch here until the mid-nineties. More than six decades later the population is sparse and scattered.

The Canadian Pacific Railway touches the lakes at both extremes, and again in about the middle, at Nakusp. The connecting links have been the railroad company's stern-wheelers. Though the lakes are long and narrow, their name comes not from their shape but from the fact, noted by Missionary-Explorer Father De Smet, of "innumerable" arrows that were sticking out from fissures in a perpendicular rock on the shore. Because of their great number, he thought it might have been Indian custom to use the fissures as targets. The native and visiting tribes fished in and hunted around Upper Arrow, but none seem to have made it a practice to winter there. On the lower lake a few families appear to have made their homes the year round.

The first white man to cruise the lakes was of course David Thompson. During the next ninety years or so, the lakes bore an occasional party of Nor'westers or Hudson's Bay men up and down; and in the sixties, as related, Captain Leonard White and his hardy SS *Forty-nine* moved prospectors and supplies through the lakes and on to the Big Bend gold diggings. The rush quickly played out and for a quarter of a century the quiet of the Arrow Lakes was little disturbed.

When in the late eighties the Canadian Pacific had completed its main line through to the West Coast, new mining excitements swept up and down the interior valleys. Prospectors popped up, as one old-timer observed, on every river and creek that flowed into the Canadian Columbia or any of its tributaries. Promoters harassed the railroad demanding that branch lines be built immediately to reach what were always described as "enormous" deposits of gold, silver, copper, or plain black coal. The railroad men, however, remained calm, and it was left to eager individuals to establish a number of local transportation lines.

Among these local ventures was the Columbia & Kootenay Steam Navigation Company, the effort of Arrow Lake pioneers, which started life with a big steam-powered catamaran built at Revelstoke (Second Crossing), then added the fine stern-wheelers *Lytton* and *Kootenay*. These steamers ran the entire lake route; and to handle traffic from the railroad to the lake at its north end, the company built a small steamer to run the river south from Revelstoke where the CPR crossed the Columbia on its way to Vancouver.

Meanwhile, the Canadian Pacific was building another cross-province line through the mountains near the United States border. This tapped the two long valleys called East Kootenay and West Kootenay, touched the Columbia's main stream at Robson, continued west to tap the Okanogan River valley, and on to join the CPR main line at the Fraser River. This was the grand strategy of the railroad. When it was being carried out, the CPR also turned its attention to providing north-and-south links to connect its two east-west lines. In 1896 it took control of the Arrow Lakes by buying the Columbia & Kootenay Steam Navigation Company which by then was operating seven steamers and a fleet of barges.

Though large and small mining booms were breaking out both east and west of them, it was the destiny of the Arrow Lakes to share in them only as a transportation route. Eastward, just over the first range of the Selkirks, lay another long body of water which delirious newspaper stories were soon calling Silvery Slocan Lake, head of the Slocan River which emptied into the Kootenay not far from that stream's junction with the main Columbia. In 1891 prospectors around the lake uncovered "almost incredibly large bodies of silver-lead ores." A typical mining camp came into being on Slocan Lake and was almost inevitably named Eldorado.

Getting ore out of Eldorado was most difficult. The first shipments of it were brought horseback ten miles down Cody Creek to the lake. They were moved in small scows to the head of Slocan, then packed in skin boats made of rawhide and dragged by horses over snow another twenty miles to a new settlement on Upper Arrow Lake that had been christened Nakusp. Here it was loaded on a stern-wheeler of the CPR fleet and taken down the Columbia to the new smelter at Trail.

At about this time a rumor got around that Nakusp was to become a smelter town. The place went into a typical boom. It quickly died, but there were large deposits of limestone near Nakusp and, within a year or so, the Arrow Lakes fleet was moving a hundred tons a day of it downriver to Trail. The Slocan mines continued to produce, but the ores no longer went to smelter by way of Nakusp. They went down Slocan Lake by CPR steamers to the Kootenay. It was a hard blow, one that Nakusp never quite forgot, and half a century later a historian of the town wrote somewhat bitterly that "it was the CPR that almost put us off the map. The proposed smelter became a myth."

The CPR had its own plan for the Arrow Lakes. We shall get to it presently, but this is perhaps the place to stress again the fact that the terrain of British Columbia was a most complicated problem for railroad builders. Nothing in the United States, unless it was Colorado, presented anything comparable. Range after range of mountains began at the Alberta border and ran on and on to the very shore at Vancouver. Between the ranges were valleys, some rich with minerals, some without; some with bench lands that might do for agriculture, others that contained little but timber.

Added to these problems was the potent threat of competitive lines, and out-and-out nuisance or blackmail railroads. In 1898, in the month of May alone, Her Majesty, Queen Victoria, by and with the advice and consent of the Legislative Assembly of British Columbia, granted the prayers of petitioners who declared they wanted to build no less than five railroads on Columbia waters; namely, the Downie Creek, the North Star & Arrow Lakes, the Arrowhead & Kootenay, the Revelstoke & Cassiar, and the Big Bend Transportation Company, the latter an all-inclusive outfit whose charter granted the right to operate steamboats, build docks, telegraph and telephone lines; supply heat, light and power to mines, smelters and refineries.

It is well worth knowing that among the incorporators of several of the roads named were William Mackenzie and Donald D. Mann whose policy, remarked a Canadian historian, was to start building short lines on an extremely low standard of quality, then to involve provincial legislatures in financing completion, usually by guarantee of bonds. A little later, the Mackenzie-Mann roads were put together to form a shoddy and notorious transcontinental which at last had to be taken over by the Dominion government and made over to become a portion of a genuine railroad, the Canadian National.

These newly chartered railroads of the nineties had to be bought off by the CPR, or otherwise discouraged. In the nineties, too, a recurrence of the old anti-Chinese spirit, common on the West Coast, was reflected in a new British Columbia law which prohibited employment of Chinese and Japanese on railroad construction and operation. The penalty for violation was set at $5 a day for each case.

These were among the problems faced by the Canadian Pacific strategists just before the turn of the century. They could not build a line up every valley or to touch every big lake. There were too many valleys and too many big lakes. They must fit the lines they did build to the terrain; they must know where freight was to come from before they built at all. They must use boats where they could to link their rails.

Once the CPR purchased the pioneer boat line on the Arrow Lakes, its plan for this part of its empire began to unfold. The first thing was a thirty-mile branch from its main line to the head of the Arrows. The branch started at the place originally known as Second Crossing where the main line railroad bridged the Columbia after coming down from the summit of the Selkirks. Second Crossing had already taken the name of A. S. Farwell, an up-and-coming town promoter who had guessed right before the CPR decided to build its branch to the Arrows. He had acquired property and laid out his townsite facing the river just below the CPR bridge. It was a good site. Farwell town was doing well, too, what with a big general store, several small shops, a hotel, a weekly newspaper, and a busy Chinatown settled by the laid-off railroad construction workers.

The Canadian Pacific sought a site for its depot from Promoter Farwell and, "failing to secure the concessions desired," as a local historian put it, bought a block of land well back from the river and a quarter of a mile or more from Farwell, then laid out its own townsite of Revelstoke. The depot was moved to the new town. Switching yards were built. Farwell became "Old Town" and began to fade. Revelstoke grew.

The thirty-mile branch south from Revelstoke had its terminus at another new town, Arrowhead, where the CPR built a long dock with a slip by which boxcars could be loaded on scows with tracks on their decks. These were taken down the full length of the two lakes and the cars transferred to CPR rails at Robson; or, they might go only as far as Nakusp and be transferred there to CPR tracks which even then were building over the range to New Denver (old Eldorado) on Silvery Slocan Lake. Canadian Pacific rails were to touch both Slocan and Kootenay lakes at other places. Convenient to both mining districts was the new city of Nelson where the railroad was encouraging construction of a smelter.

Nelson was to grow into a considerable metropolis and call itself The Queen City. It came into being with discovery of the Hall and the Silver King mines and their development by a British syndicate. The camp which, like Revelstoke, used up a couple of names before it settled on Nelson, was first known as Stanley, then as Salisbury. It was finally named not for the British sea hero but for Hugh Nelson, lieutenant governor of British Columbia. It stood on the south shore of the West Arm of Kootenay Lake, and was to vie with Trail for early importance. Few towns of the period could have had a more succinct history than that penned by one Colonel Lowery. When he got to Nelson, he wrote, "The camp was new and short of frills, boiled shirts, parsons, lawyers, and prohibition orators. It had plenty of whisky, a few canary and other birds, and several pianos. All the rest of the population were mule skinners, packers, trail blazers, and remittance men, with a slight trace of tenderfeet. The police slept only in the daytime. The first man to get drunk in Nelson was Jack Buchanan. I have no means of knowing who will be the last. Dr. LeBeau was the first physician, and Charlie Waterman the first auctioneer. W. F. Teetzel was the first druggist and Harry Ashcroft the first blacksmith. Colonel Topping was the victim of the first accident. He was stooping at the creek to get a drink, instead of drinking out of a bottle, when his .44 dropped out of his pocket and opened a crosscut in his wrist. The first dance was held in the Silver King hotel."

Nelson went ahead from the first, and its future was assured when what is now the Crowsnest Pass Division of the CPR came through from Alberta and continued on westward to meet the mainline again at the Fraser River. Many years later, when several of the district's mines gave out, and others started to send their ores to Trail, Nelson did not fade but turned to agriculture. Its fruit pack and shipments of fresh fruit have made it a notable center.

While both the Slocan and Kootenay lakes were able to supply freight from their mines, the Arrows having no mines or other industry seemed destined to remain chiefly a north-south route for water transfer of freight cars. But the CPR had plans for industry too. It attracted the eastern Canada lumber concern of Adam Hall which came to buy timber and erect a sawmill at Arrowhead. Another Eastern Canadian outfit arrived from Parry Sound, Ontario, and built an even bigger mill at Arrowhead and opened logging camps on near-by Galena Bay. The settlement at the head of the lakes grew again by addition of a shingle mill. More than five hundred men were required to

operate the mills and camps, and many of the millwork-
ers brought families. Homes and bunkhouses ranged
around the handsome Arrowhead cove and climbed the
hill in the shadow of eight-thousand-foot Mount Sproat.
A school was opened. Stores and churches came. A hotel
was built. Lumber went out by rail to the CPR mainline at
Revelstoke and in boxcars down the lakes to meet the rails
at Robson. Arrowhead quickly became of importance and
the CPR was pleased to have a sleeping car there daily
which overnight would deliver passengers in Vancouver.

Other logging camps and sawmills were established
on the lakes between Arrowhead and Robson. Nakusp
came to have one of the biggest pole and piling yards in
the province. At Halcyon Hot Springs, reputedly held by
the Indians to be the "Great Medicine Waters," a syndicate
built a sanatorium, with rows of small Swiss-type cottages;
and a bottling works was added which shipped the lithia
waters to London and even to remote parts of the British
Empire. The ailing started coming to take the cure at the
springs in such numbers that the CPR boats made Halcyon
a twice-daily port of call. Later the place was managed by
Brigadier General F. E. Burnham, much-decorated British army surgeon in World War I.

There were many other mineral springs around Ar-
row Lake. Those at St. Leon became the great dream of
Mike Grady, a mining character from Peterborough, On-
tario, who prospected the Slocan Lake country and found
a rich ledge of silver which he sold and moved to Upper
Arrow. Here he spent his pile to develop St. Leon Hot
Springs which he had come across in his prospecting days.
He first built a great three-story spa hotel. He was finicky

about lumber, and no board with a knot in it went into the structure. Then he started hand boring wooden pipes to carry water from the springs to the spa. It was a task larger than he had thought. After many weeks he gave up the idea and installed iron pipes. They turned out to be too small; the water was cold by the time it reached the hotel.

But the seekers of cures started coming. Mike got a liquor license and opened a bar. This, as old-timers agree, was a mistake because Mike himself spent too much time in the licensed premises. World War I brought a sudden halt to the flow of customers to the spa. Mike lost his liquor license. But he himself stayed on for many years, an old man now, living alone in the echoing house, shaggy as a lion, with long gray hair, whom passengers on passing steamers saw coming down from the old hotel to meet every boat, waiting for patients to take the magic waters of St. Leon. By then, the nine thousand feet of iron pipe were long since stopped up. Much later, the St. Leon hotel was taken over by others and reopened as "The Gates of St. Leon."

Fruit and berry ranchers came slowly to the Arrow Lakes and provided some traffic for the CPR steamers, the queen of which beginning in 1898, was *SS Minto*. Named for the fourth Earl of Minto, then governor-general of Canada, her hull was built at Nakusp for the Canadian Pacific Railway Company. Her fine engines, which came from Toronto, had been intended for service on the Yukon River in the then current gold rush, but were diverted instead to the Columbia.

The *Minto* was to operate on the Arrows for nigh six decades, a record for a Columbia River stern-wheeler. Indeed, she was the very last passenger-and-freight vessel to ply the Columbia's main stream on a regular schedule, a happy and sturdy anachronism when she was laid up for good in April, 1954, not because she was decrepit but because lake traffic would no longer come near to paying the cost of operation. Only then, when SS *Minto* surrendered her registry, fifty-six years after she was launched, did the Columbia River's steamboat era come to an end.

I had the great good fortune to ride her the full length of the Arrows in her last full season. We got aboard at Arrowhead after a three-hour wait. Here, where in former times a sleeping car was parked daily on the siding, ready to take Arrowheaders overnight to Vancouver, was the nostalgia that has overtaken so many villages whose life was predicated on steamboats and railroads. The CPR still maintained a dandy little depot with a well-kept flower bed, and a long pier reaching out into the bay. A vacant frame hotel stood staring blankly from beneath big old cottonwoods that shivered and rustled as cottonwoods do. Crawford's General Store was fairly busy, but it was "modern" not "country" style now. There was also a particularly graceless restaurant, though the food was passable.

The mixed train hove in from Revelstoke two hours late, bringing half-a-dozen passengers for the *Minto*, which stood smoking at the long dock. Nobody was in a hurry, least of all the *Minto*'s crew; and when she had taken aboard passengers and mail and freight, she backed away, turned and started on the 130-mile run to Robson and Castlegar at the other end of Lower Arrow Lake. In the steward's room a bright canary was singing as we pulled away. In the forward saloon was a framed map of the river dated 1919. Captain Manning, who had been on the river since 1911, was in the pilothouse.

Though she was built to be a workhorse and not a luxury boat, the *Minto* presented some few affectations of the Victorian era that in a day of grim functional design were almost elegance. There was fine grillework. There were

SS *Minto* on Arrow Lakes, British Columbia.

blue and yellow panes in the saloon skylights. The dining room was paneled. There was a big handsome sideboard. Fresh flowers stood on it and on the tables. The food was good and came in heroic portions. The day began with a thumping four-course breakfast at 75 cents. Dinner and supper cost a dollar each.

There was a wonderful surge to the *Minto*; you could tell she was a stern-wheeler and not a screw propeller by the way she moved forward. There was a pleasant exhaust, a sort of long sigh to her engines which Second Engineer Reg Barlow said were as fine as ever went into a vessel. She surged ahead, she sighed. She was an old, old lady, she knew where she was going, and time mattered not at all. We came to Nakusp after dark and there tied up for the night. I walked up a steep if low hill to the village which struck me as livelier than much larger Revelstoke, then back down to the dock. The *Minto* at night was something to put away in memory. She looked twice as large lighted up from stem to stern as she did in daytime. With the black waters of the lake beyond she stood out like a proper symbol of the era that had passed—had passed, that is, everywhere along the Columbia save here on the Arrows. She was the very last passenger steamer on twelve hundred miles of river. She was still a good boat, sound in hull and engine, but I knew she was soon to be taken out of service. Her offense was not senility, but rather that she had persisted in living on into a period when a leisurely pace is reckoned little short of criminal.

I awoke at four in the morning when bells rang and we pulled away from Nakusp in heavy fog. The gulls that had followed from Arrowhead were still with us, circling and crying in the mist. We stopped almost everywhere, first on one shore of the lake, then the other; and everywhere one looked there was a lot of scenery that made one wonder why people wanted to live elsewhere than on the Arrows.

We came to The Narrows, and I could see current here in the eighteen miles between the Upper and Lower lakes, where the shores are often less than a quarter of a mile apart. But the current soon disappeared and we were

in glassy water again. The mountains on the west gradually changed to hills, then gave way in spots to open
parklike areas. We saw many orchards close to the lake.
We stopped at Arrow Park, Carroll's Landing, Burton,
Faquier, Needles, Sherwood, Renata, Deer Park, and
Syringa Creek. Somewhere or other the *Minto* unloaded a
quantity of pipe for irrigating purposes; and here and
there we took aboard many boxes of peaches. At one lonely
place we pulled away just as a man came running down a
long slip yelling, and waving a mailbag. The accommodating *Minto* stopped in her tracks and surged ahead to ram
her nose into some high dollies obviously erected for that
purpose, then bounced off when the mailman had tossed
the bag to the lower deck.

As we neared Syringa Creek, I looked west across the
lake to see the Kettle Valley line of the CPR high in the
Monashees, a long freight crossing one trestle after another
in a stretch of mountain railroad as dizzy as one would
care to see. Shortly we came to dock at Robson-Castlegar
and the end of the voyage. We had been aboard the *Minto*
twenty-five hours, a day and a night journey through the
past that will likely hold in my memory when all other
water trips have been forgotten. Only when we drove from
the *Minto*'s freight deck up the gangplank and so onto a
paved highway was the spell broken. It was an abrupt and
a dismal end to an idyll.

The *Minto*'s end came on April 24, 1954, when she
was turned over by the CPR to the Chamber of Commerce
of Nakusp, for one dollar. Here in the village where the
Minto's hull was built back in 1898, the old stern-wheeler
was to be moored and made into a sort of community

meeting place for service clubs, Boy Scouts and other local groups. There was talk of making her lower deck into a bowling alley.

Her sister ship, the *Moyie*, also built in 1898 and put into service on Kootenay Lake, survived the *Minto* and continued to carry freight and passengers on her home waters. Other survivors of the CPR fleets are of later vintage, and none works on the main Columbia. On Kootenay was a steel and steam screw tug, the *Granthall*, which acted as relief when needed for the *Moyie*. On Lake Slocan still in service was SS *Roseberry*, a wood and steam screw tug built in 1943. The Okanogan Lake fleet's survivors included the screw tugboats *Kelowna* and *Naramata*; and the diesel tug *Okanogan*, built in 1947. All are unquestionably doomed by the ever-creeping highways. A map issued in 1954 by the British Columbia Department of Lands and Forests showed highways running the full length of Lakes Kootenay, Slocan, and Okanogan, either on one or both shores. Even the Arrow Lakes, at about their middle, had a stretch of highway; and the map also showed two other significant features. These were marked "Free Ferry." They were installed almost wholly to accommodate the trucks and other cars that are bringing the gasoline age to Upper and Lower Arrow Lakes.

Chapter 10

A Wilderness Prophet

IN THE gentle spring of 1909 there came to the foot of The Arrow Lakes a tall, bearded man named Peter Verigin. To his more than fifteen thousand followers, the Dukhobors, he was more than man. He was half pope, half king. For two decades he had ruled this Russian religious cult with shrewd understanding and, when need be, called on Revelation for aid. Now he was in British Columbia seeking land.

It is possible that Revelation touched him again as he stood on a bold headland and looked far down on the hurrying Kootenay River where it joined the more leisurely Columbia. Revelation or not, this was the place he was to choose. The spot might be called a delta. Its soil was alluvial. It was rich. Canadians and English immigrants had already proved its worth by raising fine fruits and berries here. That the place had also a dramatic setting probably played little part in Peter Verigin's decision; he sought utility and the isolation of this mountainous country. Yet Brilliant, as the neighborhood was already named, was a spectacular spot. It was at the very mouth of the Kootenay's last canyon—a smooth stretch of bottomland at the base of high and bare mountain walls that were marked here and there, eagle-high on the naked cliffs, by the futile drift-holes of forgotten prospectors.

It looked good to Peter Verigin, and no man knew better than he that he must choose well. He was here not to buy a few acres, but to establish a whole new empire for his people. Then he must move them more than a thousand miles from the Saskatchewan prairie; and they would have to change their lives as wheat farmers and learn to grow fruits and berries, even to become loggers and sawmill workers. Some of them might grumble, a few might refuse to come, but the majority would follow meekly wherever their Moses should lead them. That is the way it had always been with the Dukhobors.

The sect originated in a seventeenth century schism in the Russian Orthodox Church, and for two hundred years its adherents were shunted from one Russian province to another, beaten by Cossacks, robbed regularly by government agents, and imprisoned. Their great crime was that they refused to serve in the army of the Czar. They came in time to be vegetarians. They were nondrinkers of vodka. They did not use tobacco. Late last century the powerful Count Leo Tolstoy became interested in them. So did Aylmer Maude, an Englishman, and the Quakers. These people aided the Dukhobors to migrate to Canada. That had been in 1899, when ten thousand of them came to settle on Saskatchewan homesteads. Peter the Lordly, as he was called, joined them four years later, being delayed by exile in Siberia.*

* In 1913, when I was a newspaper cub in Winnipeg, I once saw Peter Verigin in the Manor Hotel near the CPR depot. He was

The Dukhobors proved highly successful at wheat farming, though their occasional use of Dukhobor women as field animals was a scandal to non-Dukhobors. When there were not enough horses to go round, a twenty-four-woman team was hitched to a plow and pulled it through the prairie sod. (Among the older members was the belief that many years ago, a dreadful plague had been stopped short of the Dukhobor town in Russia when "a group of maidens pulled a plow to make a furrow around the settlement.") In little more than a decade after they landed in Canada, the sect had become prosperous. They worked hard, paid their bills and minded their own business. The rub came when it was time to comply with Canadian land laws by signing individually for their homesteads. This they would not do, saying that signing would make them subjects of the British king and liable to military service. This was not true. The Dukhobors were officially recognized as pacifists by the Canadian government and specifically exempted from military duty. But they still refused to sign, and in 1907 the government acted: Each Dukhobor who had failed to comply with the Homestead Act was made to relinquish all but fifteen acres for himself and fifteen acres for each member of his family. In this manner nearly one hundred thousand acres, no little of which had been brought to the plow, reverted to the government.

This was the time when Peter the Lordly began to think of buying land outright in British Columbia and moving his people there. He urged his followers to work hard

huge, but not obese, and perhaps looked bigger than he was because of the fur coat and cap he wore. He was bearded, and the papers said he looked much like his mentor Tolstoy. I thought his appearance most imposing.

on the land that remained theirs; and he set the younger men to working for the railroads. All were to turn every penny into the community fund. They had done so and now, little more than a year later, Peter had come to the Columbia River looking for a new Canaan.

In and near Brilliant, in this spring of 1909, Peter bought lands both wild and improved which, when added to another and smaller tract at Grand Forks, a hundred miles west, totalled 14,403 acres. The price was $646,007. Indicative of the financial condition of the Dukhobors was the fact that Peter promptly made a cash payment of approximately $300,000. He had the property registered in his own name.

Returning to Saskatchewan, Peter moved through the several Dukhobor settlements, giving word that the wonderfully mild and rich country of the upper Columbia River awaited their coming. Eight hundred came immediately by special train to Kootenay Landing where they transferred to CPR boats for a voyage down the handsome lake. A majority remained at Brilliant, while the rest went on west a hundred miles to settle the Dukhobor lands at Grand Forks. Old Canadian settlers were astonished at the enthusiasm of these people and at the speed with which they erected great double houses, cleared land for gardens, and planted. Even though it was late summer, the gardens produced vegetable crops before the first frost.

A year later came another contingent. Up went a big sawmill on the Columbia water front at Brilliant, making lumber for Dukhobor buildings, with more left over for sale. In the Grand Forks colony the settlers set up a kiln and made bricks, selling part of the product to the British

Columbia government. Here, too, the colonists started grafting fruit trees and vines. A little later they were to measure their grape harvest by the hundreds of tons.

They were tireless, these people. At Brilliant they established a ferry across the Columbia. They worked like

The delta at Brilliant, B. C., where the Dukhobors settled.

ants to build a concrete reservoir that held 100,000 gallons, filled it by pumping from a mountain spring, then laid pipes to every house. In 1911 another thousand members came, and still more a year later. By 1913 there were more than six thousand Dukhobors in British Columbia. Peter Verigin took over a vacant industrial plant in the city of Nelson and soon established what became the largest jam factory in the province. The Dukhobor jams and marmalades were famous even here among the jam-loving Canadians and English.

Community living was the manner of life in the villages. All the houses were built in pairs. Each was of two stories, each accommodated from thirty-five to fifty persons. The upstairs was divided into small bedrooms, each with a window, and a doorway with a curtain. Downstairs was a general room with benches, and a combination kitchen and dining room. Every kitchen had an immense Russian oven. Back of each house was a storehouse, a bathhouse, and a toilet. A large house was built especially for Peter the Lordly, and to care for it Peter himself selected from the daughters of his people half-a-dozen young women to act as his servants and handmaidens.

All went better than well with the Dukhobors in their new homes; and also with those who remained to raise wheat on the prairies. In 1917, Peter felt the time had come to expand the sect's business with the outside world. The Christian Community of Universal Brotherhood, Limited, was incorporated under a Dominion charter. It was capitalized at $1,000,000. Peter issued the one million shares to himself and thirteen Dukhobor directors. The total assets of the company at the time of incorporation were at least three times that of the capitalization, according to J. F. C. Wright, historian of the Dukhobors.

All might have continued well had it not been for an inner sect of the group who called themselves the Sons of Freedom. These unworldly members had already caused no little trouble before the move to British Columbia. In Saskatchewan they had staged mass parades in the nude "in protest to an order to send their children to the public schools." Occasionally, and for no discernible reason, they had destroyed their own agricultural machines; they had burned their own homes and the homes of other Dukhobors. Purification, they called it.

Now, when they had come to British Columbia, the Sons refused to report births, deaths and marriages to the government. They refused to send their young to school. Three were arrested. In 1923 the first public schoolhouse in the Brilliant settlement was destroyed by fire. Two more were destroyed in the spring of 1924. All the fires were described as of unknown origin. So was the fire that destroyed the great house of Peter the Lordly. Then, in August, John Sherbinin, who ran the Dukhobor sawmill and was one of Peter's ablest and most trusted lieutenants, left the group to live as an Independent. This meant that forthwith he would contribute nothing to the community. Several others followed his example. These things were most disturbing, and they were quickly followed by an event beside which everything that had gone before paled into nothing.

On the evening of October 28—it was still 1924—a small group of Dukhobors assembled at the little railroad station beside the Columbia at Brilliant. They were there to see Peter board the cars for what he said was a routine business trip. With him was one of his several handmaidens, Mary Streliova. Peter and Mary got aboard the Canadian Pacific's Kootenay Express, where they found a seat in about the middle of the day coach. A Dukhobor man carried Peter's suitcase into the train and put it under the seat. Then he bowed and left the car. Conductor Turner signaled the engineer, and away went the train into the clear mountain night.

Ahead of the day coach was a baggage car, behind it a sleeper. In the coach were several passengers, among them John A. Mackie, a member of the British Columbia Parliament, and Harry Bishop, a commercial traveler for Swift & Company. There was a lone Chinese, and perhaps half-a-dozen Hindu men, all heading for Grand Forks to work in a sawmill.

It is worth knowing, though it merely adds to the mystery, that when Conductor Turner came through to collect fares, Peter presented him with two tickets to Castlegar, the very next station, less than two miles from Brilliant. But when the train stopped at Castlegar, neither Peter nor the handmaiden got out of their seats. The train-man nodded to Peter. "This is your station," he said.

Peter made no move. The express pulled out, and when the conductor came through again, Peter had money ready in his hand and purchased two cash fares to Grand Forks, a hundred miles farther on. At the flag-stop station of Tunnel, twenty-odd miles west of Castlegar, three Dukhobor men got aboard, were seen to nod to their leader, then settled down in a double seat six windows behind Peter and Mary. The train began to climb steadily to Farron, 3,976 feet above the sea. At Farron a cafe-lounge car was added to the train, which pulled away at one o'clock in the morning and started the long descent at a cautious twenty miles an hour, whistle mourning at the many curves, the brake shoes grinding hard.

Conductor Turner went through the day coach to check. No passengers had got on at Farron. The twenty-odd people now in the car had settled down for the night in the manner of experienced coach passengers. Turner noted that Peter the Lordly was dozing, his head bent forward. Beside him Mary the handmaiden slept, her babushkaed head on a pillow on the window sill. Conductor Turner went on ahead into the baggage car. Just then came a tremendous roar. The rear door of the baggage car was hurled off its hinges and blown halfway down the car. The lights went out. The train stopped with a jolt.

The baggageman opened a side door and leaped to the ground. The conductor and trainman, partially stunned, pushed through the splintered wood blocking the day coach, now dark save for a bright blue flame licking up from the floor where a gas main had broken. The car reeked with the fumes characteristic of dynamite. Conductor Turner looked up suddenly to find himself gazing at the night sky and its clear cold stars. The roof of the coach was entirely gone. Turner noted also that most of the north side of the coach, together with many of the seats on that side, had vanished. Conductor and trainman found eight passengers, either dead or in a state of shock, and dragged them out of the car, by then alight from the spreading fire.

The train crew and passengers looked around. One of the Hindu men was found battered and dead. Dead, too, was Mackie, M. P. The traveling man, Bishop, was dying. Mary the handmaiden, clothes torn from her body, was also dying. She never spoke. A good hundred feet from Mary lay the great king of the Dukhobors, a terrible wound in his side, one leg blown off, quite dead.

When daylight and medical aid arrived, nine passengers were found to have been killed. Many more were injured. The explosive force had been terrific. Debris was found scattered for two hundred feet along the tracks. Shreds of clothing and bits of flesh were picked up more than three hundred feet from the day coach.

The investigators, D. C. Coleman, vice-president of the Canadian Pacific Lines West, of Winnipeg, and D. W. ("Dynamite") McNabb of the Dominion Bureau of Explosives, concluded that the blast had come from within the coach and that the point of greatest force had been under or close to the seat in which Peter and Mary had been dozing. In the debris were found a dry battery and pieces of alarm clock, indicative of an infernal machine set to go off at a selected moment.

A coroner's jury said that the victims had come "to their death through powerful explosive placed in the coach through ignorance or deliberately." The "ignorance" cited had reference to the quaint practice of local ranchers and prospectors, who used dynamite to clear land and shatter ledges. Dynamite could be transported legally by rail only in a special freight car, the expense of which precluded its use by most people. Hence, individuals had been known to pack a suitcase with dynamite and carry it as hand luggage in a coach. But the dry battery and bits of clockwork in the debris would appear to demolish the rancher-prospector theory. Rather they indicate that whoever packed the suitcase which the Dukhobor man carried into the day coach at Brilliant and placed under the seat taken by Peter and Mary was preparing for something other than the clearing of land or the digging of a mine hole.

Yet, even if this likely theory be accepted, it does nothing to explain the odd business of the tickets: At Brilliant, as said, Peter bought two fares to Castlegar, two miles away. At Castlegar he bought two more tickets, this time to Grand Forks, four hours away. Why the change of destination? Was Peter trying to fool his people at Brilliant? Did the assassin suspect that Peter and Mary were actually bound elsewhere than for Castlegar?

It was baffling then, and it is baffling today. Neither rewards nor further investigation solved the mystery, and it is probable that no affair in British Columbia has caused more speculation. More than three decades after the explosion one may hear a number of theories put forward. A Son of Freedom told a casual reporter that "The government murdered Peter." Many non-Dukhobors believe Peter was blown apart by the Sons of Freedom who considered his policy about the public schools not radical enough. But many more hold the murder to have stemmed from a personal motive—common everyday woman trouble. This is suggested also by Dukhobor Historian Wright who thinks it more than possible that some young man of the colony was in love with one or another of the many pretty girls Peter selected, over the years, for his staff of handmaidens.

The death of Peter marked the beginning of a slow disintegration of the Dukhobors. His son, who became leader, was much given to the bottle and other scandalous practices. Some believe he consciously worked to undermine the spirit and economy of his people. The jam factory and sawmill were mortgaged, then lost. The finances of the group at last became so involved that the British Columbia government stepped in "to lift the burden from the backs of a loan company and place it quietly on the shoulders of the taxpayers."

For many years the province has been aiding ex-communal Dukhobors to set up as independent farmers. Schism split the sect again as recently as 1947, when one calling himself Michael the Archangel led a group of eighty to Vancouver Island. Burnings of public schoolhouses have continuously marked the Brilliant and Grand Forks settlements. So has other violence, including attacks on railroad tracks and public utilities. The Sons of Freedom established a new village, Krestova, then proceeded to burn each other's homes there. In 1953 outbreaks attributed to the Sons resulted in arrests of more than one hundred persons. The Sons even turned against the patient Quakers who at last sent one of their best field men, Emmett Gulley, to attempt to solve what much of British Columbia continues to speak of as "the Dukhobor problem."

High on the rocky headland above Brilliant stands the tomb of Peter the Lordly. It has been attacked numerous times during the past thirty years by unknown dynamiters. Each time it has been carefully repaired and it is now protected by a high steel fence and is floodlighted at night. Fruit trees and a profusion of flowers grow around the massive block of reinforced concrete and stone. From this mausoleum, hacked out of flint and granite, one looks down on the last mile of the Kootenay as it joins the Columbia; and on the vast orchards of the Dukhobors, with the great, stark, hip-roofed community homes here and there among the trees. Whether Peter Verigin was saint or charlatan, his tomb stands in a neolithic grandeur fit for the king of the Dukhobors and president of the Christian Community of Universal Brotherhood, Limited.

Chapter 11

Timber

IT is time to mention that for a century past the base of major activity along the Columbia and many of its tributaries has been timber. Timber is king here. Logs being towed in boom or raft. Logs running wild with river drivers riding and chasing them down to the mills. Deep-sea vessels with cargoes of lumber and shingles. These are the things that have characterized the river ever since the fur canoes and bateaux disappeared.

By the century's turn most of the river's larger tributaries were being served by stern-wheelers or railroads or both together; and in one way or another the source of much of the traffic had to do with timber. Not only freight, but also passengers moved because of timber. Wheat was still a big water-borne item as it had been since the 1870s. On the lower river, say between The Dalles and Astoria, the business of catching and canning salmon had grown into a large industry. But on long stretches of the main river and more than a score of its tributaries, timber in the form of logs or lumber had become the traffic of first importance. It was so in mid-twentieth century.

The most extensive forest of big trees anywhere in the United States covered the region between the Cascades and the sea. Douglas fir was the dominant species, though cedar of incredible girth grew with the fir, and in the belt near salt water were the spruce and hemlock of the so-called rain forest.

East of the Cascades were the pines—ponderosa and Idaho white. North of these in British Columbia, on a line say from Trail to Yahk, the interior spruce forest began to take over and to run on north to the muskegs.

The earliest record of logging in the Columbia's region was of that which fed the small water-powered sawmill of the Hudson's Bay Company near Fort Vancouver. By the early 1820s two white men and twenty-five Sandwich Islanders, as Hawaiians were known, were cutting trees and making them into boards at the trading post. Small amounts of this lumber were shipped out of the Columbia, but most of it was needed for Company purposes in and around the settlement. What might be called commercial logging for export did not get under way until 1848. This was at Oregon City or Willamette Falls. The mills were powered by water. Two years later the first steam sawmill in the Northwest blew whistle in upstart Portland, and export of lumber by way of the Columbia became a regular thing.

When the first loggers, many of whom were State-of-Mainers, saw the fir that grew along the banks of the Columbia, they said there just couldn't be timber that big and tall, and bragged in letters back to Bangor that it took two men and a boy to look to the top of one of these giants. Oregon pine they called it. It was neither pine nor fir, though for more than half a century it has been sold as Douglas fir. Its botanical name is *Pseudotsuga taxifolia*, meaning "false hemlock." It grows to an extreme height of 380 feet. Its average diameter at breast height is from four to six feet. Still standing not far from Astoria is a Douglas fir fifteen feet six inches in diameter, healthy and growing despite the winds and fires and bugs of a thousand years. It is a tree to give a man pause, even a logger.

One of this great fir's smaller fellows was sufficient to awe Clement Adams Bradbury, fresh from York County, Maine, when he observed its eight-foot butt and gazed up to its tip that proved to be more than three hundred feet distant. It was Bradbury who left the earliest good account of felling one of these Goliaths. On January 15, 1847, he stepped up to this tree that stood by the Columbia some twenty miles east of Astoria. Like the experienced man he was, he took in the lay of the land, spat on his hands, then started his undercut. He had not cut more than sixteen inches into the trunk when he was startled by "a copious flow of pitch that would nigh fill a hogshead." So great was the run of pitch that Bradbury quit in disgust, returning next day when the flow had ceased, and finished the job.

Bradbury's discovery was also made by almost every settler who staked his claim to forest land along the lower river. Trees to the average homesteader were just something to be got rid of. Here in western Oregon he often used an auger with a long handle to bore a horizontal hole deep into a fir, then a slanting hole to meet it. The slanting hole provided a chimney and draft when the other hole was fired. In this way a fir two hundred and more feet tall could be turned into a torch, and land was cleared.

The pitch flow was also the reason that loggers sought to start their undercuts well up the trunk of a fir. They left stumps from six to sixteen feet above the ground. They often did the same with cedar, not because of pitch but rather to escape the swell-butts of this species. Many years afterward the cedar stumps were logged and made into fine shingles.

Millions of feet of Douglas fir were felled within a few yards of shore along the lower river, then limbed and put into the water by use of hand jacks, and towed to the nearest mill, which was never very far. But logging of much of the first mile or so back from the stream was done by skid road, the Far West loggers' chief contribution to technology. These logs were too big and heavy for sleds. There was seldom enough snow for sledding anyway.

To handle them, the lower Columbia loggers first cleared a path from the riverbank back into the forest. At suitable intervals they felled trees across this path, cut them free of limbs, and sank them half-deep into the soft ground. These were the skids. Skids made a sort of track that would prevent moving logs from hanging up on rocks or miring in mud. The finished job looked something like ties laid for a railroad in Gath.

It worked beautifully. They hitched steers called bulls to the logs—five, six, even ten yoke of the animals, in charge of the bullwhacker, the teamster, possibly the master of all profane men—and pulled long turns of the big sticks, held together by hooks, over the skids that were kept slick by the skid-greaser, who walked ahead of the logs but behind the oxen, daubing thick oil on the skids that smoked from friction.

In these woods you did not "swear like a trooper," or even like a sailor. You swore, if able, like a bullwhacker. When this character raised his voice in blasphemous obscenity, the very bark of the smaller firs was said to have smoked briefly, then curled up and fallen to the ground. The team made a picture never to be forgotten, as the powerful line of red and black and spotted white swung by with measured tread, the teamster, goadstick in hand, walking beside the animals, praising them, petting them, periodically crying aloud in protest to a God who had made such miserable oxen. Behind came the big logs with a ponderous roll, presently to thunder down the landing and into the water. It all made a scene to be embalmed a century later in the murals of hotels and barrooms west of the Cascades.

It was said of skid-road logging that you could not operate more than a mile from water. To do so courted bankruptcy. By the eighties, when much of the lower Columbia's timber line had receded farther than that from water, the steam donkey engine was introduced. The bulls gradually disappeared.

High-lead logging came in. A tall fir was topped and limbed where it stood, then guyed with cables, and at its top was hung a big block or pulley. Now the tree was a spar. Through the pulley passed a rope of steel running from the donkey engine at one end to a set of chokers at the other, and the logs came in a-snorting, front ends elevated to miss the obstructions of terrain and debris. A swinging boom lower down on the spar, named for its inventor C. C. McLean, loaded the logs onto flatcars, and down the railroad they went to the nearest water.

This was fast logging. The camps grew in size. Many an outfit from the Cascades to Astoria came to put three hundred thousand feet of logs a day into the booming grounds, and some put in half a million feet. Big and bigger mills arose along the river—at Astoria, Wauna, Westport, St. Helens; at Knappton, Kelso, and Kalama. At Portland both the Columbia and the Willamette were lined with mills. Above Vancouver they whined and smoked at Camas, Skamania, Cascade Locks, and Hood River. Here, just above Hood River, the fir forest began to be replaced by the pines.

The ponderosa pine forests were scattered over huge areas east of the Cascade Range in Oregon and Washington. They reached into Idaho and southern British Columbia and western Montana. The pine belt also continued east into South Dakota, and spread over portions of Wyoming, Utah, Colorado, Arizona, New Mexico and West Texas. Ponderosa is a handsome tree with bark ranging in color from cinnamon to orange-yellow. In typical stands a ponderosa forest has the look of a well-tended park. In the region of the middle Columbia the trees run up to two hundred feet in height and average four feet in diameter.

Centering in north Idaho along tributaries of the Columbia is the Western White Pine forest. Somewhat taller and larger than ponderosa, this tree (*Pinus monticola*) has the common name of Idaho white. Its unusually thin bark makes it particularly vulnerable to forest fires.

Logging in the pine regions of the Columbia began later than in the fir districts and did not become of great importance until advent of the transcontinental railroads. Even then the rivers were the usual path of the raw product from stump to mill. Making pine lumber was the first industry at Spokane (Falls) and of uncounted hamlets that hopefully claimed to be the future metropolis of the region, or merely of a county. Up the Spokane River thirty miles from Spokane was Lake Coeur d'Alene, and a town of the same name that grew to city size on Idaho white pine. It was fed by fleets of tugs towing vast booms of logs that had been brought to the lake in Michigan style, or State-of-Maine style, which is to say on sleds (called sleighs in the West) over snow roads ice-hard from sprinkling. Horses were the motive power. The loads were slowed on the grades by hay or dirt scattered on the ice, and let down the steepest hills with the aid of a Bangor Snubber, named for the old logging center on the Penobscot.

Much the same thing was going on along the Kootenai River in Montana, Idaho and British Columbia; and around one of the largest bodies of water wholly within the United States, which is that wide piece of the Clark Fork called Lake Pend Oreille. And a little later, that swift tributary of the Snake, the Clearwater, carried annually the largest one-company harvest of pine logs down to the big mill at Lewiston.

Indeed, it was here in the Western pine country that the log drive came to have a new birth and where it survives to this day. Driving the river, any river, was for two hundred years the classic method of getting logs to the mill. When the Lake States timber gave out, the catfooted lads moved on to the Inland Empire. Give 'em a peavey or a pike pole and they were ready to fill the Kootenai, the Priest, the St. Maries, the St. Joe and the Clearwater full of logs and chase them like hounds to the sawmills. There were certain traditions the Eastern loggers brought with them to the Far West. One was that when the drive was in, a man was entitled to a bust, then and there.

"We hove-in at Bonners Ferry, Idaho, on the 12th of July, 1911, with the whole Kootenai drive," recalled George A. Newark, forty years later. He had come from Michigan to start driving pine in Montana. "We put in seventy-two days that year. Much of the time the Kootenai was bank-full, both water and logs, and we brought thirty-two million feet to the booms at Bonners Ferry. The town was ready for us. In those days, it was the custom of express company agents in river towns to have a large number of packages on hand. These might be addressed to John Smith, or Ole Olson. In any case, they all contained a gallon or so of hard liquor. You went into the agency, the man asked if you were John Smith, you said you were and paid the charges, and went out with the package. The drive was in, and no matter the local option laws, no decent town expected a man should go without his liquor at such times."

Some logs went to the mills by railroad. And there was still one more way of getting logs to the mills. This was the water-flume, an elevated trough that wound its way down the mountain, crossing ravines on high trestles, half full of hurrying water, carrying with it a sort of regimented river drive, one stick following another to the end of the flume which was a sawmill's logpond. A few flumes were from twenty-five to thirty miles long. Some outfits preferred to

215

saw their logs right in the woods and to flume the timbers and planks to the finishing mill at the lower end of the flume.

The flume also presented a cheap if dangerous method of going to town on Saturday night, though you could hardly return to camp the same way. "We'd save some good timbers to ride on," one old flume-logger recalled, "and Saturday night ease them into the trough and get aboard with a piece of edging for a balance pole, like a tight-rope walker. You had to have good sense of balance. We wore our calked boots, of course, and carried our fancy shoes and a clean shirt in a sack slung over our shoulder. Once in a while your timber would take off as though it was going to sail right out of the trough. Then it might go a long way slow and easy, maybe six miles an hour. Our flume went under several bridges, when we'd jump out, run across and drop back on our timber again. It was dangerous, but it was fun and when you were young and didn't know any better, it was a grand way to get to town. Getting back to camp was something else."

Here and there a logging flume survives in the second half of the century. So do a few logging railroads. Notable river drives continue to go down the Spillimacheen, the Priest and the Clearwater. Mostly, however, the flumes and rails, along with the horse-drawn sleds, and the Big Wheels —used for summer logging—and the river drives have disappeared. Tractors and trucks do most of the logging in the pine country as well as the fir.

From the lower Columbia, for more than a third of a century, there was periodically launched a seagoing monster that might well have come out of the mythical land of Paul Bunyan. Many a newly arrived logger was startled when he saw for the first time, or even the second, one of the Benson log rafts moving through the mists over the river like some prehistoric marine animal. These rafts took their name from Simon Benson, a shrewd logger who operated camps on both sides of the river. He was a native of Norway and he favored Scandinavians above all other loggers; and because of them, so the story goes, he was able to keep his camps running during the period of general shutdown all over the region when loggers were released for their sacred Fourth of July drunk.

Legend has it that along in late June, a barrel of whiskey arrived at each Benson camp. The head was knocked in at once, and all hands were invited to belly around with tin dippers to drink their fill. Free. Following which, naturally, no logging was done for a day or so; but, when the Fourth did roll around, a week or two later, no Swede or Norwegian at Benson's camps ever knew it. They figured they had had their Fourth, and stayed on the job, happy and working hard, quite oblivious to a calendar whose red-lettered days meant nothing to them. The crew remained intact, if a bit shaky for a few days, but Benson's camps could supply needed logs just when stocks were low in the river and the price rising.

Simon Benson had been logging the lower Columbia for many years before he built a sawmill in faraway San Diego, California, handy to what he correctly believed would soon become a great lumber market. He soon discovered that the cost of shipping logs to this distant mill was prohibitive; so was shipping them in a coastwise vessel.

One of Benson's employees came up with the raft idea. Seagoing rafts had been tried long before on the New England coast, but failed of accomplishment. They were battered to pieces. But Benson and his men went ahead. In the quiet of Wallace Slough on the lower Columbia, they built a great cradle, filled it with three million feet of logs, hitched on a powerful tug and started. In twenty days the rig made the eleven-hundred-mile voyage without trouble.

Steamer with log tow. Oxen and skidroad in foreground.

This was it. More than one hundred other rafts followed in her wake, and the Benson mill in Southern California was perhaps the only one in North America to saw lumber from logs grown in a forest eleven hundred miles away.

The rafts were cigar shaped, and they came in time to hold some five million feet of logs each, plus a deckload of shingles—enough material to build one good-sized village. A raft was thirty-five feet thick and drew twenty-eight feet of water. It was 835 feet long, or exactly 140 feet shorter

than the SS *Queen Mary* of the Atlantic. The last of the
Benson leviathans left the Columbia in 1941. Yet the river
is still a highway for logs, especially between the Cascades
and the ocean. Several billion feet move annually to lower
river sawmills and pulp and paper plants, much of it behind
diesel-powered tugs. At the far upper end of the river, above
Golden, British Columbia, millions of feet of spruce, mixed
with a little pine, come thirty miles down the roaring
Spillimacheen to follow the Columbia another twenty
miles to mills at Parson. From mouth to headwaters, the
big river is still in contact with all the commercial species
of timber harvested on Columbia waters.

Since long before white men came, the forests of the
Columbia have been periodically swept by fires. These
great old trees harbor enormous memories. In the growth
rings of their trunks one may read and plainly the record
of dry years and wet years; of sore bruises long covered, of
scars that tell of fires going back to remote times. Almost
any of these older trees has known enough hardships and
tragedy to make the troubles of generations of men seem
like nothing.

Whether or not Indians set fire to the forests to make
hunting easier is a controversy of a size not to be aired in
less than the confines of a stout book; but in 1690 either a
man or a thunderbolt started a fire that burned over half a
million acres of these woods. There were other big fires before, and more came after. In 1847, for instance, much of
the Northwest was covered with smoke from August until
the winter rains and snows fell; and the few settlers remem-

bered it as the year of dark days. In 1868, fire burned along the Oregon hills of the lower Columbia throughout much of September and October, and left three hundred thousand acres devastated. It seems to have been much the same up the river in British Columbia. An observer there wrote in 1883 of forest fires which had been burning continuously for four months along the Columbia and the Kootenay. He remarked that "in some exceptionally dry years" fires there burned from spring to autumn. Ten years later W. S. Drewry, surveying in the same general area, wrote of a great fire which "overran hundreds of square miles, and destroyed an immense amount of valuable timber, in addition to homes and personal property."

A majority of the fires west of the Cascades have occurred in the fall. On September 17, 1902, a country correspondent for the *Weekly Columbian* of Vancouver sat down at an ash-covered table in Kalama to report one of the worst to date, a disaster of whose size even he, close to the center of it, had little idea. Who he was I have no idea, but he had a keen sense of tragedy in his soul, and was thus something of a poet. His pencil moved across the sheet of paper and he wrote his lead:

> What a week ago was the beautiful valley of the Lewis River is now a hot and silent valley of death, spotted with the blackened bodies of both man and beast. . . .

He did not exaggerate. The North Fork of the Lewis, a river that enters the Columbia at Woodland, had been hit hardest of all; and now that a wan sun could penetrate the smoke which had covered much of western Washington and Oregon for a week, as well as the sea for many miles offshore, it was becoming apparent that a major disaster had taken place. Though it went into history as the Yacolt Fire, it was really a series of the most terrible forest fires white men had seen west of the mountains. Thirty-five people had been burned to death. Perhaps as many as fifty hamlets or villages had been destroyed or partially burned. Farmers and stump-ranchers by the hundreds had lost everything except their lives. Cinders fell to cover Portland half an inch deep, and the same was true of Bellingham and Seattle, and other places all the way down the map to the head of the Willamette Valley at Eugene.

This monstrous fire or fires covered some 700,000 acres and was a sight to put fear into the stoutest heart and bring total distraction to weak or susceptible minds. In the murky streets of Olympia a disheveled woman ran and screamed that Mount Tacoma was in eruption. At a camp meeting near Woodland religious fanatics cried, "Glory to God, the Last Days have come," just before they had to run for their lives.

During the awful week, and while much of Clark County was burning on the north bank of the Columbia, fire leaped up in the timber near Bridal Veil on the Oregon side. It spread rapidly to destroy a big planing mill on the river's very edge, razed the village of Palmer back in the hills, and swept through thousands of acres of fine tall green timber. One should bear in mind that this was not brush burning—but timber often taller than Bunker Hill Monument, which is a mere 220 feet high. The captain of the *Bailey Gatzert* reported that he was compelled to use his searchlight to navigate the river at noon.

The worst scars of the fires of 1902 are still to be seen

on the Yacolt Burn. The fires prompted Washington to provide for a state forester and a chief fire warden. Oregon acted to create a board of forestry. These modest steps did little toward preventing fires or controlling them. That had to wait for 1910, when a bigger and deadlier fire aroused national interest. This, too, was really a series of fires that started burning in May and continued into September. They were virtually all on Columbia waters in the pine regions of Montana, Idaho, Washington and British Columbia. Ten thousand men fought them—loggers, miners, ranchers, rangers, and soldiers. The dead totaled eighty-five. The burn covered more than three million acres. The total timber damage probably topped eight billion feet, but this is at best a guess, for the area contained widely varying stands. All of the lives were lost and much of the damage done on the two terrifying days of August 20 and 21.

An awakened public at last demanded something be done, and in 1911 Congress passed the Weeks Act which provided Federal aid to state and private forest owners in maintaining protective organizations. It was a notable effort and its effect has been encouraging, even though more than two decades later Oregon had a fire more destructive of timber than anything before.

This was the Tillamook fire which began early in the afternoon of August 14, 1933, and in ten days covered 311,000 acres in Northwest Oregon. I saw it burn and shall never forget it. The area was relatively small compared to the fires of 1902 and 1910, yet it was all old growth timber and twelve and one-half billion feet of it was devastated.

Salvage began promptly and it is still being done more

than two decades after the land stopped smoking. Reseeding and replanting as well as other reforestation measures have been almost continuously under way by the State of Oregon. The direct loss from the fire was staggering. Much greater was the loss in future forests. Men have attempted to figure this loss of productive growth and have come up with sets of figures labeled "board feet" and "dollars," but the whole matter obviously belongs in the realm of metaphysics. It is not to be computed by any known method of mathematics.

One striking fact about the Tillamook fire has been reserved to give it the accent of isolation: Of the 311,000 acres burned, approximately 270,000 acres were burned during less than twenty hours on August 24-25. This will give an idea of the speed with which fire can travel, once weather conditions are ripe, in the commonly damp climate of western Oregon, the section responsible for the nickname of The Webfoot State.

The loggers who fought these three exceptional fires, and hundreds more during the period, were footloose men. They were quite generally considered notoriously footloose men. The Northwest timber had axmen and teamsters and river drivers who had learned their trades in Maine or in one or another of the Lake States. Not too many of them ever worked in one place long enough to vote, even if they had wanted to vote. Others had been born in Sweden, or Norway, or Finland. A few were French-Canadians. A few more came from the Maritime Provinces of Canada. The one thing they mostly had in common was that they did not have any home ties. They were boomers, short-stakers, here today, gone tomorrow. After 1907, a good many of them "carried a Little Red Card," which indicated membership in the Industrial Workers of the World, a rambunctious union that advocated a dictatorship of the proletariat, staged sudden strikes in the woods and mills, and in Spokane put on a "Free Speech" fight that is still talked about. The Wobblies, as they were known, began to fade in the 1920s, and during the Depression their members joined the CIO, a few joined the Communist Party, a few foreswore all labor organizations and returned to the arms of the Catholic Church.

It was dogmatic to a majority of the younger loggers, and to many who were not so young, that at least twice a year they must go to town to get their teeth fixed, an excuse or euphemism that was accepted by logging operators as certain as Holy Writ. The Fourth of July and Christmas were the favorite periods to shut down the camps. It was then that thousands of woodsmen converged on the towns and cities. They might remain a week or a month, depending on the market for logs and their own resources. And then—back to the camps.

Not necessarily the same camp they had been working at, for many of them had developed a taste for variety. They liked to range. A young logger might start the year in one of John Humbird's camps on the Kootenai, move in April—always a restless time—to Fred Herrick's outfit on the St. Maries River, and by the Fourth be driving team for the Craig Mountain camp at Winchester. He might resume work after the holiday at a Rutledge camp out of Clarkia, jump to Bonners Ferry for Weyerhaeuser, move into Montana to work for a while for J. Neils at Libby, and before Christmas be high in the Cascades at Leavenworth for the Great Northern. It was nothing to boom and cover a couple thousand miles in one season and never to leave Columbia waters. A really dedicated boomer, who knew both the short-log (pine) and the long-log (fir) techniques, could cover five thousand miles in a season and still be on the big river or one of its timbered tributaries. He might wind up dead broke, but meanwhile he had seen a wide variety of timber and, because they were the chief hiring centers, had been exposed to the joys and sorrows of the Skidroad districts of Spokane and Portland.

The Skidroad was and is that part of any Western town that caters to the needs and urges of loggers, miners, fishermen, harvest hands, and all other itinerant workers.* It was usually near the railroad depot and the water front, a place of employment offices, small hotels, flophouses, burlesque theaters, saloons, missions, fancy-houses, and a Wobbly Hall.

Spokane's Skidroad centered at Main and Trent where Jimmy Durkin had his noted saloon. He did much of the banking business for the men from the pine camps, keeping their money in his big safe, doling it out as wanted, and making small loans to those in need. "Jimmy Durkin is a man of his word" was a saying one can still hear quoted by old-timers in the pine country. Although Durkin's place

---

* Skidroad is the right word. Its etymology is without blemish. The term originated in Seattle seventy-odd years ago when logs were hauled through that settlement over an actual skid road. Around this road grew up the saloons and other places seeking logger trade, and the district became known as The Skidroad. The word spread. Of recent years a corruption has appeared as "skidrow" and is used only by those who know nothing of what they are talking or writing about. Skidroad as a term denoting a district in a city has been in the big Webster these many years.

dispensed a fearsome amount of liquor, over his bar was a sign that warned the literate: "If Children Need Shoes, Don't Buy Booze."

The Skidroad of Portland occupied much of West Burnside Street and all of the North End. In early years a prosperous piece of it was to be found in the middle of the Willamette River, which is the harbor, where Miss Nancy Boggs anchored her floating hell-hole, a two-storied house-boat, some eighty by forty feet, the lower deck a saloon and dance hall, the upper comprising the working quarters for Nancy's stable of about two dozen hostesses. Customers arrived by rowboat from both Portland and East Portland, for the town was then two separate cities. Other sirens remained on shore, among them Liverpool Liz, who called her place The Senate; and Mary Cook, a behemoth of a woman who kept order in her Ivy Green and did all her own bouncing.

In the way of straight drinking establishments the prize of Portland's Skidroad—and possibly of all others—was August Erickson's place. The bar ran to a total of 684 lineal feet. The place occupied the best part of a city block. Art was represented by an enormous oil painting, "The Slave Market," and the slaves were not Negroes but Grecian and female—and naked. Music was cared for by a "$5000 Grand Pipe Organ." The free lunch was prodigious. Beer was five cents, whiskey two for a quarter. A regiment of bartenders, who were gentlemanly but came in dragoon size, dispensed drinks and were ready to lend a hand if the bouncer permitted matters to get out of control. The bouncer was Jumbo Kelly, a Piltdown character who weighed a bit over three hundred pounds and whose general aspect reminded customers of a gigantic and ill-natured orangutan.

Better than a hundred other establishments in Portland's North End offered relaxation in one form or another. Scattered around the Skidroad were also half-a-dozen joints called sailors' boardinghouses from which, it was reputed, drunken or drugged men were sent to sea, whether or not they wanted to go, in the lumber schooners and grain ships. In the days of sail it was the practice to discharge most of a crew on arrival in Portland, to reduce costs while the ship was waiting to load lumber or grain. Then, when she was loaded, her captain engaged a crimp to fill his crew, paying "blood money" for every man supplied. Some sailors, of course, were ready to go. Others, and they might never have been to sea, had to be shanghaied. This was where the crimp came in.

Portland had one crimp who attained international celebrity—and eventually achieved thirteen years in the pen for murder. He was Joseph (Bunco) Kelly, who once bragged of having sent to sea more than one thousand landlubbers, to say nothing of twice as many experienced sailors. Moving quietly about in the Skidroad shadows and under its gaslights, Bunco Kelly made an art of crimping. He was about five feet tall, and fully as wide. He had enormous strength. He disliked to use violence, so he said, and had his own prescription for knockout drops which were prepared for him as needed in a Burnside Street pharmacy.

Like so many professional leaders in all lines, Bunco was a man of imagination. One night when men were scarce, he picked up the big wooden Indian that stood in front of Wildman's cigar store, wrapped it in an old tarpaulin, then shouldered it up the gangplank of a British four-master that had been loading wheat. "He's a big son-of-a-bitch, and he's awful drunk," he told the skipper, "But he'll make you a prime hand." Another time, on his nightly rounds, Bunco came across eight men who were either dead or dying from drinking a concoction from a barrel they thought was whiskey in a saloon's cellar. It just happened to be the basement of an undertaker's place, the barrel contained formaldehyde and, when Bunco came along, the drinkers had passed out. In this emergency, Bunco hurried into the street, collected half a dozen hacks, loaded the dead and dying singlehanded, took them to the dock, packed them aboard a ship, and collected $50 each from a captain who believed his new sailors were merely drunk. Clods in Bunco's profession would never have conceived a $400 job from such discouraging material.

But in a later attempt to shanghai another man, Bunco found it necessary to commit murder and was sent to the Oregon penitentiary to serve thirteen years. By the time he was released Portland had long since been the subject of a Federal inquiry brought on by complaints of England, France and Germany that the city was not only notorious for abuse of international maritime law, but unsafe for any decent seaman. By then, too, steam had driven sail from the sea, the new iron ships needed much smaller crews, and the sailors' boardinghouses operated in Portland by Jim Turk, the Grant Brothers, Larry Sullivan and Mysterious Billy Smith had seen their best days.

The Skidroad was not affected, but continued to thrive as logging increased, mills doubled in size, and the ancient habits of loggers required them to blow their stakes as soon and as often as possible. Yet the Skidroad was heading toward obsolescence that crept on unsuspected. The change started when loggers got into the habit of marrying. Logging companies encouraged the habit by providing family houses in the camps. And at last, in the 1940s, the camps themselves began to disappear. Logging of course continued; it increased in volume. But the actual camp where loggers lived was done away with, and the married loggers and their families lived in or near some village fairly close to the operation, and the man of the house drove daily in his car from home to the timber, then home again.

The Skidroads of Portland and all other logging centers began to notice the lack of customers. Fewer men were coming to town. The rising new labor unions largely took over the function of the old free-wheeling slave markets or employment offices. The average age of the Skidroad customer rose by the year until a majority of the district's patrons were either pensioners, simple old soaks, or misfits at any age. The bar of Erickson's saloon, which once totaled 684 lineal feet, was gradually cut down to some forty feet. The $5000 Grand Pipe Organ was stilled. Portland's and Spokane's and lesser Skidroads still exist, but they are little more than shadowy relics of the great days when ten thousand loggers hit Portland within the space of twenty-four hours to drink, and to kick the doors and windows out of fancy-houses while the Professor beat the living daylights out of the piano in the parlor.

When this writer quit working in the timber, back in the early 1920s, steam-logging had reached its peak. So had the footloose logger. Now I am an old settler, a man out of Genesis, for I can recall when Northwestern loggers preferred Copenhagen snuff to cigarettes, when fallers and buckers used crosscut saws, when steam donkeys did the yarding and loading, and logs came down the mountain behind a puffing Shay that rocked and rattled and had a voice to frighten a cougar on the last Forty of the most remote quarter section. I thought then it was a great and wonderful era. Thirty-odd years later I know it was.

I don't mean that its social consciousness was other than medieval. It was wasteful of timber. It was dangerous to human life. It was thoughtless and careless, breeding hatred and Wobblies, spawning fires that left uncounted acres a desolate waste. The whole ripsnorting shebang was inane, often cruel, always costly from the viewpoint of society. I loved every last bit of it, not for anything it accomplished, but because it was the greatest industrial show in North America.

That era has now passed. The logging railroads were the first to go. I have ridden the locomotives or the cars of 290-odd privately owned logging railroads in four states and one province. How many remain I do not know, but they cannot number more than half a dozen for the whole area. Trucks did away with them.

The great pounding steam donkeys, too, were driven out by the internal combustion engine fed on gasoline or diesel oils. When the old-time whistle punk yanked his signal wire, the steam donkey responded with a startled cry of a quality to alert the most sluggish mind. And when it was running, it emitted sound and smoke and steam and cinders in satisfying profusion. Small, smooth quiet diesel engines did away with the big donkeys.

As late as the early 1940s trees were felled by muscular men who stood on springboards notched in the trunks and pulled the long glittering blade of a crosscut. They were mostly of Scandinavian origin—big blond men with sweeping mustaches who worked by the bushel, inch, or mile, as piecework was called. Perfection of the power chainsaw drove the big Scandies from the woods. Either that, or they learned to operate a chainsaw, a rig that will down a giant in less time than it took to set a springboard for handwork.

Almost simultaneously with the chainsaw came a far more important revolutionary change. I mean the coming in numbers of the private or company forester. He began to appear on rare occasions in the 1920s. To most logging bosses he was no more welcome than a union organizer. He knew a whole raft of fancy names for fir, pine, cedar and hemlock. He held dangerous theories among which was the proposition that, given a chance, a forest would renew itself. For a long time the forester was merely tolerated. The production man was the hero of the logging woods.

But time was taking its toll of the old-style operators, men to whom a standing, living tree was revolting evidence that their employees had failed to let all available daylight into the swamp. They died, and with them died the chief resistance to forestry. The forestry schools meanwhile went about their work more subtly: they started turning out graduates who were not only foresters but production men too. One by one these young men got jobs. Their number is now imposing. So is evidence of their influence. They are bringing to fruition the hopes of generations of honest conservationists, many of whom could not understand that sound forestry, if ever it came, was to be based less on the emotions expressed by only-God-can-make-a-tree than on hard economics.

Thus it came to pass that instead of letting his cutover lands revert to the state for taxes, the logging operator was urged by his forester to retain the land, to protect it from fire, disease and pests; and to plant and thin where necessary, all with the idea that timber is a crop to be harvested over and over like wheat or potatoes, though naturally in widely spaced cycles. Even so, these tree farms, millions of acres of which have been registered in an association, could never have come into being without the radical modifications that have taken place in the idiotic and confiscatory tax structure which for more than a century had bedeviled American timberlands.

Another thing is that the lumber industry which for three centuries was predicated on boards and timbers made from old growth forests has changed into a forest products industry. Fibre products and plastics numbered by the hundreds; the marvelous new plywoods; and finally the impreg and compreg woods—as tough as mild steel, fire resistant, decay resistant—these and other new products of the forest have taken their place along with conventional boards and timbers and shingles.

It is all good. One can welcome the many things that changed a notoriously cut-out-and-get-out industry into a stable and permanent one. At the same time, one can regret that the logging camp will presently be a thing of the past. Yet I imagine that few of today's loggers, now thoroughly and perhaps happily domesticated, regret its passing. Here and there, possibly, is one whose memory will conjure up a dawn when the sun came over the mountain to slant through the swirling mist, while the bullcook beat rhythmically on the gong and two hundred young men came stomping down the camp walks, their sharp calks clicking in the planks, heading for an incredible breakfast, a box of Copenhagen, then a thundering ride behind the Shay to where the spar-tree reared high above the big round stuff lying between the stumps. It was a great era. It already seems almost as remote as that of the sternwheelers, or even the Covered Wagons.

Chapter 12

Salmon

FROM KETTLE FALLS to the sea the Indian economy was based on salmon. The mysterious migrations of these great fish were held to be the work of gods whose moods were uncertain and had best be propitiated by prayers and often by elaborate ceremonial appeals. If you lived along the lower seven hundred miles of the Columbia or its tributaries, you depended chiefly on salmon. There were elk, of course, and deer, and other animals fit to eat, and roots and berries, but red fish was the diet just as it was the principal medium of exchange among the tribes.

Lewis and Clark encountered their first sign of salmon economy on the Lemhi, a tributary of the Salmon River which is a tributary of the Snake, which is a tributary of the Columbia. Pacific salmon were surpassing rangers. These fish which the two explorers found so far inland may well have grown mature in the high latitudes and distant waters of Alaska, but they had been born there in Idaho waters and to Idaho waters they had returned to spawn another generation, then to die. No matter the rapids, the falls, or other obstructions, including the nets and spears of the red men, these fish by a compulsion of awesome power and a memory undimmed after two or four years in foreign salt waters, simply *had* to return to an obscure stream that rose in the mountains of Idaho. It was the same elsewhere. At the Columbia's headwaters, David Thompson saw battered chinooks that had come more than a thousand weary and often tempestuous miles from the sea and God alone knew how much farther. Had some of these fish spent the best part of their lives around the island where Vitus Bering died? Had they plowed the Aleutian Trough? What an odyssey it was to have returned from a voyage measured in the thousands of miles, and what an abiding urge had prompted it.

In their Journals, Lewis and Clark noted the increasing intensity of the salmon belt. By the time they reached the mouth of the Snake, they had passed several large villages devoted to fishing; and here, on the main river, Clark made a map showing more than one hundred "fishing establishments" on the lower portion of the Snake, the Yakima River system, the Wenatchee, and another stream which probably represented the Spokane River. On their way down the Columbia they came upon whole villages engaged in making pemmican of dried fish which had been pulverized, then packed into basketlike sacks lined with fishskins. This food went everywhere, even over the Rockies, and remained in good condition for years. The sacks weighed at least ninety pounds each. The Indians told the explorers they traded what pemmican they did not need with tribes of the lower river in exchange for materials which they wanted from the Coast region. From the Cascades to the sea, the explorers remark again and again on the prevalence of salmon as native food.

Far up the Columbia, at Kettle Falls, as noted in a previous chapter, David Thompson was struck by the large village there which appeared to be devoted almost wholly to fishing and smoking fish. Thirty years later, Captain Wilkes saw the Kettle Falls fishermen take nine hundred salmon in a twenty-four-hour period; while at Spokane Falls he estimated the number of men engaged at one thousand. The natives used dip nets, spears, and traps to take the fish. Their nets were made of the inner bark of white cedar, or from the long surface roots of spruce. Willows formed their weirs. Between Celilo and the sea, the natives fished and got about with dugout canoes, a few of them fifty feet long.

When the white men began coming in numbers, they found the salmon hordes tempting. Nathaniel Wyeth, John Couch, the Hudson's Bay Company and others established fisheries along the lower river, to catch and salt salmon for export, but the business amounted to little until 1867 when Andrew Hapgood, and the Humes—William, George, and Robert—came to begin the first canning of fish in the Pacific Northwest. These men were from Maine where Tinsmith Hapgood had been canning lobster by a "secret process" he had devised. They had come first to California in 1864 and opened a salmon cannery on the Sacramento River. The run of fish there proved disappointing. There was also trouble with the canned fish exploding. After investigating the Columbia, they moved to Eagle Cliff on the north bank of that stream in Wahkiakum County, Washington. In their first year of operation they packed four thousand cases of forty-eight cans each. Next year the pack rose to eighteen thousand cases. Within twenty years they were operating twenty of the thirty-five canneries along the river. In the legendry of the river, the Humes stand out as efficient and ruthless men. William Hume built a large house described as a mansion overlooking the Columbia near Eagle Cliff, and was long known as King of the Canneries.

Canning salmon was something new. For a time Hapgood and one trusted assistant did all the cooking in a room separated from the rest of the plant by a tight partition. No one else was allowed there. Into this secret place the filled cans came through a small opening. The process was at first very crude. The bodies of the cans were cut with a pair of big shears. Each fish was butchered separately, packed into cans, and each can was a single soldering job. But the technology quickly caught up with the needs of this brand-new industry, and, long before the end of the century, a can concern in Astoria was turning out fifteen million cans annually; and the process of canning was also much improved.

Within a year of the Hume-Hapgood's first pack, Captain John West opened a cannery at Westport on the Oregon side of the river. Others soon followed, the Cook Brothers at Clifton; Sam Elmore, M. J. Kinney, and Badollet & Company in Astoria; McGowan at Ilwaco; while away up the river near the Cascades and Celilo, the Warrens and the Seuferts opened canneries. By the early eighties, thirty-nine outfits were packing salmon. This was the peak, and '83 was the top of the peak, the pack that season running to 630,000 cases, a figure that was also reached in 1895, but when a part of the catch was made offshore and not in the Columbia proper.

By the time the Columbia River Packers Association was organized in the middle nineties, Astoria had long been recognized as the center of the river's fishing industry. When young Mont Hawthorne first saw it, in 1883, "there wasn't no railroad to Astoria." Whether you got there from the north, south, east or west, you came by boat. It was quite a place. Most of it was built on piling, including the saloons which were believed to be more numerous per capita of population than in any other town in Oregon. There were several dance halls, and honky-tonk theaters, one of which had a sort of salt-water pen near the door. If you didn't have the price of admission, you tossed a big fresh salmon into the tank and were admitted to the show. A similar arrangement was to be found also at a couple of the red-light establishments, of which there were many. The major industries after dark appeared to be harlotry and shanghaiing.

The Astoria canneries were going full stride when Mont Hawthorne arrived. He recalled that the waste of fish was sickening. In the place where he worked they might heave as many as five hundred dead salmon into the river in a night. And the refuse of those that were canned was dumped too. When the tide changed, the dead fish and the offal drifted onto the beach and stayed there. After much complaint, the city felt obliged to hire men with skiffs to haul the remains out into the channel. That is, most of the remains. Enough stayed on the beach to attract bears who came to eat their fill and to cause more complaints against the canneries. The canners did not mind. It was a period when complaints of the sort mattered little. The canners provided the main payrolls of the town and could ignore ill-tempered people who considered the water-front aroma too strong.

But there was another menace which the fishermen's union and the canners rose as one to defeat: When herds of sea lions got the habit of tearing nets to pieces in their efforts to get at salmon, a dead shot, Clark Lowry, was hired to hunt and shoot the marauders.

Along the evil-smelling water front were long bunkhouses to accommodate the two thousand Chinese who were the chief help in canneries all along the Columbia. Their settlement was complete with a theater, firecrackers on occasion, and opium that was sold openly in flat round cans. Abused and bedeviled on every hand, these old men and young boys from Canton had built railroad grades, washed gold in all the diggings, and were now providing the main labor force of a new industry.

That part of Astoria called Uniontown was gradually filling up with a few Italians, a few Portuguese, and many, many more Scandinavians and Finns. The latter came in time to do the major portion of the fishing. The Chinese were not allowed to fish, ever. They filled all the inside cannery jobs, such as making the cans and cutting up the fish. A sketch artist's picture of an Astoria cannery of the time shows two score Orientals, pigtails wrapped neatly up on the backs of their necks, their faces classically impassive, going about their work in a huge room that is steaming from the cooking apparatus. Another sketch shows a few Chinese in rubber boots contemplating a room strewn with "15 tons of Royal Chinook Salmon." The Chinese were so closely allied with canning that when, some twenty years later an automatic machine was devised to open and clean fish, it became known at once as the Iron Chink. Despite its efficiency elsewhere, this machine was not used on the Columbia because of the wide variation in the size of Columbia chinooks—from five to sixty pounds. The Iron Chink worked better on fish more evenly sized. Incidentally, the technology of canning was being continuously improved, and the elapsed time between the moment a salmon was lifted from the river and the moment his meat was filling several cans grew shorter by the year, until it was said that a fish was hardly done flopping when he was inside a can.

Catching the fish in early years was done largely by vagrant fishermen, many of whom came from California; and by people who lived along the lower river and worked part time at logging. Somehow or other these crews got the reputation of being wild men, undependable in all things save hell-raising, at which they had few peers. The quality of the fishing crews began to improve in the eighties as a few Scandinavians and Finns settled in Astoria. They went to catching fish, an occupation they knew from childhood. They worked hard. They quickly learned some of the subtleties of Pacific salmon, an education that could be had almost only from empirical methods. And in the pattern of American emigration from the old world, these few pioneers from Scandinavia and Finland attracted their countrymen. In a few more years almost half of Astoria's population was made up of Finnish, Swedish, Norwegian and

Danish nationals and their American-born sons and daughters.

These were mostly literate people. It wasn't long before they could support newspapers printed in their own languages. The Finns even had a daily and a tri-weekly. Social and "benefit" lodges were formed. With them, too, the Finns brought their *sauna*, or steam-bath house, and when

Astoria fishing boat unloading at a cannery.

conventional bathrooms came in, they installed them also, but no true Finn, it was said, would let a Saturday night pass without visit to a *sauna*, of which downtown Astoria still has many.

The many Finns, together with the numerous Scandinavians, were not tardy in sensing the group action of the salmon packing houses which made agreements as to how much they would pay for a salmon; and almost from the first they had a fishermen's protective union. In time, too, these realistic people organized their own packing concerns, the first one known as the Scandinavian Cannery. The most successful, which flourishes today, was founded in 1896 as the Union Fishermen's Co-operative Packing Company.

Catching and canning salmon on the Columbia was marked for decades by periodic violence when strikes disrupted fishing or canning, or both. There were even more violent times when contending groups of fishermen fought each other over sand bars favored for operating haul seines. Fists, clubs, knives, even guns were used; and though the industry has never known the ferocity that went with the Wobbly (IWW) troubles in the logging woods and sawmills, fishing the river has not been an occupation for weaklings.

Over the years, a goodly part of the catch has been canned by outfits affiliated as the Columbia River Packers Association, organized in the nineties. This group still operates the biggest cannery on the river. For more than half a century it has also operated in Alaska.

The salmon of the Columbia are worthy the big blond men who go out in boats to get them, and of the smaller red men who used to stand precariously at the roaring fishways of Celilo and Kettle Falls to net, spear and gaff them. All Pacific salmon are anadromous, a useful word meaning that these fish are hatched in fresh water, descend to the ocean where they attain most of their growth, then return to their home or native streams to spawn. They are distinguished from Atlantic salmon chiefly by the fact that the latter may spawn more than once, while the Pacific species always die after spawning.

Once upon a time, in Indian days, any salmon in the river was considered of value, though the red men had their preferences. But since canning by white men began, only four species have been of commercial importance in the

Indians fishing at Celilo Falls.

Columbia. These are the chinook, the silver, the blueback, and the chum. The chinook is the king of salmon—of all salmon—and is often called Royal Chinook, and tyee, an Indian term for chief. It will average twenty-two pounds, and reaches ninety pounds. The spring chinook run enters the Columbia in late winter or early spring and continues through the lower river until August. The fall chinooks are more numerous but of less value commercially. There is another difference between the two runs: The spring chinooks mostly head well upriver, only four divisions of that run entering tributaries below the Cascades; but the fall chinooks are common to all the tributaries of the lower river.

Silver salmon are fall-run fish and appear in small numbers before August. There used to be large migrations of silvers to rivers entering the middle Columbia, like the Methow, Wenatchee, Yakima, and Grand Ronde, but of late years the majority spawn in tributaries below the Cascades. Silvers average ten pounds. The bluebacks come in June and July and continue upriver. They average four pounds. The lowest grade of salmon, the chum, migrate up the river's lower tributaries in the fall, and will average around twelve pounds.*

For a time it seemed as if the catching of sturgeon might grow into a large industry. These huge fish, often running well over one thousand pounds each, were occasionally taken for food by the Indians, and early settlers ate them. They were not, however, highly esteemed, and as late as 1874 the *Weekly Astorian* said that a sturgeon weighing 1,250 pounds had been taken there and was sold for twenty-five cents. That is, for the entire fish. More than a decade later, some ninety-odd tons of sturgeon were salted at Astoria. But frozen sturgeon awaited the advent of railroads and ice.

By 1888, when a railroad had come down the Columbia as far as Portland, a New York firm established what

* The names given are those used on the Columbia. Elsewhere, the silver may be known as coho; the blueback as sockeye or red; and the chum as dog salmon.

was called a sturgeon camp at Oneonta, Oregon, below the Cascades. Eighty-five tons were shipped in iced cars during the first season. Three other companies later went into the business. The sturgeon catch suddenly dwindled, and one by one the camps were closed. It was generally believed that the use of gear called Chinese lines was responsible for overfishing the river, even as far inland as Wieser, Idaho, on the Snake. A Chinese line was a real killer. It carried from two hundred to four hundred hooks. Once entangled, few sturgeon escaped. Long after the sturgeon camps closed, a few ingenious and patient fishermen made a small industry of sturgeon farms. A small bay would be staked off like a marine pasture, and into it the farmer put as many of the big fish as possible, feeding them like so many barned cattle until the market was good. Then they were hauled out, killed, dressed, and shipped. One of these pasture fish was a true whale of one thousand eight-hundred pounds. In recent years legislation has virtually prohibited the taking of Columbia River sturgeon except by Indians in reservation waters.

At the other pole from the armored monsters are Columbia River smelt. Mature smelt seldom run more than eight inches long and are so rich in fat they used to be called candlefish because a dried smelt wrapped around a wick and lighted would supply a sort of illumination. In December to February they arrive in the Columbia in such numbers as to call for editorial notice. The editorialists, and almost nobody else, refer to smelt as eulachon; and the papers send reporters and cameramen to cover the thousands of smelt-dippers who line the Cowlitz, Lewis and Sandy rivers which are the home waters of these fish. Because they do not freeze suitably, the smelt industry is mostly local. In Portland smelt become so numerous as the season wears on that one of the best stories concerns the newcomer to the region who is deluged with free smelt to the point of embarrassment, sometimes to the point of desperation, and clogs his plumbing in frenzied efforts to rid himself of enough fish to feed a multitude. But fried in corn meal, the Columbia smelt is a dish that many compare favorably with brook trout.

In regard to trout, the Columbia is the principal Pacific Coast stream of the steelhead. In the 1920s the Columbia pack of this fish occasionally totaled more than two million pounds, with another million pounds sold frozen. These figures have declined by approximately half, due in part to reclassification of the steelhead as a game fish. On the Oregon side, a part of the steelhead catch is still packed, but by far the greater portion is frozen.

Of fishing gear used in the Columbia, the gill net has always been of first importance in taking salmon. It is of record that the first gill net here came from Maine's Kennebec River and was used, in 1853, on the Columbia near Oak Point, Washington. It is basically a rectangular piece of webbing weighted on the lower side with leads, buoyed on the upper by corks, and is fished by laying it out across a section of the stream. It is then allowed to drift with the current. When fish encounter it, they penetrate as far as the region just behind the gills, and are thus caught. The gill net's efficiency varies with the skill used in laying it out and taking it in, and also in the manner it is hung. Fishermen will hang and rehang a net again and again until they believe it is just right.

There are two ways of fishing gill nets. One is constructed so that its top edge floats at or near the surface; the other, called a diver, drifts with its bottom edge on or near the bottom of the river. When the stream is muddy, a gill net is used day or night, but when the water is clear, it is fished mostly at night. Nearly all gill nets today are used with an additional net called a trammel of large-mesh webbing. This serves to catch the salmon too big to gill in the small-mesh web.

Because the efficiency of the diver-type gill nets depends on a bottom free of snags, sunken logs and other debris, the gill-net fishermen organize themselves into "snag unions" to clear the location they fish. It is said to be an unwritten and well-enforced law that the men composing a snag union have exclusive rights to that territory. The wars between fishermen have seldom been caused over gill-net locations, but have had to do with sand bars and other places where haul seines were used. Outlawed now for several years, horse-seining was a common sight for half a century. On some sand bar or other, often a mile or so from either shore, one could see six to eight teams pulling a vast net one thousand five-hundred feet long, or longer, plodding steadily through the water up to their bellies, hauling the net's offshore end, to beach a few tons of fish that flopped twenty feet on the sands. In those days, the animals were often played-out relics of the Portland streetcar system, later veterans of the fire department, and it is told that their sore feet never failed to respond to healing qualities of the water, and aged horses were much rejuvenated, living many years beyond their natural time. One seldom saw them above the first seventy miles of the river where, in season, they lived in stables built on piling at the sand bars.

In the early era of commercial fishing, Chinook Beach was often in the news because of the efforts of rival packers to monopolize this fine spot for seining. The McGowans were said to have inspired Indians to claim their legal seining rights here, while competing firms got other Indians to attack the seining claims. The matter was settled only after many years' resort to the United States courts. Another center for seining was Sand Island, and here, too, the courts had to intervene after men had been beaten and shot in the seine wars.

Then, there were the fish wheels. This device was first used on the Columbia in 1879 by the Williams Brothers, one of whom patented the idea, though the principle of a wheel had been used elsewhere previously. It was a framework with scoop nets made of wire netting. These were the buckets of the wheel, so arranged that the wheel was kept in constant motion by the current, picking up all fish that tried to swim the channel. The wheels ran from nine to thirty-two feet diameter. They were used mostly from a point above Portland to as far as Celilo Falls.

It is recorded that one wheel built near present Bonneville Dam took an average of three-thousand salmon a day during the season of 1881. By the turn of the century seventy-six wheels were turning, day and night. But they were of little use except when the surface water was at the proper height. Their use began to decline in 1900, long before both Oregon and Washington outlawed them, at which time less than forty wheels were in operation. Statistics indicate that even at the height of their popularity wheels were never a large factor in the total catch. It was the net, in one form or another, that had taken the main catch of Columbia river salmon, and gill nets topped all other types. The nets were once knitted by the Chinese, and are now made of nylon by machines.

Laying out gill nets was first done from small open rowboats. Then came sail, with the boats longer and of wider beam. This period presented something of a sight during the season. The wide estuary was alive with small craft each carrying sail and looking, as more than one observer has said, like an armada of tiny junks. In 1889, there were 2,596 of these boats operating between Portland and the mouth of the river, most of them within sight of Astoria. The first power boats came in about 1905, and later an Astoria fisherman, Matt Tolonen, started a trend by fitting a flat stern to his gill-net boat.

One of the spectacular shows of fishing the Columbia was that of the Indians swarming the rocky canyon at Celilo Falls. The first explorers saw them dipping and spearing salmon there, and they continued to dip without hindrance for nigh one hundred and fifty years more, "protected," as the terminology had it, "by a treaty guaranteeing them exclusive and perpetual fishing rights" and stipulating they might use any method they saw fit.

And it must have seemed to the Indians that here at the falls of Celilo was something the white men simply could not take away from them. This was their chief fishing ground, their source of food, since time began. They still gather there, as this is written, and many of them stay there the year around, to net and spear and gaff at will. Standing on jerry-built platforms jutting out over the boiling water, or in a basket lowered by rope down the sheer side of a cliff, they will be motionless for long periods, then lunge suddenly to bring up a whopper that calls for stout arms.

The several tribes which fish here keep what they need and sell the surplus to cannery buyers, or people driving along the highway. Fishing laws have never applied to them. Celilo, as the legend goes on millions of picture postcards, is "the Indians' happy hunting grounds where they may catch the big Chinook salmon in any way they choose."

That was all well enough when it was written, but it was written in sand. A dam is rising not far below Celilo at The Dalles, and it will soon bury the falls so deep in a lake that not a ripple of their fury will trouble the surface. The redskins have been defeated once more, this time not by the United States Cavalry, but by the genial dam builders of the United States Army, Corps of Engineers. Custer is revenged again. And if the Indians at Celilo should persist in their age-old liking for salmon as food, then they may buy it in cans, by the case if need be.

Chapter 13

Two Men Named Hill

MANIFEST DESTINY prompted the City of Portland to stage a Lewis & Clark Centennial Exposition that opened its gates on June 1, 1905, and continued for nearly five months. Letterheads and other stationery of business firms displayed a fine scene of the intrepid explorers, complete with fur caps and powder horns, being ushered into a gorgeous Pacific sunset by a flag-draped Columbia. Charles Warren Fairbanks, vice-president of the United States, was on hand to deliver the opening speech, paying homage to the expedition which among other things had brought the great River of the West out from the fogs of mystery.

Another speaker at the festivities was James J. Hill, the railroad man from St. Paul, Minnesota, whose Great Northern already crossed Washington from Spokane to Seattle. Now, while viewing the marvels of Oregon's first big fair, Hill took occasion to remark that he had a good mind to "help with the development of this wonderful state." The remark was made quietly enough, even casually, but word of it electrified everyone and nobody more than it did E. H. Harriman, who was not present but happened to control the Union Pacific and Southern Pacific railroads, both of which met in Portland after threading Oregon from the east and the south. Harriman felt with some reason that Oregon was *his* empire.

Both Hill and Harriman were empire builders. They had been fighting each other for years, during which Hill managed to get control of the Northern Pacific and also of the Burlington System. Harriman's Union Pacific reached Portland by the water-level route through the Cascades and occupied the south bank of the Columbia. The north bank of the river from Pasco to Vancouver, opposite Portland, was still virgin of rails. When Harriman got news that Jim Hill planned to "help with the development" of Oregon, he knew immediately where the development would begin. Harriman happened just then to be in hospital recovering from an operation, and he called Hill by long distance telephone, according to a pleasing if perhaps apocryphal story, to say that he, E. H. Harriman, was gaining strength daily and was quite ready to meet any of Hill's development plans.

Discovering at once that Hill's engineers had already been quietly locating a route between Pasco and Vancouver, and that grading and construction crews were already at work, Harriman acted with the speed that had made him feared. He organized two paper concerns, the Columbia Valley Railroad and the Cascade Railroad, and sent engineers and a battery of his most accomplished legal talent to fight it out in the field and the courts. At every spot where a Harriman survey crossed a Hill survey, Harriman applied to the United States Land Office, under right of eminent domain, for certificates to lay track. Some were refused but others were granted, producing delays highly satisfying to the Harriman forces.

Though these and other tactics slowed the Hill progress, Hill was not called "The Empire Builder" for nothing. His lawyers fought off the legal attacks, and his field bosses continued to make grade and lay rails. Harriman put track crews to work. While the court battles continued, the track crews took it upon themselves to make war on each other. Fists, pickhandles and rocks were the weapons; and two or three times dynamite was used to destroy equipment. A sort of truce came late in 1906 when Harriman at last conceded victory to Hill. The last spike of what Hill named the Spokane, Portland & Seattle Railway was driven in 1908, when it was announced that the Great Northern and the Northern Pacific would use the new road jointly. Hill then bought the Portland-Astoria road built on the Columbia's south bank from Portland to the sea. He established an ocean terminal near Astoria, bought two vessels for the run to San Francisco, then put on a special boat train from Portland. All of which was for the sake of competing with Harriman's Southern Pacific rail route to California.

Harriman retaliated. He began buying a right of way to extend his Union Pacific to Puget Sound, and started to dig a tunnel to get out of Portland and another tunnel to get into Tacoma. Hill understood such tactics. Having weighed the possible results, he agreed to double-track his own line to Puget Sound and permit Harriman to run his trains over it.

The battles for the North Bank, for Astoria, and for Puget Sound were over, but not the Hill-Harriman war; this was to continue until after both principals were dead. They were still very much alive when Hill started what old-timers in the region still refer to with happy nostalgia as the Deschutes Railroad War.

The Deschutes rises high on the east slope of the Cascade Range and flows north to empty into the Columbia a few miles above The Dalles. In 1909, when Jim Hill turned his attention to it, the Deschutes flowed two hundred miles through a region almost bare of population, a country of great lonely open spaces marked by lava fields, boulders, buttes of obsidian and other volcanic remains, and sagebrush. A few homesteaders here and there persisted in remaining, but many more had given up and gone elsewhere.

Once upon a time, during Oregon's early heyday of railroad excitements, the Deschutes region had been staked out, at least on paper, by promoters of railroad mirages. One of these was called the Oregon Trunk. It had long since been forgotten by 1909 when Jim Hill secretly bought its only tangible property, which was an elegantly printed charter. With this instrument in possession, Hill sent his famous locating engineer, John F. Stevens, into the central Oregon country through which the Deschutes hurried on its way north to the Columbia.

Posing as a sportsman devoted to fishing, and under an assumed name, Stevens found the Deschutes wonderful fishing. He called on the scattered homesteaders, a jovial man obviously enthralled with everything pertaining to this isolated country. It was, he remarked, a sportsman's paradise, and he had a mind to buy himself a good piece of it. This he proceeded to do very cheaply, getting options on a tract here, another there, most of them along the river. Then he disappeared.

It was soon announced in the papers that Mr. Hill was

about to build a railroad into central Oregon from his newly completed line on the north bank of the Columbia. He would bridge the big river at Wishram. The branch would take off to follow the Deschutes upstream 165 miles to Bend. Building a railroad to get to Bend may have sounded odd to most Oregonians. They had never heard of Bend. It had a saloon and a blacksmith shop, and possibly a population of a hundred. The announcement did not sound odd to Mr. Harriman. He knew well enough that Bend was not the goal; that Hill planned to build to Bend, certainly, and right on through Bend in a direct line to San Francisco, a city which Harriman meant should be served by no "foreign" railroads.

Again Harriman moved with characteristic speed. He chartered a Deschutes Railroad Company. He brought the celebrated engineer George W. Boschke from Galveston where he had just completed the famous sea wall. Boschke was told to build a railroad from the Union Pacific tracks on the Columbia to Bend—or to wherever it might appear Hill was heading. Hill had the east bank of the Deschutes. Harriman's men took the west bank.

Now began what turned out to have been the very last of the old-fashioned railroad wars. Not just battles in the courts or in the stock market, but out on the rights of way. The Deschutes war was fought by opposing forces representing the two foremost railroad kings of their time.

All supplies for the big crews had to be toted overland a hundred miles or more. Over the sand and sagebrush went the ten-horse teams, the wagons piled mountain high, wending their way into and out of canyons, disappearing briefly into coulees, appearing again, moving on over the crumbling lava, turning out around buttes that had been cooked into black glass in some forgotten era, heading for the end-of-steel. The camps prohibited liquor, but on paydays the boys could find boot-leggers lurking behind the nearest butte, and the nightly chorus of coyotes was drowned by the howling of liquored gandy-dancers.

Day by day the work went on, but sporadically with interference. Charges of unsuspected dynamite went off while opposing gangs fought for track room in a narrow canyon. Boulders that had not moved in centuries suddenly started to roll. Men were killed, more men were injured. A boxcar of supplies was splintered. Here and there, on some high ledge of rimrock, sharp-eyed men lay prone with rifles, watching the scene below for hostile moves; and high above the sharpshooters the ever-present buzzards moved lazily on motionless wings, seeing all, possibly wondering at the strange invasion.

At Mile 75, where the contending forces were getting truly desperate, a telegram came to the Harriman camp for Chief Engineer Boschke. It purported to have been sent from Galveston, Texas. It said: SEA WALL HAS BROKEN. COME AT ONCE. Boschke ignored the fake message. The war on the Deschutes went on, and Harriman's men won an important battle: They had managed to get option on a right of way from a homesteader named Smith. A court held that Smith had proved right to his land, that the option was valid. There was no other way by which either railroad could move on toward Bend save over the Smith homestead. Hill was obliged to halt his crews and to arbitrate. He had met his match.

In agreeing to a truce, Hill promised to build no farther than Bend and to permit Harriman to use the line to that place. Jim Hill himself was on hand for the last spike, which was driven in October of 1911. He made a few remarks to the effect that he was happy "to lend a hand to the Union Pacific and Southern Pacific in opening up the country," adding that if those two lines were not prepared to go ahead "then we will take the load ourselves." Hill was seventy-three. He was also the last of the old-time railroad barons. Harriman had died shortly after he imposed the Bend truce.

The Hill-Harriman struggle continued. Hill died at last in 1916, by which time Bend was growing into a thriving lumber center, getting logs from the slopes of the Cascades. Hill died too soon to see his Great Northern's extension south from Bend to connect with the Western Pacific over which GN trains could reach San Francisco. By then the Great Northern, along with many another railroad, had started to pull up the tracks of numerous branch lines and to board up only too many depots on their main lines. The highways were taking heavy toll from the rails. Neither Hill nor Harriman died a moment too soon.

There remains something more than a footnote to the Hill story, even though Jim Hill himself had nothing to do with it. It concerns what is possibly the most durable and surely the strangest structure that has been raised anywhere along the big river. A highway tourist or the traveler by Union Pacific, on the south bank of the Columbia in Oregon, may lift his eyes in wonder, when approaching a place named Biggs, to gaze upon this imposing piece of irony known through the Pacific Northwest as Sam Hill's

Castle. It stands grim and lonely and high on the Washington side, overlooking uncounted desolate miles of sharply chiseled waste, but with the redeeming waters of the big stream in their deep gorge far below. No tourist or traveler can fail to see it, and the stranger is sure to ask what it is. He will almost certainly be told in the best of faith that it was "built by old Jim Hill's son, Sam, in memory of his mother and for her named Maryhill." It would be difficult to compress more misinformation in so brief a sentence.

Maryhill castle was one of the myriad projects that occupied the lively mind of Samuel Hill, a native of Deep River, North Carolina, who in 1888 married Mary, one of the seven daughters of James J. Hill, the Empire Builder. When he conceived it isn't known. Actual work on its construction appears to have started about 1913. It was still incomplete thirteen years later when an authentic queen was imported from Middle Europe to pronounce its dedication.

The reasons for erecting this costly and improbable pile in the vast nothingness of the mid-Columbia were never clear. Probably they were not clear even to Sam Hill himself. At different times over the years he gave various explanations: It was to be some sort of cultural center; again it was to be an international museum; then it was to be a fortress to stop invaders of the United States who, so Hill specifically stated about 1920, would be Japanese warships; still again he thought of it as a "universal school for all the people."

From the first, however, he called it Maryhill; and though Mary was the name of his wife, Jim Hill's daughter, she refused steadfastly to come near the place and apparently never saw it even from a distance. If this was a crushing commentary on a million-dollar or maybe two-million-dollar memorial, Hill never let on. The memorial remained and remains Maryhill to this day, and it is also the place where Sam Hill, a sociable man, achieved the ultimate social triumph of his life. The only thing that really mystifies Oregonians and Washingtonians is why "Jim Hill's son" chose such a remote and generally inaccessible spot.*

Maryhill Museum.

In his later years Sam Hill probably earned the epithet which conventional people apply to the imaginative. He was an eccentric. Yet he happened also to be as shrewd a

* Although three decades later it was still fairly remote, Maryhill Museum of Fine Arts, as it is now called, was generously endowed by Sam Hill and is open much of the year. Its interests are varied. There are excellent collections of native Indian arts and artifacts; firearms; royal robes and other relics of Romania; textiles; and many paintings and pieces of sculpture. It attracts a steadily increasing number of tourists and Northwest people; and one can hope that in time it will outdraw even Grand Coulee Dam as a place to see.

lawyer and all-around fixer as old Jim Hill had on his staff, and he was a pretty good financier on his own account. Born in the South of Abolitionist parents, in 1858, he went with them to St. Paul on outbreak of the Civil War. He was sent to Germany for schooling, then to Harvard from which he was graduated in 1879.

Admitted to the Minnesota bar in 1880, a period when Jim Hill was fighting all manner of legal wars and needed the best talent obtainable, Sam joined the railroader's staff. The elder Hill found young Sam quick to see the right spot for an attack and to be aggressive in carrying it through. He was personable, too, being tall and handsome; and it was easy to charge his sometimes excessive ebullience to his youth. Yet, he understood thoroughly how to choke a short-line railroad into submission, how to outsmart town promoters who sought to stop Progress by withholding a right of way, and how to gentle a recalcitrant legislature.

Then, in 1888, Sam Hill married Mary, his employer's oldest daughter. He was elected head of the Minneapolis Trust Company. His law practice grew. His many investments and speculations turned out enormously well. Harvard University made him an Overseer. Business took him often to the western portion of his father-in-law's railroad empire and there he began a lasting love affair with the Pacific Northwest.

His passion was Good Roads. It is generally conceded, in both Oregon and Washington, that Sam Hill played a dominant role in speeding the coming of highways in those states. Meanwhile he traveled extensively all over the world. He liked to say that he walked with kings and princes—indeed, with queens, and he was inordinately proud that he was an officer of the French Legion of Honor, a commander of the Belgian Order of the Crown, and a member of the Order of the Sacred Treasure of Japan. He was more than proud that he was one of the Queen's Body Guard of Romania. A particularly handsome decoration and rosette came with this honor.

On one or another of his extended stays in the Northwest, he acquired seven thousand acres of barren land in Washington's Klickitat County and started the project that is Maryhill. Material and supplies came in by his father-in-law's Spokane, Portland & Seattle Railway; and that accommodating line was glad to put up a modest depot and name it Maryhill. A large crew of men arrived and went to work.

The first thing was a sort of hotel, Meadowlark Inn, to house the upper-echelon employees and also the guests who, so observed an admiring guest, were "to be classic scholars, road builders, riflemen—the kind of friends Teddy Roosevelt might have chosen for his Dakota ranch."

For a time it appeared that the seven thousand wild acres of Maryhill might be populated with and worked by European peasants. At one period Sam Hill reported that a whole colony which he described as "Belgian Quakers" were to come over to settle on the estate and raise something or other. Again, it was a group of Swiss who were coming. Rumor had it that scouts for both the Belgians and the Swiss did come to Maryhill, looked it over, said No, and went away.

Yet, peasant or no, there was going to be a castle anyway. Up it went, three stories of it, concrete and stone and tile, on the edge of a precipice some nine hundred feet

261

above the Columbia. Poplars were planted in a rectangle around the castle. A lane of the same species inclosed the long approach. Getting up there was, to be sure, a task that would have been less suitable for the sea-level Belgians, who never came, than for the Alpine Swiss who stayed away. A steep winding road led up from the railroads; and, in time, led up from a ferry landing on the river. There was never anything like a traffic jam on the road to the castle.

The years passed serenely. The gangs of workmen rose or fell in number according to the current whims of Sam Hill and the condition of the labor market. World War I was fought and finished; and Sam Hill emerged from it as one of the most decorated civilians by reason of his good works among the Allied powers.

Then, one day in 1926, Sam Hill announced that Queen Marie of Romania was going to dedicate Maryhill castle. It wasn't quite finished yet, he admitted, but it had walls and a roof and would do for a dedication. Well, a newspaperman wanted to know, what *was* it, anyway—a convent, a monastery, a hotel, or what?

"I may make it a museum," he heard Sam Hill say. "An international museum of fine arts. And a library. It will be a school of all the people. The farmer folk could come here to find solution to their problems." Many years later the newspaperman recalled that Sam Hill's reference to "farmer folk" had given him more amused reflection than almost anything in his experience. For one thing, where were these farmer folk to come from? Could any farm folk in Oregon and Washington spare the several days that would be needed to get to and from this remote "school for all the people"? It was obvious that Sam Hill was still thinking, not of American farmers, but of peasants or serfs. It was just as obvious that this hulking fortress stemmed from his youthful memories of some castle on the Rhine.

Another newspaperman asked Mr. Hill, now that the castle was finished, or nearly so, would he not bring his wife to live here at Maryhill? "No, no," cried Mr. Hill in a *non sequitur* of some complexity. "She loves the city and the quiet life." Maryhill strikes most visitors as quiet enough for a recluse.

Then, one gray autumn day in 1926, here she came, Queen Marie of Romania, granddaughter of the late blessed Victoria of England, complete with entourage which included the aged Loie Fuller, in her day an international celebrity, darling of the Folies-Bergère, and inventor of the serpentine dance. And at the head of the entourage, you may be certain, was Sam Hill, rosette in lapel, bubbling like a boy at a circus which, indeed, it was.

Lucky Portland, being only 114 miles from Maryhill, and hence the city nearest to it, prepared for the event in Second Coming style. The city was decorated. The main arteries were cleared of traffic for the entry of the Queen. No such mob had ever assembled in the town. The royal party was properly fed and, despite Prohibition, properly wined, or at least sufficiently wined to promote a face-slapping between two male members of the party in regard to matters of protocol, making an incident highly pleasing to Oregon's commoners.

Getting to Sam Hill's castle for the dedicatory ceremonies may well have caused the Queen to reflect on the life of the pioneers. But she was game. After all, Portland felt, she had to be since she probably got a thumping good honorarium for her efforts. Most Americans, seeing large advertisements with Queen Marie's picture tied to some cosmetic, might be excused if they thought that she had picked up many an honest dollar for her country while in the United States.

One may wonder what went through the Queen's mind as she stood by the pile of stone and cement that was Sam Hill's unfinished castle and looked in four directions. Though her eyes were keen and she could see for many miles, she saw naught but rock and sagebrush. Her logical mind must have asked: Why this Maryhill, well beyond the limits of where even God apparently had ceased to care?

Yet, the good queen dedicated more than she could have guessed. Sam Hill had built better than he knew. The kingdom of Romania has long since disappeared. Sam Hill's castle, high on the stark cliff above the big river, still stands, weather-beaten, it is true, by the hell-hot zephyrs and icy winds of the Columbia River gorge, but stanch enough, a sort of Gibraltar defying the passage of time that otherwise would dim the great name of James Jerome Hill, who died as said in 1916, and wholly obliterate the lesser names of Louis W. Hill and Samuel Hill. Louis, son of the Empire Builder, died April 27, 1948, at St. Paul. Sam Hill, son-in-law of the Empire Builder, died February 26, 1931, at Portland, and his ashes were placed in the characteristic tomb he had prepared for them on the lonely canyon wall at the foot of Maryhill.

"Sam Hill," said one who knew him well, Frank

Branch Riley of Portland, "was a great guy. He was charming, filled with enthusiasm, the complete extrovert. He was blessed with a vanity that was captivating. I fancy that Jim Hill's harder-headed, and maybe harder-hearted, son Louis was often bemused, possibly often annoyed, by the performance of his handsome, virile and volatile brother-in-law, with his tremendous flair for the dramatic and the spectacular."

So long as it stands, Sam Hill's somewhat melancholy pile above the Columbia River gorge will likely assure all three Hills of some measure of regional fame. What does it matter if the public never does get the business straight? It is magnificent irony. There she stands, Maryhill—as almost any native or long-time resident will tell you—there she stands, a lasting monument *"to his beloved mother erected by Sam Hill*, a son of Jim Hill," the Empire Builder, whose Great Northern-Northern Pacific trains roar through the canyon below it. . . .

The irony of this by now indestructible piece of misinformation is not lessened by the fact that Maryhill is best observed from the trains of the Union Pacific Railroad, a portion of the railroad system put together by Edward H. Harriman, Jim Hill's most notable business enemy.

Chapter 14

New Pioneers at Longview

BY THE turn of the nineteenth century the pattern of towns and cities on the main Columbia had been pretty well established. Metropolises had congealed into the several molds that were to be listed as populous places in the census reports. A few of the old trading posts and forts had changed their ways of life and managed to survive as conventional towns. Both river boats and railroads had played parts in the growth or decline of many places. The many mirages of town-plat promoters had vanished almost completely, leaving few remains other than their preposterous maps growing brittle in the collections of historical societies. By 1900, to use a convenient date, it was obvious which places were to enjoy a municipal life of some permanence. It was generally conceded that the pioneering of new cities was a thing of the past.

For this if for no other reason the city of Longview, on the Washington side of the Columbia, is notable. It came into being a quarter of a century after pioneering had gone out of style. It grew quickly, though far from haphazardly, into the third city on the main river. It was as rigidly planned a town as the national capital had been, though neither state nor Federal government had anything to do with it. And neither river boats nor existing railroads played a part in its birth.

It is unlikely that present generations will see another birth like Longview's. It was conceived and whelped in what has been called the Aspirin Age of the 1920s, a time of marvels without end, when not even the sky was the limit, when normalcy was near to fantasy, and Men of Vision were as highly regarded as were the Old Testament prophets in biblical times. This "Model City of the 20th Century" was the grandiose dream of Robert Alexander Long, already past seventy when he dreamed it, a native of Kentucky who with his associates had built up an immense business in the Midwest as the Long-Bell Lumber Company of Kansas City, Missouri.

Long was a pious man, markedly humble in religious matters but in no matter humble elsewhere, to whom came his great dream at a time when the company he founded back in the 1870s was facing a shortage of timber for its mills in the South. In 1920 he called a meeting of his board of directors in what, characteristically enough, was named the R. A. Long Building and, after two prayers and a reading of the 67th Psalm, got down to business. Did they favor liquidation of the Long-Bell Lumber Company; or a move to the Pacific Northwest where timber was plentiful? If one reflects on the fact that the 67th Psalm is basically a prayer for the enlargement of God's kingdom, it is not surprising that the board chose to move the company into the region of mighty firs, vast cedars, even vast hemlocks whose tops sighed and murmured a good 225 feet above the ground.

Timber cruisers were engaged. They liked what they

saw in Cowlitz County, Washington, a region that drained into the Columbia, at a spot about halfway between Portland and Astoria. No man to shirk responsibilities, Long himself and three high officials put on cruiser clothes and went into the woods to see. He and they were convinced. Here was a forest fit for giants to fell and make into lumber. From the Weyerhaeuser Timber Company, the Long-Bell people purchased several billion feet of virgin timber on seventy thousand acres.

Mills must be built for the harvest, and when the news leaked out that a big outfit from the South was looking for a manufacturing site, the go-getters of chambers of commerce up and down the lower Columbia went into action. Long-Bell men were harassed to build here, to build there; and taken to view the lands available at Astoria, at Portland, and many places in between. But on the recommendation of their chief and able engineer, Wesley Vandercook, the Long-Bell officials chose a broad and soggy stretch of lowlands bordering the north shore of the Columbia where the Cowlitz River enters it.

The only habitations were a few weathered and aged farm buildings. Once upon a time it must have seemed as though this spot, then called Monticello, might become a city. In 1852, a convention of settlers here had voted to petition Congress to create Washington Territory. When this had been done, the new legislature was happy to form Cowlitz County and to make Monticello its seat. But floods came, and during the 1860s much of the small yet proud settlement was washed down the river. The court-house was not rebuilt, nor was much else. Monticello faded from the maps.

In the summer of 1921 the advance crews of Long-Bell started clearing the heavy brush from the site; and Engineer Vandercook put gangs to diking the place and installing an elaborate drainage system. J. C. Nichols, landscape architect of Kansas City, came to plan the several residence sections, the boulevards, avenues, and common streets; and the lakes and fens and sunken gardens. For this was to be no typical sawmill town. It was, said R. A. Long, whose enthusiasm grew by the month, to be a planned city—a city planned for beauty, planned for the health and happiness of its citizens; planned just possibly with the thought that it might become the metropolis of the Columbia and all its region.

The place was doubtless preordained to be called Longview. There were already nine Longviews in the United States, (there were also nineteen Monticellos) and apparently no one took the trouble to learn that one of these Longviews stood in Benton County, Washington, on the north bank of the Columbia. It was a flagstop on the Spokane, Portland & Seattle Railway. It had a post office and not much else. Yet it was officially on the map of the Post Office Department.

When these facts somehow became known to the Long-Bell people, they were much dismayed, and worried. As well they had a right to be. A wealthy corporation is generally considered fair game for blackmail, and here was an outfit not only wealthy but "foreign." The Post Office Department would not permit two Longviews in one state. All of Long-Bell's promotion plans were based on the new city's being Longview. If the citizens of the older Longview were as grasping for an easy dollar as only too many other residents along the lower river had proved to be, then it was going to cost Long-Bell a pretty penny to have the only Longview in Washington.

The few citizens of the older Longview, however, were men of good will. When Long-Bell attorneys came to them with the predicament, the three families genially agreed to give up the name and Postmaster R. M. Kline-felter promptly signed a petition to the Department asking that Longview be changed to Barger. Before the delighted Long-Bell men left the older Longview, one of its citizens casually mentioned it would be a fine thing if their tiny depot could be equipped with some sort of covered platform that would keep the mail bag, tossed from moving trains, out of the wet. The Long-Bell men heartily agreed with this modest suggestion and were happy to expend the sum of $25 for just such a platform.

"The only thing cheap about Longview," wrote John M. McClelland, Jr., historian of the new Longview, "was the name." The record indicates as much. To begin with, Long's plans for the town were rather grand. Then there was the almost universal urge felt by small owners of land to soak-the-company, any company, which obviously needed a bog or a barren for any purpose whatever. For instance, the far from valuable fourteen thousand acres of the site of Longview, cost Long-Bell almost exactly $125 an acre more than the wildest native would have dreamed possible. Long-Bell officials also made some errors that could not be charged to local greed: the dike around the city, so they figured, would cost no more than $817,359. Actually it came to $3,250,000. There were many other items which came much higher than Long-Bell estimates.

The three existing railroads in the vicinity, which were the Northern Pacific, the Great Northern, and the Union Pacific, agreed that they would not welcome to their pooled tracks the trains of Long-Bell logs on Long-Bell cars pulled by Long-Bell locomotives. If these roads were not to share in the transportation, then Long-Bell had better run its own trains elsewhere. Whereupon, Long-Bell organized a subsidiary, the Longview, Portland & Northern, which never got to Portland and ran only a few miles north to the Long-Bell logging camps. This unforeseen item came to something like $5,400,000, no little of which was spent laying track up the west side of the Cowlitz River to the woods headquarters of Ryderwood. The LP&N required a new bond issue. So did construction of the two great sawmills. The city paving, the sidewalks, and the lake and park developments, all cost more than their estimates, and doubtless more than was reasonable.

Meanwhile, the long established and none too attractive town of Kelso, across the Cowlitz from Longview, invited the new city to join it and form one municipality. Longview begged to be excused. A long feud began. Kelso people and many others considered Longview, in spite of its big ideas, to be simply another company town, of which there were many in the lumber industry of the Northwest. Newspapers in Cowlitz County took delight in heckling every plan or move in the new city. At least two of these papers were frankly blackmail sheets, waiting to be bought off. The Wobblies, just then preparing for what turned out to be their last mighty effort to capture Northwest camps and mills, set up an IWW hall in Kelso, sent organizers into the district, and carried on their special kind of guerilla warfare, denouncing Long-Bell as a pack of slave drivers out of the South.

Longview moved ahead. The *Daily News* was established. A fine six-story hotel arose, the Monticello, and Joe Knowles came to do the murals for its lobby. This was the same old Nature Man who, many years before, had gone naked into the Maine woods as a circulation stunt for the Boston *Post*, and created a sixty-day sensation and an immense number of readers for the paper. Joe tried to repeat this success later in the Oregon woods, for Mr. Hearst, but was defeated by circumstances beyond his control: his stunt had barely got under way when most of Europe blew up in war. It also blew Joe out of the news. He turned to his talent for art, establishing his home near Ilwaco at the Columbia's mouth, and in Longview's new Monticello Hotel did some effective murals of covered wagon trains, of Indian fighting, of bull-team logging and other characteristic Western subjects.

Because Longview was being planned with the greatest confidence for a population of anywhere beyond fifty thousand people, it quickly took on the aspect of a city of magnificent distances. Here stood a fine big business block surrounded on all sides by expanses of vacant lots which quickly filled with weeds and the rubbish of careless citizens. Paved streets might run two hundred yards through the section designated as downtown and not pass any business. In the several carefully planned residence areas, the pavement ran on and on, with here and there a rather pretentious home that seemed to accentuate the loneliness of this apparent infinity. A small lake, named for Sacajawea, the Indian heroine of the Lewis & Clark expedition, was dug out of a slough, beautifully landscaped with trees, ornamental shrubs, and waterways remindful of Boston's fens; and there it lay, remote and silent, visited by passing fowl and breeding, so heckling newspapers announced, more mosquitoes and bigger ones than were ever before seen on the Columbia.

Imposing schoolhouses were built. Long himself gave funds for one and for a public library building done with

The Long-Bell lumber mill, Longview, Washington.

red brick in Georgian style. A brick city hall arose, complete with tower and clock. These and other public buildings, including the library and the hotel, were grouped around a landscaped Common which, almost inevitably, was christened R. A. Long Park.

Then, one day in the summer of 1924, the "biggest sawmill in the world" cut its first log. It did so to an audience of many thousands attracted by circuslike promotion. But the saw did not enter the log until a band,

273

prompted by R. A. Long, had played "Nearer My God to Thee." A governor, a United States Senator and a congressman, together with a full admiral and other dignitaries, were on hand to sing the praises of Mr. Long The Builder. And to climax four days of Longview's Pageant of Progress came nobody less than the Reverend Billy Sunday, to deliver an inspirational sermon. Shouting that he "wouldn't preach outdoors for anybody but God and R. A. Long," the latter of whom paid the evangelist $500 for coming, Sunday gave a rousing performance which was reported under a famous headline in the IWW paper: LONG-BELL HIRES JESUS-MAN TO QUIET SLAVES.

Although few places on the Columbia ever faced more troubles than those which quickly surrounded Longview, they were not due to labor difficulties. For one thing, the town's population was attracting far too few permanent residents. In an attempt to remedy this, Long-Bell footed the large bill occasioned by full-page advertisements in the *Saturday Evening Post*, the *Literary Digest* and other national periodicals. Another difficulty was A. Ruric Todd, an opportunist of adventurous ways, who turned up to apply for the job as manager of the Longview Chamber of Commerce. His application was not accepted, whereupon he moved into Kelso and prevailed on businessmen there to promote a campaign for the Port of Kelso.

As a site for new public docks to service deep-sea vessels, Todd selected Carrollton Channel. This was in the Columbia and was several miles from Kelso, but it was also safely outside the boundaries of Kelso's now hated rival across the Cowlitz. Longview sensed the danger and hurriedly set out to convince the commissioners that a site near the Long-Bell mills was the logical place for public docks. A. Ruric Todd got himself elected mayor of Kelso. He wrote handbills and pamphlets denouncing the Longview site. He called mass meetings. Criminal libel suits were filed against him. So was a recall, and after five months in office he was ousted by a slim majority. Just then Thomas J. Dovery, owner and editor of the *Cowlitz County News* of Kelso, was shot and killed by parties unknown while returning home at night from a meeting of the Public Welfare League. Dovery's paper was in the midst of the turmoil. His murder was generally believed to have been perpetrated because of his support of Todd and the Port of Kelso campaign.*

While the mystery of Dovery's murder still blanketed both Kelso and Longview with fear and apprehension, the First Christian Church of Kelso broke into warring factions. Pastor Charles L. Thornton, a Todd supporter, was locked out of the building. Suddenly, on a Thursday night when the closed structure should have been open for regular prayer meeting Third Street in Kelso filled with men and women. Armed with a crowbar and rope they advanced on the church, ripped open the locked doors and then, singing "Onward Christian Soldiers," ushered the Reverend Mr. Thornton and his wife inside and took possession. By then, the Longview-Kelso feud had become almost a continuous news story in the Northwest press. Both towns were getting more publicity than they wanted.

---

* It was not. Fairly conclusive evidence assembled long after the murder indicated the shooting had been incidental to an attempted robbery.

Now came a genuine queen from Europe to add a new note.

This was of course Marie of Romania who, as related, was on a visit to the United States. She was heading for Portland where she was to visit and dedicate Maryhill for her old and good friend, Sam Hill. The Queen's Western tour was being handled by President Charles Donnelly of the Northern Pacific Railway, and one day he got a letter from R. A. Long, chairman of the Long-Bell board, suggesting that the fine new city of Longview, with a brand-new railroad station, would be pleased to entertain her highness; and called especial attention to the fact that Longview was on the Northern Pacific line over which the royal party would travel from Seattle to Portland. So it was, but the Queen sent her regrets.

This was no way to treat the City that Vision Built. Mr. Long decided to make an issue of it, and harassed Donnelly until word came that the Queen would indeed stop at Longview. When this became known, Sam Hill, the Queen's old friend of World War I days, blew up. He had different plans for Marie. But the Queen, or Donnelly, or somebody, had given the word, and the royal word could not be broken. So, on the fog-ridden morning of November 4, 1926, and at the un-Christian hour of seven o'clock, the Queen's special rolled into Longview, Mr. Long's brass band cut loose with an approximation of the Romanian national anthem, and Queen Marie was taken to see the biggest sawmill on earth. One hour and twenty minutes later her train was rolling up the Columbia for Portland.

The Queen's visit was a sort of gala interlude. Long-

view's troubles continued. Frederick J. Bannister, elected
president of the Long-Bell Lumber Company in 1921 when
Long became chairman of the board, suddenly resigned
and brought legal action against the corporation, alleging
that vast sums had been diverted from the Long-Bell treasury "in an attempt to promote and force the growth of
a large and populous city"; and specially that these vast
sums had been used "in the building and paving of miles
of roadway, the development of an extensive boulevard
and park system, the development of civic centers, the establishment of lakes and lagoons, and the erection of a
luxurious and extravagant hotel." These were unkind
words to speak, and you may be sure they were read with
much satisfaction by the considerable number of Longview's enemies; the come-latelys were to get their come-
uppance. It did not work out that way. The suit was
brought and tried in Missouri and was at last settled in
the Company's favor by the supreme court of that state.

Despite his liking to see his picture in the papers, and
of making certain he was in the exact center of any picture,
and his inordinate desire to have his name attached to a
company, to a city, a street, a library, a school, a business
block or two, and almost anything else that needed naming, R. A. Long did not intend Longview to be a one-
company town. Industries were actively sought. During
the 1920s a plant went up for the Longview Fibre Company, another for the Pacific Straw Paper & Board Company, both of which used wood chips from the Long-Bell
mills. Then, in 1927, the Weyerhaeuser Timber Company,
the biggest forest products concern in the United States

and from which Long-Bell had bought much of its Western timber, decided to build in Longview. It erected three immense sawmills, later added a sulphite paper mill, and established a research laboratory from which since has come the techniques for manufacturing many new products from so-called mill waste.

The coming of Weyerhaeuser, providing a new payroll as large as Long-Bell's, appears to have been the chief item that was to assure some permanence to the new city. Yet the town's troubles were not finished. The business of the bridge came next. It seems originally to have started as an idea of the State of Oregon whose engineer recommended that a five-span bridge, 159 feet above water, be built across the Columbia between Rainier, Oregon, and the new city of Longview. Portland did not want a bridge there. It would, according to horrified spokesmen for the river's metropolis, be a grave obstruction to traffic on the lower Columbia. All of the Portland papers, except the *Oregonian*, referred to Longview as the "synthetic city." Portland's mayor declared "we must win in order to protect Portland and the Columbia Basin" from this dreadful span.

Seattle got into the battle. It automatically supported Longview against Portland. The Longview Bridge Company was formed with Wesley Vandercook, Long-Bell's engineer, in control of 51 per cent of the stock. The bridge was built, with the height raised to 195 feet, and completed in 1930, and tolls set. Instead of bringing an income at the rate of $500,000 a year, as expected, the tolls totaled less than one-third of that amount. The Depression was making itself felt. A "reorganization" of the bridge company had no effect on business, or finances. Much later, the State of Washington was induced to buy the structure, which had cost some $6,000,000, for $2,250,000, and continues to operate it as a toll bridge.

In the depths of the Depression, when the biggest sawmills in the world, along with most other sawmills, were running on part time, and the Long-Bell Lumber Company appeared to be facing certain bankruptcy, Longview was brightened somewhat by Mrs. Minnie (Ma) Kennedy, mother of the remarkable and perhaps even notorious Aimee Semple McPherson, the founder and female pope of the Four-Square Gospel. Ma Kennedy herself was a talented evangelist and, following a series of indecent and well-publicized rows with her daughter, she removed from the incomparably lush atmosphere of Los Angeles to set up a temple in Kelso. Ma preached both salvation and damnation. She also liked outdoor exercise. She bought a horse, named it Billy Sunday, and stabled it at the Longview Riding Academy when she was not out for a canter along the bridle paths around Lake Sacajawea. Once she rode Billy into the lobby of Hotel Monticello where, so it happened, a news photographer was waiting. It made a dandy picture in the papers. Though Time was running out on the Aspirin Age, it was still not too late for Longview to enjoy Mrs. Kennedy as something of a local personage.

And then, though she was in the autumnal era of her life, Ma announced to the local newspaper boys that she had fallen in love. Those were the exact words. She went on with little urging to describe in some detail the lucky man whom she identified as "Mr. G. E. Hudson of New

York City." Then, "What a man!" she cried. This remark was welcomed by the local press, and by the United and the Associated press services. Pretty soon Ma called the boys again and said she and What-a-Man-Hudson were going to be married right in Longview. The story went all over the country. Longview might be in the economic dumps, but it was still a lively place.

The wedding of Ma and What-a-Man was scheduled to take place at two o'clock on a Sunday afternoon. But for some reason or other, and just possibly in order to make the Sunday papers, Ma shifted the hour, and the radiant couple were married Saturday evening, on the banks of Lake Sacajawea under what, said a story in the Longview *Daily News*, "were the rays of a pale June moon." The event served to put Longview's name in papers even in places like Chicago, New York and Boston. In Longview it was soon forgotten in the gloom that thickened as the days passed, as wages were cut again, and the workday reduced.

The Long-Bell Lumber Company had managed to break even in 1929. A year later its books showed a loss of $2,600,000. A minority group of stockholders, charging mismanagement, sought to place the company in receivership. A Federal judge disallowed the receivership, remarking that for sixty years the Long-Bell firm had enjoyed an unsullied reputation for honesty and fair dealing; only a world-wide depression had brought it, along with many other great enterprises elsewhere, "into a sea of troubles." The company was permitted to reorganize, and thus weathered the bad years. By then R. A. Long was dead.

But Long's great dream of his old age, Longview,

was to justify itself. Twenty-five years after its founding it was without question the leading forest products city in the United States. Its population had never grown anywhere near the size its builder had expected of it. But its 20,339 citizens lived in as attractive a city as can be found along the Columbia; and there are many nonresidents who consider Longview to be the most beautiful town in either Oregon or Washington. Those vacant spaces have been filled, yet there is still no crowding, though that seemed to be approaching in mid-century. The place plays a large part in the life of the Columbia, which serves as log ponds and booming grounds for its sawmills, and as a transportation lane for incoming logs and outgoing lumber. Ships from all over the world dock here to load timbers, boards, and wood fibre products, and pulp and paper. They come also to load other things, including a sizable amount of aluminum made in Longview.

Kelso is no longer an enemy. It grew because of Longview, and even speaks well of the Long-Bell Lumber Company which once upon a time only too many Kelsonians held to be nothing but another of those soulless corporations which, so a disgruntled Kelso editorialist once wrote, would soon feel the wrath of God in the form of a Columbia River flood like that "which years ago destroyed the arrogantly proud settlement of Monticello that stood where Longview now stands, and washed it down to the sea."

It looked, for a few anxious days in 1948, as if the Kelso prophet might be right. In the greatest floodtime in sixty years the Columbia arose in May and, for more than a thousand miles along its course, wrecked homes, farms, bridges, warehouses, factories, sawmills; it wiped out completely the wartime city of Vanport, near Portland, causing several deaths and millions of dollars in damage. For at least a quarter of a century before 1948, it had been said often that in case of flood, then Longview could not survive. It would be the first to go. The 1948 waters climbed the miles of Longview dykes, while the more timid citizens took to the hills. But Engineer Wesley Vandercook's bulwarks held, while many other communities up and down the rampaging river suffered varying damage. Longview had survived the economic and political dangers of its formative days. Now it survived the wrath of waters.

Chapter 15

Canals, Locks and a Dam

EVER SINCE history began, people who lived along a river have felt the urge to control its flow, or at least to impose some sort of partial discipline on its vagaries. It was so with the Nile. Thousands of years later, the Oregon pioneers who came down the Columbia never forgot the experience. To the last they remembered the tragedies due to its wild dashings, and the heart-breaking labor of the portages around the falls of Celilo and the Cascades.

Those who came by sea were immediately harassed by the dangerous bar at the river's mouth, by the treacherous channel after they entered the stream and again, if Portland was their destination, by the islands which all but blocked entrance to the Willamette. And once farms and towns had been settled, the river had a way of suddenly rising above the highest visible or known watermark and washing buildings and crops down to the sea.

Farther up, in the long stretches between Walulla and Canada, and somewhat later in time, were the wheat ranchers who had at first marveled that they could plow and sow the bunch-grass lands and raise fifty bushels to the acre; but within five or six years discovered the moisture stored in the soil had been exhausted and ten bushels was an average crop. These men were victims of a disaster nothing but water could alleviate; and the only water was that of the Columbia, flowing past their powdery acres at the bottom of a canyon from three hundred to five hundred feet deep. Most of them must have dreamed of getting water somehow, yet it was a dream. They went away.

Then, there were doubtless imaginative men who looked at the surging power that came hurrying in such volume from the snows and glaciers of a vast region that included the high backbone of the continent and wondered, even if idly, how this immensity could be dammed and made to turn turbines. They were bold men, who thought of such a thing, for the Columbia is obviously an arrogant piece of water. There is nothing yielding about it, nothing submissive, nothing that could even be called considerate.

No matter the idle dreaming about flood control, and irrigation, and power, and navigation canals, the first actual improvements of the river were the little portage tramways which were soon changed into steam railways, at the falls of Celilo and the Cascades. Brief mention has been made earlier of these projects. The first was a one-mule and one-car job built in 1851 on the Washington bank around the Cascades by Hardin Chenoweth. For 75 cents a hundred pounds he moved "emigrants effects" from the steamer *James F. Flint* above the rapids to the brig *Henry* below. This was the same flimsy artery which in 1855 helped to speed Army troops upriver. It was somewhat improved by the Bradford family who bought it from Chenoweth and added new cars and more mules. A rival tramway was soon established on the Oregon side.

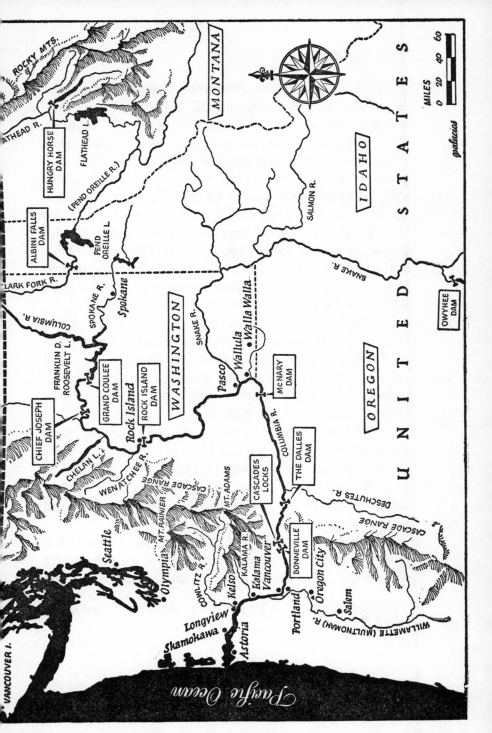

The Oregon Steam Navigation Company was quick to understand the significance of portage railroads. The company owned most of the boats, but not the transfers. The tramways became notorious for delays. Too much freight was "lost" during the short portage. The OSN complained vainly, then bought the portage outfit, added strap rails and a little cableless locomotive, the Pony, which operated on four connected drivers.* The company also built a ten-mile railroad from The Dalles City to a point just above Celilo Falls. This was something of a notable portage. To ensure presence of a train to meet every boat from above and below, the company strung a telegraph line along the track. When the agent at Celilo wired that a boat had hove in sight, the train at The Dalles, steam ready, set forth to meet it. The Dalles-Celilo line worked pretty well, though it had continuous difficulty from sand blowing over the rails. It later became a part of Villard's, and still later of the Union Pacific's, system, when it was extended from Celilo to Walulla.

The Cascades portage line continued to operate until the flood of 1894, when much of it was washed away and the remnant sold to a cannery that used it to move salmon from the fish wheels to the plant. By then, the long heralded project of Cascade Locks was well along toward completion.

It came to be said of Cascade Locks that only the most ancient pioneers could remember when the project was started. This was of course a gross exaggeration due

---

* This first locomotive in Oregon is now displayed in front of the Union Station at Portland.

to offended local pride. Yet, in all truth, Cascade Locks was a long time building. Discussed seriously as early as 1870, Congress four years later authorized Army Engineers to survey both the Cascades and Celilo with the idea of building canals and locks at those places. The Engineers recommended that the Cascades project be undertaken. Time passed. In 1876 Congress appropriated $90,000 to begin work. Work began. It went very slowly. More money had to be appropriated. When the original construction contract expired late in 1879, and the locks were still far from done, an extension was granted. This was soon abrogated and the Federal government purchased all of the contracting firm's equipment. For the next twelve years, the work went ahead, if that describes it, with hired labor. In 1892, the desperate government, apparently very tired, was glad to turn everything over to the firm of Day & Day and give them a contract to complete the job.

On November 5, 1896, or two decades after actual work began, Cascade Locks were declared ready. Several hundred excursionists passed through the three thousand-foot canal, and its lifts, on the *Harvest Queen*, the *Dalles City*, *Sadie B*, and the *Sarah Dixon* which had a cannon bolted to her deck and let go at proper intervals. Veterans of the river recalled the several captains who had taken their ships over the rapids in days past. In 1882, the *R. R. Thompson*, Captain McNulty; the *Elvira*, Captain McKenzie, and the *Mountain Queen*, Captain Troup, all came through what Lewis and Clark called "the Great Shute"; and later other skippers brought the *Gold Dust* and the *D. S. Baker* safely over and into the lower river, while

Captain Troup repeated his earlier exploit, this time in the celebrated *Hassalo*. It was generally agreed that those had been the days of the giants.

Cascade Locks had its busiest year in 1905, when 1,417 boats went up or down, and carried a total of 133,-070 passengers. By then demands for a canal and locks at Celilo had been made by a group organized in Portland as the Open River Association. Working with wheat growers of eastern Washington and Oregon, and of Idaho, the new association's battle cry was Anti-Monopoly. The Monopoly was alleged to be the Union Pacific Railroad: it charged far too much to move wheat to Portland for transfer to deep-sea carriers.

The next move was to organize the Open River Navigation Company which put three boats on the upper river to compete with the railroad in moving wheat and made arrangements with the Regulator Line, below Celilo, to take the cargoes from the portage railroad terminal to Portland. It is interesting to know that the Regulator boats had been purchased by James J. Hill who was invading the Union Pacific's territory with his Spokane, Portland & Seattle Railway along the north bank of the Columbia.

A result of the Open River-Union Pacific competition was an astonishing revival of shipping and passenger service on the river between Portland and ports not only on the upper Columbia but on the Snake. Within a short time the Open River Navigation Company was operating the *J. N. Teal*, the twin-stacker *J. M. Hannaford*, the *Inland Empire, Twin Cities, Norma, Spokane, Lewiston* and the *Joseph Kellogg*. It was most heartening to see so numerous a fleet running the Columbia and the Snake as though there were no railroads anywhere near the river. It was little short of a miracle to the decaying river hamlets which the railroads had by-passed. It was agreed by all that the Open River idea had brought steamboating back to the Columbia where it had been all but obliterated by the railroads. A few fanatical river enthusiasts went so far as to say that the railroads would never be able to compete with boats as wheat carriers. The rail business would wither. When the Celilo Canal and locks were finished, sagebrush would soon cover the tracks, sand and tumbleweed would bury the little depots, and the wayside watering tanks could leak unseen and be damned to them.

The Celilo job was authorized by Congress in 1903, and the Corps of Engineers given the go-ahead. The Engineers had already done a great deal for the lower river by constructing a twenty-five-thousand-foot jetty at the Columbia's mouth which quickly cleared the accumulations of silt and resulted in a depth of thirty feet across the bar that had been dreaded since Captain Gray's time. (A second jetty, finished in 1917, deepened the channel entrance to forty feet at low tide and widened it to four thousand feet.) Now the engineers moved to the grimly dramatic ledges and boulders above The Dalles where the river boiled and roared for more than ten miles below Big Eddy. For nearly twelve years they blasted and drilled a path around the rapids. By 1915 it was ready, a ditch sixty-five feet wide at the bottom and some eight miles long, with turnouts for vessels to pass each other. Its eight feet of water was enough for any steamboat that might conceivably need to get into the upper river.

The festivities occasioned by the opening of Celilo

Canal occupied the best part of a week and were marked with boats going up and down through the locks, and some rousing oratory by officials and friends of the Open River Association: "Our faces are still set to the future, and we must never falter or tire until from the mountains to the sea our great river is free as the air we breathe. . . ."

It was indeed true that the great river was now free from what for a generation had been declared was a railroad monopoly. Yet, it became gradually clear that shippers of wheat, as well as passengers, were in no haste to use the boats of the revived river fleet. For a time the Open River Navigation Company managed to keep fairly active with excursions from Portland and other lower river points to the new canal, but passengers soon diminished. A fine paved highway was being built up the south side of the Columbia from Portland and almost immediately it became the most talked about piece of road in the Northwest. From the headlands like Crown Point marvelous views of the river were to be had. The many little creeks tumbling straight down the mountain walls broke into Latourell, Multnomah, and Horsetail falls, to name a few. At Mitchell's Point was the superb daylighted tunnel that was compared favorably with the famous Axenstrasse in Switzerland. The new highway passed around mountain shoulders, curved into and out of deep ravines, and performed a figure eight such as few automobile tourists had ever seen. All in all, the Columbia Gorge Highway as it was named, was one of the most spectacular drives in the United States. "Kodak as You Go" had become a slogan. Camping and picnic grounds, many of them free and provided by men of the Mount Hood National Forest, added to the attractions. For nearly forty years the visitor to Oregon was told he had seen nothing unless he had driven the Columbia Gorge Highway.

But down below, on the river, the wheat traffic did not increase. It diminished almost as quickly as had the passenger traffic. The boxcars of the Union Pacific and the new Spokane, Portland & Seattle railroads were getting the business in wheat. The highway was getting the passengers. The high ideals and great expectations of the Open River Navigation Company faded. Its boats were retired, or sold to others. The new owners did no better when they tried to operate above The Dalles, and one by one the boats were retired again, or transferred to the lower river. By 1920 the canal and locks at Celilo lay virtually idle.

When I first saw them in 1923, the Celilo Canal and its locks looked to me—a stranger then and with little knowledge of the background that had brought them into being—they struck me as the ultimate fantasy of Federal spending at its worst. Stretching out to the horizon in this bleak region of vast distances lay a ribbon of steel-gray water confined by stone, metal and cement. Everything about it had the perfection of geometry. The bright green of the lawn by the locktender's house was an arresting sight in contrast to the desolation on every hand, a desolation that mounted to the tops of the stark hills and crawled on and on as far as the eye could reach. Over all, too, was a hush—a complete silence such as I imagined had blan-keted this scene as soon as the din of some prehistoric volcanic explosion had died and its sizzling lava had cooled. True, one could hear the noise of the falls, but it was muted, all but drowned by the immense quiet of this life-less country. It seemed to me a place of the greatest lone-liness, and I wondered what the boys of the Engineers—and their wives—had said, when among themselves, about a tour of duty at Celilo Canal. I was told by a friend at The Dalles that no craft had passed through the locks in three months.

Yet, Celilo Canal came in time to know some of the activity it was built for. Not stern-wheelers but steel barges pulled by propeller tugboats hauling wheat downriver pro-vided much of the new traffic; and even more came from the movement upriver of oils and gasoline carried in the special type of barges generally credited to Kirk Thomp-son, a well-known riverman. The locktenders at Celilo at last had some locktending to do. Almost one million tons went through in 1941.

The Celilo Canal and the North Jetty at the river's mouth were the last major improvements by government agencies on the Columbia in two decades, or until com-pletion of Bonneville Dam in 1938. Bonneville, however, was not the first dam across the Columbia. That distinction belongs to the dam at Rock Island, below Wenatchee, built by the Puget Sound Light & Power Company. In 1929 this alert outfit purchased land less than six months before the stockmarket crash that heralded the long depression of the 1930s. It was granted a license to construct a dam and build a power plant. In spite of many difficulties, the com-pany went ahead full tilt, and in 1931 this first dam on the Columbia was completed.

By the time Rock Island was producing power, the Corps of Engineers was under way with an over-all survey of American rivers. The general idea was to develop all resource potentialities, including navigation, flood control, irrigation and hydroelectric power, namely, all of the things which generations of men had dreamed of applying to the streams they lived on or by. The Engineers' study appeared as the "308 Reports" and involved, among other streams, a survey of the Columbia system such as had not been made before.

After pointing out in their recommendations that vessels of various size were blocked only at Kettle Falls, although there was need for an improved channel through various rapids, the report added that any dams should be built not for navigation alone but for "multiple purposes." They would help to maintain an even flow throughout the year. They would permit slack-water navigation for long stretches. They should supply water for irrigation; and they should generate electricity.

Work on the first unit started in 1933 on a dam named for Captain Benjamin Eulalie de Bonneville, French-born graduate of West Point whose career has long been a matter of some controversy and which, in any case, made him a prominent figure in the old Oregon Country through his dabbling in the fur trade and later by reason of being the first commandant at Vancouver Barracks, Washington Territory. Bonneville Dam was built just below the falls of the Cascades around which the canal and locks had been completed in 1896. Extending from Bradford Island to both banks it is a structure in three parts. Across the main channel a spillway dam regulates the height of water in the reservoir behind it. Across the falls between the island and the Oregon shore are a powerhouse and penstocks.

Next to the powerhouse is a lock to handle vessels up to eight thousand tons. The lock is seventy-five feet wide, five hundred feet long, and it raises a ship fifty feet in a single lift.

At last the "Great Shute" of Lewis & Clark, the place of labored portage alike of trappers, immigrants, and steamboat freight and passengers, lay untroubled in the quiet waters behind Bonneville Dam.* The dreaded barrier was gone. On July 12, 1932, the lock was opened to pass the *Charles L. Wheeler,* which proceeded upriver to be the first deep-sea vessel to dock at The Dalles and to make that long rapids-fenced town a port of the Pacific Ocean, 189 miles distant. Transmission of power from the Bonneville turbines started in 1938.

Not only the Great Shute disappeared in the impounded waters. With it went the physical evidences of the Bridge of the Gods which most condescending white people referred to as a "favorite myth" of the Indians. This was a natural stone arch under which, so the natives told the pioneers, the canoes of their ancestors had floated in the days before the various gods who inhabited the Cascade Mountains had got to warring and started throwing smoke, fire and boulders, to the end that the bridge collapsed and forced the river into a new channel. There is considerable geologic evidence that something like this did happen. Whether or not it did, the theory was given wider circulation by a romantic novel, *The Bridge of the Gods,* written in nearby Hood River by a young preacher,

* It might trouble the somewhat pompous Captain, who pronounced his name in two syllables, to know that the dam is almost invariably called Bonn-e-ville.

Frederic Homer Balch and published in 1890. It has been periodically reprinted. The dam waters also covered an extensive submerged forest, the stumps of which were occasionally twenty-five feet tall, well preserved, and included both fir and pine trees.

Possibly the greatest interest shown by the public in Bonneville Dam were the arrangements for the migration of salmon. There are three fishways, one at each end of the spillway dam, and one across the face of the power-house. Each consists of a collecting system, a fish ladder, and a pair of fish locks. Each ladder is an inclined flume forty feet wide in which are installed a series of fish weirs. The weirs create successive pools, each a foot higher than the next one downstream. The ladders circle around the ends of the dam and powerhouse, permitting adult fish heading upstream to reach the higher water above the dame. The volume of water flowing down the ladder is regulated to induce the fish to swim rather than leap from one pool to another.

It is the fish-counting stations that attract most visitors to the dam. Near the head of each ladder is a small house beside a pool in which is a picketed barrier with three openings. The counter in the little house can open any or all of the gates. The floor of each gate is painted white in order to light the forms of the fish as they pass quickly across it. This makes identification by species easy for the trained personnel in the counting stations. It also does a great deal more; it gives visitors the feeling of participation, even if only as watchers, in the incomparable mystery of salmon migrations. There they are for a brief moment, big fish and medium fish, moving across the patch of white paint, heading for home waters, for procreation, and death.

Because there is little movement of fish at night the counting is limited to daylight hours. During the peak of a salmon run two counting stations are usually operated on each ladder. Each species is listed separately. All counts are recorded hourly. More than nine million fish were counted and identified during the first ten years after completion of Bonneville Dam. The average annual count included 359,054 chinooks, 127,431 steelhead trout, 72,834 bluebacks, 9,437 silvers, 1,600 chums, 22,426 shad, 13,458 carp, 132,730 suckers, 59,750 squaw fish, plus miscellaneous bullheads, crappies, bass, and sturgeon. There was also an average of 105,128 lamprey eels counted annually.

Climbing the ladder at Bonneville Dam is one of several brilliant descriptions in *Return to the River*, a fine and sensitive book about salmon by Roderick L. Haig-Brown. "The ladder," he writes, "was a curving quarter-mile length of fast-flowing water that drew down across the island from the slough behind the powerhouse." He then singles out two fish and tells of their efforts to find their way to the bottom of the ladder, then how they worked their way up easily, going from pool to pool in the bright water, until they came suddenly to the dazzling light reflected from the counting plate. It was too much brightness. The two fish turned and fled into the dark of the pool; but presently they were back again, swimming slowly and cautiously, investigating; and now they crossed the white plate without panic, while "a dozen pairs of human eyes made the brief sight their own, for all time." The two salmon passed quickly through the remaining steps and out into the slough. They would meet no other obstacle

until they came to the dip nets of the Indians just below
Celilo Falls.*

Because the fish ladders proved satisfactory, the operation of Bonneville's fish locks, or lifts, has not been necessary, but they are there in case of emergency. The downstream migrations of fingerlings go over the spillways, or
pass through the turbines, or are conducted through four

Bonneville Dam.

by-passes provided with entrances at points at which fish
are most apt to arrive at the dam.

After the fish going upriver have passed Bonneville,
they climb similar ladders at The Dalles Dam, at McNary,
and Rock Island, but when they come to Grand Coulee,
they are at the end of the line. (When it is finished, Chief

*Celilo Falls seemed in no danger of being submerged when Mr.
Haig-Brown wrote, or when his book was published by William
Morrow & Company in 1941. The Falls have since disappeared in
the waters of The Dalles Dam.

Joseph Dam will technically be the end of the line for migration, but this will change nothing because no salmon-run streams enter the Columbia between the two structures.) Mechanical devices could have been installed at Grand Coulee to permit fish to pass on to their native streams above the big dam; but it was thought better to try transplanting. How this was done, and its results, were told by Alphonse Kemmerich, regional fishery management co-ordinator for the Fish and Wildlife Service.

Beginning in 1930 [said Mr. Kemmerich], adult salmon and steelhead migrating up the Columbia were trapped at the Rock Island dam fishways, then transported to the four tributaries entering the main river below Coulee dam and upstream from the point of their inception. These were the Wenatchee, Entiat, Methow, and Okanogan rivers. Approximately 50 per cent of these adult fish were held in specially designed ponds, artifically spawned, and the resulting eggs incubated in three hatcheries constructed in the Wenatchee, Entiat, and Methow watersheds for this purpose. This program was continued throughout the succeeding four years.

Beginning with the 1944 migration all barriers to upstream movement of adult fish were removed from the fishways at Rock Island dam. The adult salmon and steelhead returned and successfully spawned in the newly adopted streams where they were hatched or reared five years previously, thus completing their life cycle.

A portion of the adult salmon returning annually to the Wenatchee, Entiat, and Methow rivers are artificially spawned and the resulting young fish handled in these hatcheries. This combined production from artificial and natural sources has resulted in the successful transfer and maintenance of chinook and blue-back salmon of the upper Columbia.

The comparative average of annual runs, during the period 1933-1943, before the experiment was started, and during 1950-1954 afterward, were chinook 8,045 and 22,717, for blueback 17,015 and 101,858, and for steelhead 3,110 and 3,453.

In regard to ships, Bonneville's locks have proved adequate to all needs, even when river traffic rose sharply during World War II. Only 162,000 tons went through in 1938, the first year of operation. One and a half million tons were lifted or lowered in 1952, and since then the annual tonnage has averaged close to that figure.

Bonneville to the eye is a handsome dam in a hand-some setting. The green timbered Cascade Mountains rise abruptly on both sides, and from the heights the structure, with blue quiet water above and foaming white below the spillway, has been a favorite with airborne photographers. It is significant not only because it was the first govern-ment-built dam on the main Columbia, but also because it was the first project of the so-called Reports of the Corps of Engineers, a document which in two decades has changed the river almost beyond knowing. If all of the recommendations of the Engineers are carried out, then the work of taming the Columbia has hardly begun.

The second step in the 308 Reports was Grand Coulee. This in turn has been followed by others which have come to completion one after the other so rapidly as to affect the lives of almost everyone along the lower five hundred miles of the main river, and along several of its tributaries.

Chapter **16**

The Dam Era Begins

ⓦ ONE OF the several recommendations in the 308 Reports of the Army Engineers had to do with the immense geographical oddity, already mentioned, called Grand Coulee. A dam across the Columbia at this point, said the report, could be used to pump water into Grand Coulee itself and there store it for irrigation as needed. The structure would be a multiple-purpose affair for hydroelectric power, irrigation, and flood control. It would also be an aid to navigation above Grand Coulee by wiping out the many rapids and falls between the dam and the Canadian border.

Grand Coulee is one of scores of abandoned river channels in the plateau that lies east of the Cascades in Washington and is roughly bounded by a line from Spokane to Walla Walla. This particular coulee got its name from the fact that it was a thousand feet deep in many places and some fifty miles long. That makes quite a noticeable canyon in desert country. We have seen how it impressed the pioneer explorer, Alexander Ross, when he stood on its floor to look into infinity. This much-traveled man was all but stricken dumb and to his Journal could remark only that Grand Coulee was "the wonder of the Oregon country."

Over the years many another man looked at Grand Coulee to ponder how it came into being. Geologists hold it to be a gigantic river course made by the Columbia when ice dammed its natural valley in this region and caused it to overflow and cut a new channel. Fifty miles long, this ice-age river bed widened to three miles, then plunged from the top of four-hundred-foot cliffs. Climatic changes melted the ice barrier. The Columbia returned to its original course. The coulee went dry. Where the diverted flood fell over the high cliffs at the far end of the coulee are now the Dry Falls, rated one of the geologic wonders in the United States. "The Dry Falls," wrote Fred O. Jones, former geologist for the Bureau of Reclamation at Grand Coulee, "beg one to imagine the violent river which at one time plunged and thundered as one of the largest waterfalls ever to operate on the earth's surface."

Over the years other men looked at the Grand Coulee to ponder not only how it came into being, but what if anything could be done with it. One of these was Billy Clapp, a short, plump and cheerful attorney who operated his law business, such as it was, from a two-by-four shack in Ephrata, the modest sun-baked hamlet of five hundred souls that was the seat of Grant County. It was a dusty and windy county. Little rain fell there. With a great deal of toil, settlers around Ephrata had managed to raise fruit on patches irrigated from deep wells. Jesse Cyrus platted the three-block townsite and named it, according to one story, for the Biblical Ephratah which may have been simply another name for Bethlehem. The Ephratah-Bethlehem of old was known for its many cisterns.

For all its wells, however, Grant County's Ephrata was in the middle of a boulder-strewn desert, and no subject was of greater interest there than the possibility of irrigation. The citizens had been holding on and waiting and hoping for moisture for seventeen years when Billy Clapp got his idea about Grand Coulee. He had been looking at the coulee for a long time. The extreme southern end of the great dry canyon was almost within Ephrata's corporate limits. "Why," he mused aloud one day, "why couldn't we build a big dam at the other end of her and make the river run right down the coulee and give us some water?" In this remark of Billy Clapp, according to a favorite legend that also has some documentation, was the genesis of the vast project that came to fruition more than two decades later.

It was quite natural that the Ephrata lawyer should have irrigation on his mind. In Grant and other adjacent counties water had been the first topic of conversation since settlers came. For at least seventy years men had known what a little moisture could do for this powdery soil; and irrigation in the Yakima and Wenatchee valleys had been done on a scale and with sufficient success to encourage similar projects elsewhere.

Back in 1846 Dr. Marcus Whitman had dug a ditch to divert water from Doan Creek to the wheat field and garden plots of his mission near Walla Walla. A year or so later the Oblate Fathers used water from Ahtanum Creek to irrigate their newly founded mission. The grains and fruits and vegetables of both ventures were prodigious. And so it went. The early settlers in all of the arid counties either did something in the way of irrigation, or they went away from there. There were no two ways about it; you got water somehow, or you moved.

The first big-scale project was promoted by John F. Oakes, president of the Northern Pacific Railway, much of whose land grant through this desert was worthless without water. Oakes picked a forty-four-year-old ditch-and-dam builder from Montana, Walter Granger, to scout the sagebrush and jackrabbit country of the Yakima valley. Granger found the prospects so good he agreed to build the first ditch on an option permitting him to buy railroad land at $1.25 an acre. Out of this deal came the first stretches of the Sunnyside Canal, a highly successful piece of work that touched off many more efforts. In the Wenatchee district the Great Northern Railway effectively encouraged and even financed a number of canal networks that paid off well.

Federal agencies like the Geological Survey and the new Bureau of Reclamation became active. The latter proposed, surveyed and carried out a sizable project in the Okanogan valley, then went on to many more. The Indian Service took charge of the Wapato job on the Yakima reservation which brought 136,000 acres into production.

Private and semiprivate groups were organized to build small dams, canals and ditches; and in time these combined to weave a maze of conflicting rights and claims. Water in this aridity was virtually life. Men fought, sued, and shot each other because of water. Communities warred and split because of water. A shallow trench with finger-deep water rippling along it was reason enough to shout Glory, or to bring the sheriff. Valves were opened by agencies described as "parties unknown," and sticks of dynamite

303

went off in the night to wreck the work of months. The community that did not get water was a community doomed.

The conflicts turned so bitter and the canal finances became so muddled that the state legislature set up irrigation districts for the administration of water rights. By the time of World War I, the State of Washington had stepped in to refinance some forty-odd of the irrigation districts that were facing bankruptcy.

This was the period when Billy Clapp of Ephrata, which had never shared in the state or other water projects, came up with his proposal for Grand Coulee: Why not fill its fifty miles with water to be drawn upon as needed? It was Rufus Woods, editor and publisher of the Wenatchee *World* who, while in Ephrata looking for ads and news, got Clapp to expand on his idea. It was something to light the imagination of the ebullient newspaperman. Next day, which was July 18, 1918, his *World* appeared with a front-page editorial bannered "Two Million Wild Horses," which was either Billy Clapp's or Rufus Woods's estimate of the unharnessed horsepower of the Columbia River.

The editorial went on to say that it was "a well established fact" that the Columbia's course had once upon a time run down Grand Coulee. Then it cited the proposal of Billy Clapp which contemplated "turning the Columbia into its old bed by construction of a giant dam." This would reclaim some two million acres of waste land in Grant and adjoining counties, said the editorialist warming to his subject, and also "develop water power approximating Niagara Falls."

It all looked fairly simple to Editor Woods. "When the dam has been completed to such a height that it will run down Grand Coulee," he remarked, "the job will be about completed." That's all there was to it. Neither Woods nor Clapp knew that the floor of the coulee was a good six hundred feet above the river; or that any dam high enough to divert the river into the coulee would back up the Columbia so far into Canada that the Arrow Lakes, the city of Revelstoke, and perhaps even Boat Encampment would disappear in the monstrous lake behind the dam. Little details concerning the project were matters for the dam builders, not for big-idea men like Billy Clapp and Rufus Woods.

Although World War I was just then going into its last great fury before the armistice, and most Americans had eyes for little more than dispatches from France, the *World*'s editorial created a stir in eastern Washington where war had to share the front page with anything that concerned water. Much of the comment occasioned could have been crystallized in a remark by R. S. Steiner of Waterville, a judge of the superior court. "Dam the Columbia!" he wrote the *World*. "Verily, Baron Munchausen, thou art a piker." Yet, no matter the wild-blue-yonder flavor of the *World's* editorial, it was William M. Clapp, to cite his full name, who was "the direct lineal ancestor of the particular effort which resulted after fifteen years of travail in the start of construction" of the dam across the Columbia at Grand Coulee.*

* So wrote George Sundborg in *Hail Columbia* (1954) an excellent and detailed if highly opinionated account of "the 30 Year Struggle for Grand Coulee Dam."

The "fifteen years of travail" were a struggle between determined and opposing forces who came to be described as "the pumpers," or those who favored the dam at Grand Coulee, and "the gravity men" who wanted no dam at the coulee and believed that the way to get irrigating water was a canal to the desert from Albeni Falls on the Clark Fork in Idaho, a major tributary of the Columbia. During some fifteen years of contention, both sides attracted thousands of partisans. Legislatures and even Congress were periodically in an uproar. Treachery and venality were among the lesser crimes charged. At times it came to seem as if Grand Coulee were an emotional thing as bitterly resented and supported as once had been the name of Arkansas. "Change the name of Arkansaw? Sir, better to change the constellations in their orbit. . . ."

The literature devoted to the construction of Grand Coulee Dam, including its "heroes" and "villains," according to the point of view, is of a bulk to dismay anyone except the truly dedicated. It has been estimated that a definitive shelf of Grand Coulee books, pamphlets, magazine articles and newspaper stories would run to more lineal feet, or greater poundage, or would by any other measure far exceed all other writings which for a century and a half have been devoted to the discovery, exploration and exploitation of the Columbia and all of its tributaries from source to mouth. This is so chiefly because it was the greatest battle to date of the continuing war between public and private power interests. Public power won the battle. Grand Coulee was built. Among them all perhaps James O'Sullivan came as near as anyone to being the father of

Grand Coulee Dam.

a project for which at least several hundred men worked devotedly, even fanatically.

Born in 1876 at Port Huron, Michigan, Jim O'Sullivan was a former lawyer and college professor whose lively imagination was enthralled by the idea of Grand Coulee. It was he, as one writer put it, who "organized the daydream" of Billy Clapp of Ephrata, who "focused the diffuse energies of promoters like Rufus Woods," and marshaled supporters "like the Grange, the public power people, the unions and veterans" into "an effective alliance to reward the friends of the dam and punish its enemies." * Before his death at seventy-three, in 1949, Congress passed a bill affixing O'Sullivan's name to one of Grand Coulee's subsidiary dams which was "to create a 47-square-mile reservoir for irrigation waters."

Construction of Grand Coulee began in the fall of 1933. It was going to be quite a job. Jobs were just what was needed in 1933. Breadlines were the longest that had been seen this century. For the next decade thousands of men had jobs on what the papers liked to call "the biggest thing on earth." By January of 1942 the dam itself and the powerhouse were done. Six months later a sheet of water poured over the spillway. The reservoir was filled. Its lake extended 151 miles back to the Canadian boundary.

Though the Army Engineers had built Bonneville Dam and had in their 308 Reports recommended Grand Coulee, the latter was made a project of the Bureau of Reclamation. Possibly nothing since the Erie Canal received comparable notice in the press which was kept more than well

* *The Dam,* by Murray Morgan, 1954.

informed by a small army of Federal publicists. Visitors were taken on tours all over the project; and a tour lasted anywhere from six hours for a casual look to two or three days for the full treatment.

Readers of newspapers and magazines were informed that this was "the largest concrete structure in the world." From bank to bank the dam stretched fourteen city blocks, or four thousand three hundred feet. It rose five hundred feet from foundation. It had a "useful storage" of five billion acre-feet. The ultimate capacity of its power plant was given as 2,160,000 kilowatts. Because most of these measurements are quite meaningless to most people, the thoughtful publicists used comparison: The crest of the dam was almost twice as high as Niagara Falls; all the buildings in Rockefeller Center, New York City, could stand on the surface of the spillway, and there would be exactly three acres left over.

It is big all right, but it has to contend with too much space to *look* big. Set in the midst of appalling distances, it appears like a play dam of children, lost in the terrifying wastes that are now threaded with transmission lines. More impressive is the lake behind the dam. Directly into this body of quiet water pours the great volume of the Clark Fork which was once considered to be the main Columbia. The Spokane River comes in, too, and many lesser streams like the Sanpoil and the Kettle. The dam changed everything on the Columbia for more than 150 miles upstream. All towns and farms that were less than 1,310 feet above sea level had to go. That was the line along which the shore of the lake was to lie.

It turned out that eleven towns large enough to support post offices had to go. The old settlement of Kettle Falls moved upgrade a little way to Meyers Falls, then its impolite citizens, who outnumbered their hosts, voted to change the name of the place to Kettle Falls. Other towns that disappeared from their original sites were Marcus, Boyds, Keller, Peach, Lincoln, Gerome, Gifford, Daisy, Harvey, and Inchelium. Some moved to higher ground. Others were merely abandoned and passed from the maps. Altogether, including ranchers, more than three thousand people had to pull up stakes and get out ahead of the rising waters behind Grand Coulee Dam.

While the old towns were in process of moving or abandonment, new settlements arose, places like Mason City, Grand Coulee, Grand Coulee Center, Elmore and Electric City. They grew quickly, filling up and overflowing with the men and families who followed construction jobs as a usual thing, or who were glad of any sort of job in the worst years of the Depression. These mushroom places also attracted others less interested in jobs at day labor than in "business opportunities" such as pool halls, barber and beauty shops, beer parlors, taxi stands, stores, and places whose merchandise is not commonly identified in the yellow pages of telephone directories. The swarming population lived in just about everything from "company" houses and barracks to trailers, auto camps, tents, and huts built of tin cans. Every desert shack on every abandoned homestead for many miles was occupied.

Eighty-odd men were killed at the dam. Some were drowned, others electrocuted. Others died from falls. A few were caught under trains. On March 17, 1937, it looked for a moment as though a mass tragedy was coming. Just as work began that day, sirens let go to warn that the big cofferdam was leaking. A bit later one of its cells burst, and water, dirt and rock roared down into the pit where two men escaped death and swam to safety. Thousands of men worked at diking while every available pump went into action. They were at it the rest of the day, and all night, hauling truckloads of tumbleweed, sandbags, old cable, sacks of cement, even mattresses snatched from bunkhouses, to stem the leak. The dam was saved by a close margin.

Fifteen years later, when it had long since been a working dam, Grand Coulee had another narrow escape from disaster. Because of what a reporter termed a "constellation of circumstances" a flood burst within the dam structure, which has eight miles of tunnels inside its bulk, and swamped the powerhouse, threatening to ruin the turbines. The accident happened because a dam employee "pushed the wrong button" and let a part of the Columbia run wild within the dam's corridors. The Pacific Northwest "teetered on the edge of economic catastrophe while a handful of desperate engineers fought the icy flood in the innermost recesses of the structure." Catastrophe was averted, but people in all parts of the Northwest knew something had gone wrong with the power center of the region.

When the generators started going off the line during the flood, men were laid off at the Bunker Hill & Sullivan mine and smelting plants in the Coeur d'Alene country of Idaho. Work was cut at the Potlatch Forests plant on the Clearwater. In the aluminum plants at Spokane, Tacoma and Vancouver, technicians were faced with the problem of keeping the cooking vats hot as the flow of power from

Grand Coulee was reduced. Housewives in three states were asked in hasty radio announcements to "Eat cold cuts tonight. Don't wash the dishes. They are having trouble at Grand Coulee." It was indeed trouble they were having. When it had been remedied, one of the men who had helped remarked of the Columbia: "That's one hell of a strong river." *

Whatever the cause of the accident, or its cost, the marked and immediate if only temporary loss of power impressed the Northwest as nothing else could have done with the importance of Grand Coulee Dam. Most people had read, of course, that Grand Coulee was the greatest powerhouse in the world; that it "won World War II" because it supplied the energy that made the aluminum for 60 per cent of American planes; and that because of it, too, the government atomic plant was established at Hanford, within easy transmission distance from both Grand Coulee and Bonneville dams, of which more later.

Yet just because she had read these things, it did not follow that a housewife was not dismayed when she was told not to wash her dishes because there was a lack of power to run her washer or light her kitchen. All she knew was that here on the Columbia was the mightiest source of electricity imaginable. In the industrial field, the many brown-outs were chargeable less to the one accident at the dam than that to the fact that all of the power plants in the Northwest were insufficient to operate the combined load of the old and the new plants at full capacity. As this condition was made known, industrial users were indignant, or alarmed, or both. Like the housewife,

* *The Dam,* by Murray Morgan.

they had come to believe that power in the Northwest was unlimited.

The outcome was a demand for still more sources of power. If more power meant building more dams, then build them. This is what has been going on ever since. The end is not yet in sight.

The main reason for the brown-outs was the immense and mysterious establishment which is now generally known as the Hanford atomic works. What Hanford's power load may have been, or is, is still a secret; few people can estimate how many kilowatts are required to produce a pound of plutonium-239, which is the product made in this isolated and carefully guarded plant set in the wastes less than a hundred miles from Grand Coulee.

The Hanford plant began to form late in 1942, under a thick haze of mystery that did not lift the least bit until three years later when the President of the United States announced that Americans had just destroyed the Japanese city of Hiroshima with an atomic bomb, adding that this weapon had been the product of two plants, one on the Tennessee River, the other on the Columbia. It was only then that people got an idea of the importance of the Hanford project which had started operation as the White Bluffs Military Project, then became Hanford Engineer Works.

At the beginning of things, in 1942, the few people who lived in Hanford started to wonder what besides dust and sand was in the air when Army officers, many with stars on their shoulders, arrived. It is improbable that more than a handful of Washingtonians could have said where Hanford was. It was not to be found on the automobile route maps of the time. But these many military men suddenly hove into the hamlet in December. They made trips into the desert which surrounded Hanford on all sides. You may be sure they were questioned by curious residents; but they were as uncommunicative as they were courteous. They went away. In February, 1943, other Army men came in force, to say that they were going to need perhaps 440,000 acres, or 631 square miles, of Benton County's desert. It would be used for a project the government had in mind. Then they started condemnation proceedings against approximately 2,000 property owners. Those who refused the prices offered were told to start suit in Federal court. But everybody must get out at once. They did get out, and no one of them could guess why.

It now became known that the Du Ponts of Delaware were coming to build some sort of gigantic plant for the government. Many Hanford people immediately jumped to the conclusion that the plant was for making aluminum, a metal that was very much in the news of the Northwest where two plants to make it were already being built. Along with this supposition went another—the Hanford sands were heavy with alumina, or bauxite, or whatever substance it was that went into the manufacture of the light metal so much in demand.

Not a few of Hanford's owners of real estate thought they were being hornswoggled and charged that the Army men were acting as a front for Du Pont in order to secure land cheap. Resentment became so marked that Colonel Harry Kadlec, public relations officer on the job, called a community meeting at which he told the embattled Hanfordites that the virtually unlimited volume of sand in Benton County did not contain enough alumina to make a single coffeepot of, say, six-cup capacity. Well, then, asked a property owner, if Du Pont wasn't going to make aluminum, then what was the product? Colonel Kadlec couldn't answer that one. Maybe he didn't know.

But the original population on 440,000 acres of sand moved out on schedule, and the first of 60,000 workers began to move in. They were recruited by government agencies in all parts of the country. The agents were hard put to tell what sort of work was to be done; and their job was not lightened when rumors got around that a new and terrible kind of poison gas was to be made at Hanford. Yet the workers were hired, and they moved in waves to the Hanford Engineer Works. They laid out 345 miles of highway over the shifting sands. They used 360,000,000 feet of lumber to whack up offices and barracks. They poured 800,000 yards of concrete. At the peak of activity, in mid 1944, 51,000 workers lived in Hanford alone, while thousands more came to work daily from tents and trailers and auto courts within a radius of sixty miles. Nearby Richland grew into a sort of company town.

It has been estimated that of the thousands who worked in and around the fortlike plant at Hanford, less than a hundred knew what was going forward. But everyone there, working under what seemed "security" conditions close to fanaticism, came in time to feel the mystery which enveloped the place. The mystery cleared somewhat, as related, in August 1945, after President Truman reported that two large cities of Japan had been wiped out and more than 150,000 persons killed by two bombs of a new type which had been fashioned at secret projects in Tennessee and Washington.

War's end brought rapid demobilization. Everywhere the huge cantonments began to fade. But activities of what became officially the Atomic Energy Commission increased many times over. Hanford was not permitted to fade. The blanket of mystery was lifted briefly, but security conditions remained only a little changed. A year after end of the war the government asked General Electric to take over and operate Hanford Engineer Works. It did so. Just what has been going on there since is not specifically known, although now and then the veil is raised a little. General Electric announced, for instance, that the buildings at Hanford were being heated by the hot water incident to producing atomic power. It is also known that the several great vats set in the Benton County desert are used to cool substances which are both hot and "hot"; and that the processing water must be stored for a time before it is diverted back whence it came, into the Columbia, lest it raise the river's temperature and Geiger count to a dangerous point.

For the rest, it was public knowledge that General Electric had asked the Atomic Energy Commission to authorize a dual-process reactor which the company said would not only produce plutonium, but give off electrical energy which would be used to supply Hanford with all the power it needed. It might even contribute excess electrical energy to the Northwest Power Pool.

This idea, it quickly appeared, had both friends and enemies. It became a political matter of such heat that many believed it could not be settled except by an act of Congress. In the meantime, Hanford remained by far the biggest industrial plant in the state of Washington, according to Ralph Cordinier, General Electric's president who also happens to have been born at Walla Walla, almost on the edge of the Hanford desert. As a youth just out of nearby Whitman College, young Cordinier used to sell toasters and washing machines to the few people in Benton County. Since his company came to manage Hanford, Cordinier has been at the plant often. James Stevens wrote of him: "Call Ralph Cordinier Sagebrusher, and he will know what is meant, and like it. . . . He also represents today's uses and tomorrow's prospects for the partnership of Columbia River power and human enterprise."

Of all of today's uses and tomorrow's prospects in regard to Grand Coulee, none is to be more easily seen and appreciated than irrigation. A million and a quarter acres of so-called wasteland has been marked for reclamation by water. Generous samples of this area have already proved the observation made three quarters of a century ago by Lieutenant Thomas W. Symans, U. S. Army, who wrote that the soil of this desert was rich enough to provide bountiful harvests if moisture could be added to it.

Grand Coulee's irrigation project, as outlined by the United States Bureau of Reclamation, embraces an area about one hundred miles north and south, and sixty miles east and west. The land lies south of the dam and north of Pasco where the Snake meets the Columbia. Eighty per cent of the irrigable land in this area is privately owned. All of it has been surveyed, classified and appraised. The

317

appraisals are based on dry-land values, and not because it is to be watered. It is worth while knowing that all land eligible to receive water is protected by antispeculation restrictions.

The plan to use the coulee itself as a reservoir for irrigation headwaters was mentioned earlier. When the dam was under construction, the first of "the 12 largest pumps ever built" was installed at the pumping plant at the dam. Others have been added since. Each has a capacity of 700,-000 gallons a minute. They lift water 280 feet from the lake behind the dam into the canyon of the coulee where dams have formed a reservoir twenty-seven miles long. This is called the equalization reservoir. From it the water flows by gravity, plus some supplemental pumping, through a system of canals. A second reservoir, in effect an extension of Moses Lake, catches the runoff water from irrigated lands in the northern end of the project for re-use on lands to the south.

Somebody in the Bureau of Reclamation figured that Grand Coulee's two bigger irrigation canals are each longer than the Potomac, and that the main canal alone could hold the flow of the Niagara River. This is a good use of comparison. Even more effective is a statement from the same source that when all of Grand Coulee's canals and laterals are completed, some years hence, they will stretch 4,500 miles.

On May 29, 1952, the first irrigating water from the Grand Coulee reservoir started to flow when Mike Strauss, Commissioner of Reclamation, turned a valve-control wheel and let a froth of white go tumbling down the dry ditches that spread across project farms near Moses

Lake. "Here this afternoon," he said, "we celebrate the addition of the equivalent of a new state to the nation. . . . Our country is now about to reap harvest from the desert."

There can be no question as to what water will do for the desert of the Grand Coulee country. More effective than the statistics of crops grown is what the eye cannot help but see in passing through the region. After running for mile upon ghastly mile through veritable desolation, one plunges suddenly, and with no more warning than the fleeting legend on a roadside sign, into a prodigal greenness of startling fertility. One such sign says "Quincy Valley Columbia Basin Project 120,000 acres." Then comes the lush vegetation which even in a more naturally favored region would be marked, but here in the midst of volcanic and glacial wastes will astonish almost anyone. Has it come to pass that the mountains have dropped down new wine, that the hills flow with milk, and all the rivers flow with waters? One's memory almost invariably recalls dim Biblical passages about an oasis, or reflects on the American West's first great irrigators, the Mormons, who made their State of Deseret blossom as the rose.

On this reclaimed land one sees combines working in high heavy wheat on acres which day before yesterday were bunch grass and sagebrush, the home of jackrabbits and of as many rattlesnakes as the rabbit population would support. Or the crop may be one of many fruits or vegetables. The never-ceasing winds still blow hot or bitter, according to season, but they have been tempered now and they carry less dust and sand. Perhaps one should not call it Eden, though many a weathered homesteader has called it as much after reaching into his memories of other times and other places.

The size of farm units varies from ten to 160 irrigable acres. Prices have been kept low, ranging from $2.50 to $20 an acre. But other costs are high. The Bureau of Reclamation's men have been careful to point out that a family should have at least $7,500 before moving to a tract, and expect to put in another $13,000 or so before it is fully developed. There has been no shortage of applicants. As a new block of farms was opened, there were usually several thousand farmers waiting. Drawings are held to determine the order in which applicants shall be examined.

The basic plan for the Grand Coulee project was that the sale of electric power would pay a little more than three fourths of the cost of irrigation and that the remainder would be repaid by the farmers settling on the project. It was also believed that the cost of Grand Coulee Dam, as well as the other multipurpose dams that have since been built or are building on Federal account, would eventually pay for themselves through the sale of power and irrigated land. Time alone will tell if these expectations are to be fulfilled.

Long before construction was started on the Bonneville and Grand Coulee projects, a group of men interested in navigation on the Columbia formed the Umatilla Rapids Association to urge construction of a dam that would drown out the white-water shallows between Walulla and Umatilla. Though better navigation was the main reason cited, the proponents thought the dam should generate power to irrigate the region round about, and any surplus energy be sold to home and industrial users. The first meeting of this group took place in 1920. Thirty-four years later the wanted structure, named for Charles McNary, by then a long dead United States senator, who with others had been active in getting the dam's authorization and appropriations, was ready for dedication by the President of the United States.

The long history of this dam at Umatilla Rapids may give needed strength to the proponents of other delayed dams on the Columbia. The idea of McNary Dam appears to have been discussed locally as long ago as Woodrow Wilson's first administration. Organized efforts were started during Wilson's second administration, and continued on through the days of Harding, Coolidge and Hoover; on through the three administrations of Franklin D. Roosevelt. At last, in 1946, in Harry S. Truman's time, when Guy Cordon had succeeded to the late Senator McNary's seat, Congress appropriated funds to begin work.

Work, however, did not begin at once. Cordon carried on the fight with vigor and at last, in 1948, the Army Engineers were told to go ahead. One day in September, 1954, President Eisenhower came to throw the switch, which is the equivalent of driving-the-golden-spike which marked the heyday of the railroad era. There must have been several thousand men and women in the great audience at the ceremony who were yet unborn when the dream that became McNary Dam was first organized.

McNary Dam cost some $281,000,000. It was to contribute about twice as many kilowatts to the Northwest Power Pool as Bonneville, and almost half as many as Grand Coulee. Its single eighty-six-foot-wide lock lifts vessels into a lake sixty-one miles long. Umatilla and Five-Mile Rapids are now safely under deep water. Around the lake lie approximately 244,000 acres of arid land that will be irrigated by pumping. Although the very bulk of Grand Coulee overshadowed McNary Dam, the latter project called for some notable feats of construction, among which were the relocation of no less than eighty-two miles of railroad and twenty-four miles of highways, in order to put them above the new water line.

By the time McNary was producing power and locking ships and speeding salmon up its ladders, there remained two uncompleted dams on the main Columbia. One was under way near The Dalles and was named for that city. The other was at Foster Creek Rapids fifty-one miles below Grand Coulee and was named Chief Joseph in honor of a noted Nez Percé leader. The Army Engineers were building both dams.

As originally planned the Chief Joseph was to be primarily for power, though it may possibly be used also in connection with the Grand Coulee irrigation project. Many another dam has been proposed, and all were somewhere between the dream and the actual beginning of construction. One of these still abstract dams already has a name, John Day, from the Oregon river that enters the Columbia. Another is at Priest Rapids just below the Rock Island dam of the Puget Sound Light & Power Company near Wenatchee.

A page of type could hardly list the many dams that have been proposed in recent years for the Columbia's tributaries. Some of these, like the project at Albeni Falls on the Clark Fork in north Idaho, were almost completed.

Another, on the Kootenai at Libby, Montana, was still on paper. Far up the south fork of the Flathead, also in Montana, the Bureau of Reclamation had completed the high Hungry Horse Dam which rises 564 feet above its foundation. On the lower Snake, between Pasco and Lewiston, three dams have been recommended by the Engineers. Farther up this stream is the site, or rather the sites, of the most controversial project of the Columbia River system. This is a dam or dams in Hell's Canyon, a subject that has long since entered the bewildering fog of politics.

Almost any map of the Columbia River basin issued since mid-century, save for route and road maps, has been spotted with a variety of lines and symbols marked either "Proposed Dam" or "Recommended Dam." These appear on the Columbia and most of its larger tributaries. They also appear on tributaries of tributaries. Doubtless some, maybe all, of them will be built in good time.

What is certain enough is that Bonneville and Grand Coulee dams changed much of the Pacific Northwest as nothing else since the coming of the covered wagon trains. Those two projects also had an effect in touching off what in future years will surely go into the history of the Columbia as the Dam-Building Era. In mid-twentieth century that era bids fair to continue until the great river and many of its tributaries have become a series of enormous lakes marked at their outlets by turbines and possibly by irrigation canals.

It is not to be supposed that the Canadian portion of the stream will remain unharnessed very long. The Kaiser Aluminum & Chemical Corporation of America has proposed to Canadian authorities that it be permitted to construct a low dam at the foot of the Arrow Lakes, near Castlegar, for storage of water for use by the company in the United States. Already authorized by Congress is a dam on the Kootenai at Libby, Montana, which, if built, would form another storage lake largely in Canada. Then, there is the much-discussed project of a true monster of a high dam on the Big Bend of the Columbia north of Revelstoke. This would involve capital supplied by private power interests in the United States.

Any or all of these projects are subject to approval by the International Joint Commission. The business is further complicated because British Columbia officials seem to not be of one mind. At times they have apparently been unalterably opposed to "giving U. S. interests water which might be needed for British Columbia's own provincial hydro development in the future." At other times they have seemed anxious for Americans to get on with their projects.

But the Dominion (federal) government is not at all convinced that American involvement is desirable. In an address not long ago at Spokane, General A. G. L. McNaughton, chairman of the Canadian section of the International Joint Commission, remarked on what to him was obviously loose talk about "surplus" water. "Please do not think," he told his American audience, "that there is going to be power in Canada which will be surplus and to spare. This is certainly not the case, for the more carefully made predictions show that only a comparatively short time remains until we may expect that all of our economically available hydro power will be in use."

Possibly these remarks may have been a warning. A little more than a year later it was announced quite casually at Ottawa, the Canadian capital, that the dominion government was studying the feasibility of diverting "surplus" water from the Columbia to the Thompson River. It was a startling idea to the American interests who wanted to use the Columbia's "surplus" water. But as an engineering job it was wholly within reason. By tapping the big river somewhere near Downie Creek, thirty miles north of Revelstoke, its waters could be led by tunnel and natural fall less than twenty miles to reach an arm of Shuswap Lake, which is the headwaters of the South Thompson which, in turn, is a major tributary of the mighty Fraser. The Fraser would lead the "surplus" Columbia waters to the sea at New Westminster, British Columbia.

Though it hasn't yet been mentioned, and may never be officially brought up, diversion of the main Columbia is not the only possibility open to Canada, should she feel in the mood. At Canal Flats, a mere ditch would serve to send the Kootenay racing over the mile of level plain into Columbia Lake. Then these mixed waters of Kootenay-Columbia could be diverted in turn, as already mentioned, by a low dam across the Columbia near Downie Creek on the Big Bend—and so on to the Thompson, the Fraser, and the ocean.

It is wildly unlikely to happen. If diversion of the Kootenay would make all but worthless a dam at Libby, Montana, it would also play hob with the great orchards and fruit ranches around Kootenay Lake in British Columbia. Diversion of both the Kootenay and the main Columbia, into the Fraser River system, would be a catastrophe to Washington and Oregon, including their many dams and powerhouses and irrigation networks.

It is perhaps reasonable to hold that he who owns a headwaters does not thereby own a whole river, but he assuredly does stand in a mighty nice position to discuss matters in relation to it. Since 1909 the United States and Canada have had a treaty on regulation of the Columbia River. It was made at a time when navigation was uppermost in the minds of the parties to the treaty. Navigation on much of the Columbia has since become a subject for antiquarians. And the Columbia's primitive beauty, the solitudes of its continuous woods, the sound of its dashings—these things are cherished by comparatively few people, commonly regarded as old-fashioned sentimentalists in a day when "Progress" is weighed in kilowatts, just as it is measured in miles of paved highway. So, the Columbia is really no longer considered as a river in the classic manner, but as a source of hydroelectric power. One can hope that both good will and farsighted statesmanship will attend discussions of the International Joint Commission which has quite suddenly become one of the most potent bodies in North America.

Chapter 17

The River as Powerhouse

![decorative thistle ornament] IT WOULD be tempting to ponder what in the middle of the twentieth century would seem most striking about it to the man who first navigated the Columbia. I think the changes might appear little greater to David Thompson who ran the river in 1811 than to men who did not see the stream until a century later. A bridge here and there, steamboats, villages, and the locks at the Cascades, these were the major things which up to 1911 had changed the life and looks of the river. The river itself still flowed as wild and free as it had when, by the grace of God and seven paddlers of the Northwest Company, Thompson had voyaged from its headwaters to its mouth. Almost another quarter century had to pass before what Webster defines as "a natural stream of water larger than a brook or creek" was made to change its function, even its shape, and above all the manner in which men looked at it, from a flowing highway to a powerhouse.

After Thompson cruised it, the river waited 120 years before a dam crossed its path. This was at Rock Island. Because the State or Government becomes steadily more powerful in mid-century, and we tend to demand of it

327

more than used to be our fashion, it should be remembered that this first dam on the Columbia was the work of private enterprise. Since then, however, Government has completed three great dams across the stream, two others are all but done. All these are on the main river. And a map issued by the United States departments of the Army and the Interior, entitled "A Comprehensive Plan for the Development of the Columbia Basin," shows what else is in store for the main stream and its tributaries. On it are little red oblongs, marked either "Authorized Dam" or "Potential Dam," blocking the Snake at many places, blocking the Clark Fork, blocking the Kootenai, the Okanogan, the Spokane, and lesser tributaries like the Cowlitz, the Lewis, and the John Day; and blocking tributaries of tributaries such as the McKenzie, the Clearwater, the Salmon, the Blackfoot, and even the Hoback, and the Gros Ventre rivers in Wyoming. It is incidentally a tributary of the Gros Ventre, Fish Creek, which is the most easterly of the Columbia's waters.

These authorized or potential projects on the American river numbered 106 as long ago as 1948. How many may have been added or subtracted since then is no subject to speak of with any certainty. Political and other pressures for and against are too wayward to gauge the outcome. As to the Canadian river, the proposals for dams, and for diversions of water were still to be considered potential, yet there could be no doubt but that before the decade of the fifties had run its course, the river above 49° would like the river below have started to take on the look of a series of lakes and the function of a powerhouse. Between the headwaters and the international boundary the Columbia has its greatest fall. In the first 520 miles it drops from an elevation of 2,670 feet to 1,292 feet, or well more than half of its total fall.

Except for stretches here and there, it is possible to go by highway or lesser roads from the mouth of the Columbia to its headwaters at Canal Flats. In many places, of course, the road and the river are not within sight of each other; and most of both shores of the Arrow lakes are without highways, or even common roads. Yet in this fact is nothing to give heart to those who happen to love the river as a river, as a "natural stream of water larger than a brook or creek." The highways creep a few miles more each year. Car-ferries are added, or bridges built. And at last, in 1954, the last stern-wheel passenger boat has to be retired.

As one of the comparatively few old-fashioned or reactionary people who love the Columbia as it was more than as it is, or as it is likely to be next year and the year after, I like to believe there will come a day when Americans and Canadians will tire of automotive wheels. This belief is unquestionably founded more on wish than on any sign that such a miracle could take place. But say that it did. It would have no effect on the modern function of the river as a powerhouse, or as an irrigating reservoir. It could, however, bring about a return to the river as a place of recreation.

When I first looked upon the 150-mile long reservoir behind Grand Coulee that is called Lake Roosevelt, and the long if lesser lakes behind the dams named Chief Joseph, Rock Island, McNary, The Dalles, and Bonneville, my first thought was that here were proper waters to cradle a whole fleet of stern-wheelers. These vessels would not try to compete with land carriers of freight or passengers. They would be for recreation only. They would be built to operate with steam, and their lines and appointments would follow the style of the nineties. Generations unborn when the steamboat era ended on the river could get something of an idea of what travel was like in the times of the *Harvest Queen*, the *Bailey Gatzert*, and the *Minto*. It is not difficult to work up enthusiasm for the idea, but the whole thing collapses when one reads the casual announcement of some automobile maker or other that next year's model will have three hundred horsepower and do one hundred and twenty, or thirty, or thirty-five miles an hour. No, the time for recreation by return to the river by stern-wheeler is not ripe. Barring an extraordinary change in human nature, it never will be ripe.

Brief as the time of man is, compared to the river's measurement of time, man will go on to modify the Columbia in every way he can, and thus change the many homely and frail little civilizations that flourished at one time or another along its banks and on its waters. Everything possible will be disciplined, "improved" and "modernized." I never feel quite so old as I do when I contemplate how little of the Columbia I knew thirty-five, even twenty-five, years ago is left. Nor quite so lonely as when I brood on a past which so few others even know about. What I mean here is the past which began when Captain Gray entered the stream at its mouth; or better, the past which began when David Thompson had completed his navigation of its entire course. The Columbia's past began at different times at each end, and at still another time in its middle reaches, with Lewis and Clark noting its beginnings there.

There is of course no way to retrieve the past, or to hold fast to the present, save in the shadowy world of word and picture which at best calls for an exercise of the imagination if it is to make history live. The process of transforming the Columbia has grown so swift that there are already hundreds of miles of it that are wholly unrecognizable. Rapids, falls, bends, eddies, deltas have disappeared. So have the sites of Indian encampments and trading posts. Hamlets and towns of respectable size have gone under. Only too many of these geographic features and man-made landmarks disappeared before anyone had troubled to preserve them in word or picture; while the knowledge of others, such as it is, is comprised of a few lines of doubtful or even garbled prose in some homemade local history pamphlet, or a dim photograph spotted with acid, creased, bent and torn, and identified as "Taken Feb. 4th." *Which* February 4th? It appears to have been a credo of both amateur and professional photographers to note carefully the month and day a picture was taken, but never to mention the year.

Or, consider the return of a native of Marcus, come to show his children where he was born almost within sound of the roar of Kettle Falls. For a decade Marcus has been sixty feet under water. The new Marcus will hardly do. It is two miles away and it is not the historic old place where stern-wheelers were built and launched, and near which stood Fort Colville dating from Hudson's Bay Company times. Marcus is one of a numerous company of river towns that are no more, even to their sites.

It is certain that there are a great many people who had rather look at a big dam, with its powerhouse, transformers and networks of wires marching away in all directions, than to see a weather-beaten if historic hamlet where Captain Leonard White built his *Forty-Nine* and where, if legend be correct, Captain George B. McClellan, attending a party at the Bay Company's post, put one arm around the neck of Factor Angus McDonald, to whisper, "Mac, my proud father, too, was at Culloden," just before he slipped from the sofa to the floor.

The thousands who each year visit Grand Coulee and Bonneville, Rock Island and McNary, Chief Joseph and The Dalles, are indicative of the abiding interest in the Columbia's dams. Thousands more go to see the dams on the tributaries all the way from the Hungry Horse on the South Fork of the Flathead in northern Montana to the Detroit on the North Santiam in Oregon. The Columbia River system in mid-century was perhaps the scene of the greatest activity in power dams and irrigation reservoirs in the United States, and in which Canada was about to join.

There is still a primitive wonder along the main Columbia, mostly from the foot of the Arrow Lakes to the headwaters. And there are also magnificent stretches of the river elsewhere, places which outlanders declare, often grudgingly, to be unequaled in grandeur. For many years now, the chambers of commerce in the Columbia basin, along with assorted booster clubs, have spent millions of dollars publicizing the river as a "scenic playground." By the very nature of their goals, the same groups have also been the loudest proponents of dam building. If they have sensed any conflict between their aims, they seem not to have admitted it in public. Perhaps there isn't any conflict. Perhaps the increasing number of dams is as much a magnet for what are called "tourist dollars" as the now decaying Columbia Gorge highway used to be.

To attempt to halt "Progress" is to deny the passage of time. One may wish, however, that before it is too late Progress along the Columbia will include a few markers to the end that those who come to look at the river next year, or the year after that, will learn more about its past than is common to a people much of whose leisure is spent rolling along highways. New England long ago discovered that its glorious past was a fit subject to interest tourists. Today hardly a village in the six Yankee states does not display a marker or sign calling attention to some historic spot in the neighborhood. The same is true of New York and Pennsylvania. The Potomac River is justly famous for its markers. So is many another stream, no few of which have had far less an influence on history than the Columbia.

There are already a handful of markers on the Columbia. There should be perhaps a hundred more, for the river is long, and a couple of hundred signs calling attention to historic events would not burden twelve hundred miles with too much roadside literature. In many stretches, too, such signs would be something of a relief among the shrieking panels celebrating cigarettes, soft drinks, shaving cream, hotdogs-one-foot-long, motels, hotels, dine & dance, snake pits, dens of horror, trout ponds, fox farms, Jesus Saves, automobiles, and gasoline; signs warning of Crossroads, Logging Trucks, Deer on Road, Impaired Clearance, Steep Hill, Keep Single File, Soft Shoulder, Narrow Bridge; and cards asking for votes for sheriffs, mayors, councilmen, senators and congressmen, all of whom were long since elected to office, or were defeated.

What events or persons should be memorialized by markers along the Columbia ought to be suggested by people in the several neighborhoods. This book will make no suggestions. Instead, its next and last chapter will look at the river as it appeared to one who last followed it, by highway, ferry and stern-wheeler, from its headwaters to its mouth, in the mid 1950s, when it coursed through the turbines and over the spillways of four dams, and when two more mainriver dams were all but completed.

Chapter **18**

The River at Mid-Century

WE CAME to Canal Flats over Highway 95 from the south, crossing the Kootenay to the brief gravelly plain which separates that already powerful stream from the headwaters of the Columbia. It was a bright morning in September. The arch of the sky was blue from the summit of the Rockies to the ridge of the Selkirks. The unpaved and rather nondescript hamlet ranged for two short blocks along the base of a mountain that rose almost straight up from the east shore of Columbia Lake. The lake is not visible from here. The rest of Canal Flats, its suburbs, were a sawmill and rambling bunkhouse, and small homes scattered at random among the scrub pines.

There was nothing imposing about Canal Flats. It obviously could have done with a paint store. The oblongs and false fronts along its one street were beaten and weathered. They had the composite character of the Northern frontier in pioneer times. Yet I felt an immediate attachment for it, not as a municipality but for what these few acres of plain had meant in the life and times of the Columbia River. There was a satisfying feeling of remoteness about it, too, a sense of the ultimate. One could go no further.

Over this flat David Thompson had carried his canoe a short distance to find in wonder another stream that flowed in the opposite direction from which he had come. Over this flat another man had dug a ditch and sent one river racing across it to join the headwaters of another. Through the ditch still another man drove a vessel from its native waters to ply ever after in the headwaters of the Columbia. As though these things were not enough to distinguish this place, there had been another noteworthy event here in prehistoric times when a season of flood had permitted Pacific salmon to swim across the flat and enter the Kootenay, and to live ever after landlocked in that river. Surely, Canal Flats stands alone. It is unique.

The stark lines of the little village seemed softened in the haze of autumn. I noted the post office, a couple of general emporiums, a hardware store that seemed to offer mostly toys and novelties, a restaurant with a particularly loud jukebox, a hotel, and a building that housed fire-fighting equipment of the British Columbia Forest Service. A little west of the village, set in a marsh beside the abandoned canal, was an isolated and demounted boxcar, painted CPR red. This was the depot and its newly painted sign said Canal Flat.

At the post office Postmistress Alice Renwick said there had never been much agreement about the name. The railroad station had it Canal Flat. So did the Forest Service. But Mrs. Renwick stamped a letter to show me that to the Dominion of Canada, at least, the place was Canal Flats. Various official maps of the province show the name in both its singular and plural spelling. David Thompson had called it McGillivray's Portage, for a friend.

Later, and for a few years, it became Grohman's Flats, for him who dug the canal.

The Canal Flats post office was interesting on several counts. Part private home, part public office, the postmistress was also a mistress of fine needlework, several pieces of which I was privileged to see. The bulletin board presented photographs of the recent coronation of an English queen. It carried notices of a timber tax sale, a Canadian

Columbia Lake near Canal Flats, British Columbia.

Army recruiting poster, and a sign that said to Keep Canada Green. On a letterhead was a neatly typed notice: "Dr. George A. Duthie (M.D.) will be in Canal Flats on July 2, at 9 A.M., in the Bunkhouse on the Second Floor." I learned that Dr. Duthie was a partner of Dr. K. J. Williams, a veteran physician long esteemed around the Flats, whose office was at Invermere, a little way down the Columbia.

At the Columbia Hotel, operated by Ranny and Jeanette Macdonald, I learned that next to lumber the chief industry at Canal Flats was supplying guides for big-game hunters who come here from all parts of Canada and the United States. Business had been so good, said Mr. Macdonald, that six months' notice was needed to make certain of a guide in season. The guide's minimum charge was $30 per day per hunter. Guides did not want parties of less than three hunters, or for less than fifteen days. The guides supplied everything needed except guns, ammunition, and sleeping bags. All guides in the province are classified by the government. Each is allotted a specific area. What a Canal Flats guide means when he speaks of big game are mountain goat, bighorn sheep, and bears, both black and grizzly. There are also two or three species of deer, and some large cougars.

So much for the headwaters village of the Columbia. Leaving town to head north on the highway, we passed the forlorn railroad depot in the swamp and stopped to see the famous canal and one of the old locks built of logs and squared timbers, now moss-grown and rotting, overgrown with poplar, and oozing water which, in spite of an old dam a little way to the east, I supposed was trickling through from the Kootenay, which is normally from six to eight feet higher here than Columbia Lake.

It was here in the boxcar depot that M. J. Lorraine lived while building the seventeen-foot bark that was to take him to Astoria, and result in a book with a title fitting the subject: *The Columbia Unveiled, Being the story of a trip, alone, in a rowboat from the source to the mouth of the Columbia River, Together with a full description of the country traversed, and the rapids battled, By an old*

voyager and whitewater man, M. J. Lorraine, C. E., M. Am.
SOC. C.E. The book was published in 1924. The voyage
began on the morning of June 13, 1921.

A CPR section hand named Brede helped Lorraine
carry his outfit from the boxcar depot to his little shipyard
by the canal and stow it in the boat. Lorraine was delighted
to find that his five hundred pounds of gear, plus his own
weight, caused the vessel to draw no more than five inches
of water. Being a thorough man, he did not start his trip
on Columbia Lake, but here in the old canal at the Flats.
He found that the water did not increase much in width
because it was still pretty well confined by the old canal ex-
cavation, but the depth increased considerably due, he
thought, to a constant accession from springs. "In about
three-quarters of a mile," he noted, "Columbia Lake was
reached and a broad vista, heretofore partly hidden by the
timber, unfolded itself to my view. Ahead, on both sides of
the valley as far as the eye could reach, was a grand succession of mountain peaks, their summits capped with snow
and ice." Ahead of the old whitewater man, too, were five
months, 1,264 miles, and 435 pages that closed with the
observation that "my arrival at Astoria was THE END
OF A LONG ROW."

My own and less hardy row continued along the highway north of Canal Flats to a fine high bench overlooking
Columbia Lake, a good place to stop and see the headwaters. The sight is all one could wish, this clear cold beginning of a great stream which has the misfortune to rise
at so high an elevation as to brand it indelibly for the
harnesses of power and irrigation. Its east shore is the sheer
side of a mountain. Its west shore, where I stood, was the

start of foothills that quickly grew into the tumultuous confusion of the Selkirks. A sign, pointing to the lake, said this was the "Source of the Columbia River which Empties into the Pacific Ocean at Astoria, Oregon." The inevitable cutup had placed a "C" before Astoria, which fitted him for a career in television, but some person of good will had tried and almost obliterated the excruciating letter.

We dined that evening and stayed overnight beside the lake at the huge log home of the Carmichaels, Bill and Elsa, as civilized a place and company as one could wish for. The Carmichaels stayed here the year round and in season provided meals and accommodations for visitors. I went down to the shore to sit a while on a log and contemplate this headwaters of the river. One may sit here for long periods and hear only a loon. There was no echo of the din of the dam builders who were so busy at their work a thousand miles downstream, no faint sound of the fleets of trucks you knew were roaring beside the river from Castlegar to Trail; from Trail to the boundary; from the boundary to Grand Coulee—and so on the whole way to Astoria. This quiet by the lake seemed like safety. Yet you had best not feel anything like assurance. You might come to believe you were alone, unless you had let your eye wander to read a sign beside the road from Canal Flats. It said in good grammatical English to Please Drive Carefully; and another on a little bridge warned that the structure would not support trucks of more than so many tons burthen. These were portents. And no longer than a week before, the Carmichaels had played host to a party of American engineers who said they were heading for the Big Bend

of the Columbia where they and Canadian engineers were
assessing the possibilities of a dam near Mica Creek, which
is little more than two hundred miles from the headwaters.
. . . No, there is no hiding place. One begins to understand how the Indians felt.

Next morning we soon passed the first bridge over the
Columbia below the lake. This was near a roadside place
called Totem Pole. The stream here was swift, shallow and
clear, perhaps twenty feet wide. Near the highway is Fairmont Hot Springs and a sort of resort with cottages, bath-
houses, and an open-air pool. The river presently spreads
into marshes that continue a few miles to Lake Windermere, which I had been told was stocked with Kamloops
trout, and the hamlets of Wilmer, Athalmer, Windermere
and Invermere. Near Invermere Point is the first Historic
Monument on the river, marking the site of Kootenae
House, to use the spelling of David Thompson who founded
this post of the Northwest Company. It was the first trading post west of the Rockies. It was also the post which, as
related, did not deal in the stuff "of many evils." No
trapper red or white could get rum at Kootenae House.

Just below Lake Windermere a road turns east to what
used to be Sinclair Hot Springs, but has now taken the
name of Radium, and continues through Kootenay National Park to the CPR resorts at Banff and Lake Louise.
We did not take the turn, but kept on north along the river
and at a less-than-hamlet named Brisco discovered that the
stream was now enough the Columbia to bear its name. On
a fine big barn one could read that this was the Columbia
River View Farm. The next sign that came into view was

on the little red railroad station labeled Spillamacheen, where the river of the same incomparable name comes tumbling down foaming from high in the Selkirks.

These Selkirks are suitable monuments to the great names of the Canadian Pacific Railway Company, both in its financial and operational departments, and of other British notables. The highest peak is 11,113 feet above the sea and is named for George Mercer Dawson, director of the Geological Survey of Canada. The best known is Sir Donald, a 10,808 monolith that honors Donald A. Smith, the Scottish boy who became a knight, then a lord, meanwhile heading the Hudson's Bay Company, the Bank of Montreal, and sitting as Senior Director of the CPR. There is also Mount Sir Sanford (Selwyn), named for a CPR director, and Mount Rogers for the bewhiskered engineer who laid the route through the mountains. The Van Horne glacier takes the name of the CPR's great operating boss. One of the lower peaks in this high range is named for Jove, another for Napoleon, thus establishing an interesting ratio of values.

For twenty miles or so below Spillimacheen village the Columbia is a driving river, carrying the logs that have been cut thirty miles back in the Selkirks to the sawmill at Parson. Voyager Lorraine had quite a time of it along here, being obliged to drag his boat over a series of booms strung across the stream from bank to bank. He did not complain of the obstructions, even when, because the bottom land was flooded, he had to cut his way through a forest of willows. He was somewhat bemused, however, for he passed more booms and a big sawmill and continued on, not realizing this was the town of Golden. He did see and feel the added surge here where a swift stream entered the Columbia. It was the Kicking Horse, coming from the summit of the Rockies. Before he knew it, Lorraine was well along into the Big Bend. Seeing a lone depot on the right bank, he hauled ashore to learn that it was Moberley, a section-gang station. Golden was six miles to the rear. Rather than paddle against the swift current, Lorraine struck out on foot up the railroad track for the metropolis of the region. He needed to buy a rope for lining down the rapids ahead.

Lorraine counted five hotels in Golden, three large general stores, two banks, and a newspaper. Its population of fifteen hundred made it the largest town on the Columbia east of the Selkirks. I was disappointed that he did not mention, in his *The Columbia Unveiled,* Thomas King, the Marshall Field of the Upper Columbia. Perhaps in his haste to get a lining rope, which he did, and a gold pan which he wanted but failed to find in the town, Voyager Lorraine did not meet Mr. King.

Thomas King's General Store has been a fixture at Golden since 1886. Tons of its merchandise in the early days came by way of Canal Flats from Montana in the very *North Star* which Captain Armstrong had driven through the canal to ply ever after between the Flats and Golden. King went to work in the store in the nineties, bought an interest in 1905, and later became the sole owner. When I met him, Mr. King at seventy-four was a wiry man of medium height, snow white hair, blue eyes, and ruddy complexion, who had served for many years as member of the provincial parliament. He recalled that when he came to Golden a good deal of placer mining was going on in the neighborhood. At night, he said, the Selkirks winked in the dark from the many campfires of the prospectors. In his office was still a fine set of scales for weighing gold, but they had not been used in many years. Logging, along with the CPR payroll, is the main support of Golden today. The town is on the main line, and it was a delight, in a day of highways and cars, to see no less than four long passenger trains stop at the Golden station, and possibly four, maybe more, freights pass through the town.

Mr. King remembered the young Presbyterian missionary, Charles William Gordon, who had the pastorate here in the nineties and also preached occasionally at Donald Station in the wilderness of the Big Bend. Many years later Gorden was influential in promoting union of Presbyterians, Methodists and Congregationalists into the United Church of Canada. But he is more widely remembered as "Ralph Connor," author of the Glengarry novels, and *The Sky Pilot*, on which he was working when he was stationed at Golden. I was delighted to know that the author of *Glengarry Schooldays*, which enchanted youngsters of my generation in New England, had carried a light in the Big Bend country.

When I came to see it, there was nothing else left anywhere else on the Columbia that even remotely resembled Thomas King's General Store at Golden. It was a big two-story affair that faced the railroad from the main street. The ground floor was piled high with almost everything one could think of. If there was anything missing, then it was to be found in the cellar, an immense cave of catacomb dimensions; or on the top floor, which was stacked with clothing, boots, yardage, and Hudson's Bay blankets; or in the warehouse attached to the store, in which were vast piles of bagged flour, sugar, and salt; kerosene lamps and lanterns to light the Columbia all the way to Canal Flats, and enough cant dogs to arm all loggers on the Spillimacheen. There were also four other large warehouses.

The office, with fine gingerbread work and a half-door, presented a jumble of ledgers, daybooks, files, guns, a few stuffed birds and animals, a really huge safe, and the gold scales. The stairs to the upper floor took off from the middle of the store and were ladder steep. There appeared to be enough clerks busy to staff a dozen supermarkets. The entire place had exactly the right look and smell to proclaim that Thomas King, the patriarch of merchants on the far upper Columbia, was above all an individualist who was not to be hounded by fad or fashion into transforming a wonderful emporium of classic character into just another copy of a glib modern merchandise mart.

The Big Bend begins at Golden. For two hundred miles the highway passed through a primitive forest such as nowhere else on the river. At Donald Station, where Gordon-Connor had preached, the river and highway parted for a few miles, while the railroad followed the river to Beavermouth, then it too left the stream to begin its climb over the Selkirks. When nearing Kinbasket Lake, the highway suddenly went to pieces at a huge wide sweep of gravel, scattered boulders, downed trees, and the assorted debris of floods of the Sullivan River which here enters the Columbia. The road was barely perceptible, weaving its way gingerly around obstructions and crossing the main channel of water by a low timber bridge. Looking east, the Sullivan appeared to pour directly out of a wall of the Rockies.

345

I thought it as astonishing as anything seen around the Big Bend, which is something of a region of primitive astonishments and drama.

We came to the lake named for Chief Kinbasket of a local tribe, and stood to marvel that so lovely a place seemed virtually unknown to outlanders. Both the Selkirks and the Rockies have closed in and the lake is hemmed and shadowed by some of the most formidable peaks of

Sullivan River on the Big Bend Highway, B. C.

either range. One who has seen Kinbasket needs not trouble himself if he has not seen the famous Lake Louise or, for that matter, seen the Alpine Lakes of Switzerland. It is a little beyond words, and it is just as well to leave it to the painters and the photographers, though I fancy it is a little beyond them, too.

But the reason Kinbasket is unknown really is clear. It has been available by highway only since 1940. The Big Bend Highway is often cursed by the people who use it most and who have called it "a highway of sorts." The implication may not be unjust, but that there is any sort of highway around the Big Bend is a triumph and a credit to the engineers who laid it. Yet the automobiles of thousands of tourists have been put aboard railroad cars at Golden to be taken over the Selkirks to Revelstoke at the other end of the Big Bend, and thousands more have been loaded at Revelstoke and unloaded at Golden. Gasoline has thinned the spirit of the Cariboo Trail as it has the urge which caused men and women to walk from the Mississippi to Oregon and California.

Another thing has left the Big Bend to comparatively few: there is nothing "fashionable" here; the Big Bend is not talked about. Couple that fact with an imperfect highway and you have the good fortune to find at least two hundred miles of country where no billboard offends the eye and where, indeed, there are almost no inhabitants, save for a stray trapper or prospector.

Out of Kinbasket Lake the Columbia roars into twenty-four miles of almost continuous rapids. Whitewater man Lorraine, who rode them safely through, charted them in fifteen sections, and found what he termed their character to range from Minor through Medium to Great, this latter an adjective he used sparsely throughout his voyage. Eight of the Kinbasket falls rated the respect of Great. The traveler by highway will not likely doubt Lorraine's adjective. The rapids are to be seen here and there through the woods from the highway, and one is almost constantly aware of the sound of their fury. Far below in the canyon they boiled white from fall and speed, and the echoing cliffs sent up a roaring such as is not to be heard on the Canadian river again until perhaps at the brief if terrible plunge at the Dalles des Morts.

At Boat Encampment is the apex of the Columbia's northward surge. Here it bends suddenly around the end of the Selkirks and starts south. Here, too, a bridge crosses it and the highway moves to the east side. This is the place

Boat Encampment, British Columbia.

to which David Thompson first came by way of Athabasca Pass through the Rockies and the Wood River which enters the Columbia here at Boat Encampment. On a rockbound knoll by the river is a monument to Thompson which was dedicated on September 6, 1953, when it was unveiled by none other than Thomas King of Golden, Member of the Legislative Assembly. The text of the monument's plaque relates that Boat Encampment was a point of transshipment in fur-trading days for almost half a century, that it was by-passed by the railways and "made accessible to visitors by completion of the Big Bend Highway in June 1940."

Ten yards from this chaste memorial stood, and probably stands, the incomparably incongruous object of the Big Bend. It is a monstrous and hideous wooden head with a wooden hat on it. The features looked to one dazed visitor like those of a once notorious Italian prize fighter named Primo Canera. On this thing is a sign. "Don't Be Wooden-Headed," it reads, and "Drive Carefully." It is a striking example of how an urge to commit Art and do good can result in a singularly loathesome object whose effect tends to unsettle the most careful driver. In twelve hundred miles I saw nothing so revolting as this hand-carved monster at the top of the Big Bend, and I have often wondered not who made it but who placed it fair in the middle of this stately wilderness. Possibly it will not matter much, for long. Twenty miles below Boat Encampment a small hurrying stream named Mica Creek enters the Columbia.

When I saw it, Mica Creek had just become the most talked-about of any creek that flows into the river. This was the place where somebody or other proposed to dam the Columbia. And there, already in the middle of the Columbia, was a huge scow of machinery, guyed stoutly by cables to both banks. Men in a steel longboat were moving near the scow. On the east shore was a typical camp of an engineering party, perhaps a score of tents, with smoke from a cookstove, and washings hanging from lines. What a day or two before I had dismissed as a fantastic rumor now took on the uneasy look of possibility. *They had even come here.* I did not stop to ask the engineers what they were up to, but left Mica Creek with the feeling that a good piece of the Big Bend was about to be obliterated. Meanwhile, I reflected that Boat Encampment was 1925 feet above sea level. Between there and Canal Flats the Columbia dropped 650 feet. Between Boat Encampment and Revelstoke it dropped another 506 feet. Even a man ignorant of dams and engineers needed to know no more. I could see in the near future the waters backing up around the Big Bend to cover the memorial at Boat Encampment, and wondered how high the Mica Creek dam would have to be to send them on to flood Kinbasket. It was certain, of course, that the very material it was made of would save the hand-carved monstrosity. I fancied him floating around in the reservoir behind Mica Creek Dam, bobbing up and down, admonishing the men in the powerhouse to drive carefully, frightening the jays and the owls and growing, in good time, into a legend that will make him a lost totem pole of the ancient chief Kinbasket, a handsome piece for the souvenir postcard trade.

Driving on toward Revelstoke, we saw many signs of small mining ventures, and at one place a sign pointed up a creek and said Samson Mines, Limited. This creek may have been the Goldstream River which, in the early days of this century, seemed destined to be another Klondyke. A big outfit moved in, laid a railroad, blasted mountains, and drilled out a lot of ore, then suddenly dropped everything and went away. I saw only one person in the eighty miles between Mica Creek and the outskirts of Revelstoke. He was bearded, tanned to leather, and he sat motionless by a half-collapsed cabin near the road. I took him to be a survivor of one or another of the many rushes that have taken men to the Big Bend since the 1860s.

At Revelstoke, Earle Dickey told me of the romance that has been associated with the Big Bend. His late father had come here with a CPR construction crew when Revelstoke was Second Crossing, and he himself was born here

Revelstoke, B. C., looking down from Mt. Revelstoke and across to Mt. Begbie.

in the nineties. We sat on the bank of the river while he told me that in his youth the Big Bend's very name was magic and mystery. He saw smooth-shaven men leave Revelstoke for the diggings, to return six months or so later with beards a foot long. They were wonderful. Some of them could show a little gold dust, others some few pieces of rock that glittered. In either case, he said, boys of his generation were sure that the whole Big Bend country was

351

fairly plated with gold. That was a certainty. Legends emanated from almost every creek that flowed from the high Selkirks into the Columbia. Young boys heard them and believed every word. Just because nobody ever brought out more than enough gold for a passable spree made no difference. The Big Bend was to Revelstoke boys the land of Ophir and Bonanza—lost mines, sourdough, and colors in tin pans.

"That was all true up to 1940," Dickey said. Which was when the highway around the Bend was completed. Dickey had driven up to see this idyll of his boyhood. "It turned out to be one of the greatest letdowns I ever experienced," said he. "The region suddenly changed into just another place for automobiles to go. It was no longer the Big Bend of my youthful imagination. What I had to do was to put the Big Bend into a separate compartment of my mind—a sort of deep-freeze, to keep the legend as it was when I was young, and safe from the indecencies of tourists and Sunday picnics." He did not think that a dam at Mica Creek would change his feelings about the Big Bend. "It was already ruined for me when the highway got there," he said.

No town on the river has a more dramatic setting than Revelstoke. Its horizon are mountains in full circle, peaks of all shapes and heights, many of them snow-capped the year round. One fancies the prospect pleased Lord Revelstoke himself, who was head of the house of Baring & Glyn, which took a bond issue of the Canadian Pacific Railway Company in 1885 when, says an official statement of that company, "the financial outlook was blackest." Milord's name is also honored by Mount Revelstoke National Park, an area of one hundred square miles through which the Royal Highway leads to the summit of the Selkirks. The dominating eminence, however, is Mount Begbie, which has a park of its own. Revelstoke's lively Board of Trade stages an annual Golden Spike Days festival which has reference to the official completion of the CPR, an event that took place on November 7, 1885, at Craigellachie, twenty-eight miles west of the town. Revelstoke also claims to be "the pioneer ski centre of the West."

Our drive to Arrowhead was broken by a ride on the government free ferry across the Columbia, a cable affair which is operated by the current. The one settlement along here was scattered around a sawmill and named Sidmouth, a remarkably untidy place even for a wilderness lumber operation. But a few miles more brought us to hushed, nostalgic Arrowhead, head of the Lakes, and the snug handsome little CPR depot, I. R. Allardyce, agent, with its well-kept garden beside the tracks.

Twenty-five hours on SS *Minto*, as related, brought us to Castlegar-Robson at the foot of the lakes, a voyage of wonder that is no longer possible.* The Dukhobor settlement of Brilliant was quiet enough, yet tense, for nearly a hundred of the sect at nearby Krestova were in police custody for various reasons, including the usual mass-nudity and arson charges.

At Trail, Jack Lunney, editor of the *Daily Times*, said that this newspaper was started in 1895 as the *Trail Creek*

* In January, 1955, at Castlegar, the Interior Tug and Transport Company, Limited, was putting the finishing touches to a new prefabricated motor vessel, described as of 95-passenger capacity, which was to run the Lakes.

News, dropping the "Creek" in 1901 when the city was incorporated; and becoming a daily in 1928 when its present name was adopted. Mines and mining, of course, have always been the subject of most importance in the news columns here, and none could have had more appeal than that having to do with the Rossland mines. During the depression of the 1930s, when Trail's huge smelter was running short-time, several employees of Consolidated asked for and were granted permission to prospect the several old diggings in Rossland that had long since been abandoned. At least four or five of the boys did better than well by striking rich veins of gold that had been overlooked. They came out of the venture, not millionaires, but with several hundreds of thousands of dollars a piece. It was the perfect rags-to-riches story, free of the qualifications of long years of labor and nearer to the sudden riches of the Count of Monte Cristo; and also much better because it was *gold* rather than the same value in mixed and murky ores like zinc, copper and lead. It gives one to wonder if a sequel might not be written about the possibly hundreds of prospectors, inspired by these few fortunates in the "played out" diggings of Rossland, who may still be sinking futile drifts in the craggy terrain between Trail and the United States boundary.

On his voyage down the Columbia in a rowboat in 1921, old whitewater man Lorraine had run all rapids or lined them until he came, just below the boundary, to Kettle Falls. One look at these convinced him it was time to portage. There were two tumultuous channels, and "it meant sure disaster to run or line either of them." Either presented a sheer drop of twenty-five feet. This was the famous fishing place of the Indians which disappeared when Grand Coulee Dam was built. Once past the falls, Lorraine in his boat would go his way some 150 miles down the river and past villages whose sites are now under water. Through his eyes one may have an idea of what the Columbia was like just before the dam-building era began. His was not the last boat through, but it will do. Lorraine was an observant reporter of the things which most interested him.

The portage around Kettle Falls took him past an old stable which, so a Farmer Brigham told him, was built in 1811 by the Northwest Company; and nearby were the ruins of the fort. A little way on was a deserted structure which had been a Jesuit mission, built in 1837, of the "Most smoothly-hewn logs I ever saw"; and although not a single nail held the building together, the walls were still upright, sound and substantial. The portage was for a little less than two miles, where the boat was put back in the Columbia.

The next fast water was Grand Rapids which were "to be feared by the navigator as much as any other" on the river; but Lorraine, determined "to dodge no difficulties," ran and lined the mile or so of rough going, and camped that night near the Colville Indian reservation. Next day he paused at Inchelium which he found to be "three good-sized general stores" and little else. That day he passed Driftwood Island with its crown of derelict logs stacked like jackstraws. Below the village of Hunters, he ran into the worst storm he was to meet on the river and was forced to camp on a gravel bar partially covered with willows.

355

By morning the storm had blown away, and so had his boat. It was not to be seen. In it were his camera, typewriter, guns, clothing, provisions, cash—in fact everything except his tent and the oars. Taking a rough trail on the east shore he trudged along for six miles, to find his boat caught and held on a riffle. Making her fast, he took to land again and got a farmer, Jim Lincoln, to go in a wagon with him to where he had left his gear on the gravel bar. This turned out to be something of a task, for the riverbank was steep and the going and returning to the boat consumed three hours.

But time was not the essence, as Lorraine remarked, and a day later he was running a series of swift water stretches near Gerome, and through the "high and tempestuous breakers" of Spokane Rapids, to camp in a deserted cabin below White Rock. It was here he heard the noise of a motorboat coming upriver. He hailed her to shore and found the crew to be Earl Houston and a Mr. Fitzgerald, returning from towing a raft of logs to the sawmill of Ike Emerson, at Barry.

In spite of its name and its "unsavory" reputation, Lorraine decided to run Hell Gate. "I confess to a slight feeling of uneasiness," he recalled, "and removed my boots and outer clothing, in case of an upset." No sooner was his boat shooting down the narrow canyon, however, than "all unease fled, and mind and body was alert and active." After the ordeal, he reflected on how well the Reverend Samuel Parker had described the mental stage of a boatman when running whitewater. Parker, a Congregational missionary, had run the falls at the Cascades back in 1836, and remembered the experience with obvious pleasure.

The sensation of fear which he felt when his bateau came to the falls, he wrote, immediately subsided "before the power and magnificence of the rolling surges and the roaring breakers." He advised those whose energies of body or mind needed arousing to try navigation of the Columbia at high water. Their powers, he promised, would thereupon "be invigorated for almost any future enterprise."

Lorraine himself seems to have been invigorated by the run of the Hell Gate. He went on to take Box Canyon and Monaghan Rapids in stride, and did the same with Mahkin Rapids which were "nothing more than a little rough going." He passed the mouth of Foster Creek, where later the Chief Joseph Dam was to rise, and stopped briefly to visit the town of Bridgeport. Here he saw an odd vessel, the square-nosed stern-wheeler named for the town, and whose master was Captain Fred McDermott. Lorraine remarks that SS *Bridgeport* was the only steamboat on the Columbia between the Arrow Lakes and The Dalles City. He made camp on a beach at Brewster which he mentioned was "a town just outside the Indian Reservation." What he calls the right side of the river, meaning what in its north-south reaches would be the west side, was spoken of by residents of the region always as the "Indian Side" of the Columbia, in reference to the several reservations.

It seems a little odd that Lorraine devotes but two lines to Grand Coulee and they are not to marvel, but tell only that it was formed by ice and erosion in prehistoric times. Apparently he did not stop to look at the much-publicized natural phenomenon. Even then, in 1921, however, engineers were on the ground; and in view of later developments it is significant that he found a party of them "engaged in sinking holes to test the underlying formation at a site six miles above Barry," and added that "a diversion into the Grand Coulee, to the south, is contemplated."

Lorraine, a civil engineer himself, talked with these engineers and from them learned that other dam sites under consideration were at Kettle Falls and the Little Dalles. But what was to be "the largest dam in the United States," he learned, was planned for the foot of Priest Rapids. (In 1955 a Priest Rapids Dam was still in the future.) This dam, he wrote, would so change the character of the river as "to render impossible a duplication of my feat of navigation." This gave him no little satisfaction to contemplate: "I will probably be the last, as well as the first, to make a complete, continuous descent of the Columbia River."

More than thirty years after Pathfinder Lorraine made his continuous descent, I drove a hundred miles down the east shore of the lake that backed up behind Grand Coulee dam to drown the rapids, remove landmarks, and obliterate the villages mentioned in his logbook. We followed the highway, leaving the main Columbia near Gerome. We crossed the Spokane on a bridge, and saw that this stream, too, was no longer a river here but an arm of the lake behind Coulee Dam. At Davenport we turned west, to head for the big dam; and I wanted to stop along the way at Creston which, once upon a time, and if only for a brief moment, was on the front pages of newspapers all over the United States. *Harry Tracy had been run to earth here in Creston.*

Up until August 4, 1902, Creston was merely one of

the hundreds of hopeful settlements that "got the railroad" but never grew. Perhaps once in the age of man, and never oftener, it seemed the vagrant fancy of Fate to select one or another of such forgotten places to become, for an instant, the outstanding place in a whole region, to be talked about and sometimes to be looked at in pictures, in distant parts like Chicago, New York, even London and Paris. There was no rule for these things. Man could not plan them to happen. They happened in spite of man, and almost never were they of any advantage to the community. For a moment, however, they lifted some peaceful or merely dreary crossroads into the white heat of headlines.

Creston was and is wheat country and, on that far away August 3, a wheat rancher named Oscar Lillengreen drove into the little village to get shaved. He found George Dodd's barbershop fairly seething with talk, not about wheat or prize fights, but about Harry Tracy. Word had just come to Creston that Tracy was hiding out on a farm near the village. Tracy was the most notorious bandit the Northwest has had. In the sixty days previous to this August 3, he had escaped from the Oregon penitentiary, had evaded more than one thousand militia troops of Oregon and Washington, and numerous posses of deputies and their bloodhounds, and had made his way, on foot, by stolen buggies and commandeered boats, from Salem, Oregon, north across the Columbia and on to Olympia and Seattle, and so—or such was the talk in Dodd's barbershop —and so to the wheat fields near Creston. The Oregon bad- man had covered a good five hundred miles. On the way he had found it necessary to shoot and kill seven men, four in Oregon, the others in Washington.

Creston's town marshal, Charlie Straub, said there was sure enough a reward of $4,000 for Tracy dead or alive. By the time Lillengreen was shaved, he and Straub, with fellow townsmen Maurice Smith, Joe Morrison and Dr. E. C. Lanter, were ready to set out to take Tracy. They hired a rig at the local livery stable, stocked it with ordnance, piled in themselves, and struck out for the Eddy ranch a few miles from the village.

Tracy was there all right. Shooting started at once, and the outlaw took into the yellowing wheat. Blind shooting went on for a while. Night came on. The five possemen were in no haste; they meant to divide that $4,000 five ways, and not less than five ways. They had the wheat pretty well covered on all sides, and thus they sat out the night. By early morning they were not alone. The crowd around the field had grown to more than four hundred armed men. No sound came from the wheat. At daylight, the five possemen moved slowly into the tall grain, guns ready. There in the center of the field was Tracy, dead enough, lying on his back, a Winchester across his chest, a Colt .45 in his right hand, a big hole over his right eye. It was clear he had shot himself in the night rather than bleed to death from a leg wound, obviously the shot of one of the five barbershop possemen.

In the enormous crowd at the wheat field and in Creston village were reporters from the major cities of the West Coast, from Chicago and New York. There was at least one photographer, and the first piece of business after discovery of the body was to pose the dead thug on his left side, gun in hand, trigger on finger, with the tall wheat as background, to make a picture that was to sell in postcard size by the hundred thousand. Creston, population 216, was in headlines across the nation.

Characteristic phenomena of the United States appeared immediately. A Tracy Cocktail was advertised in saloons. Two or more women suddenly appeared, each with the claim she was the widow of the great man. Within two weeks a melodrama with Tracy as the leading character had taken to the road. The five possemen were interviewed for their attitudes in regard to crime. Incidentally, they got their reward and were able to split it five ways. "For my part," Posseman Lillengreen told this reporter many years later, "for my part it come in handy. The wheat crop wasn't very good that year."

For one great wonderful day the population of Creston rose by well over 550 per cent, and almost as quickly returned to its normal figure which half a century later is about the same. Yet Tracy did not die wholly in vain. He supplied a most interesting topic of conversation that has lasted into the present. First in dime novels, later in true-crime magazines, and now in the comic books, Tracy lives on as King of Badmen, the Lone Bandit, the Oregon Outlaw.

It was windy and cold when we drove into Creston. The one street was deserted. So too was the stark little false-fronted structure where the five possemen had assembled before setting out to get Tracy. In the tavern next door I was told that the current proprietor, Harve Johnson, was away on an errand. I returned to look a moment, noting on the shop wall a deerhead that could well have been an artifact of 1902, when men were men and were shaved in Creston by George Dodd. Then we drove on to Grand Coulee.

After viewing the dam, which I had visited before, we struck out for Bridgeport on the Columbia. It was a drive over as desolate waste as could be seen in the Columbia River basin. The region is a high plateau. Not a tree, not even anything that could be called shrub, softened the terrain. There was virtually no traffic. The wind was bitter, even in mid-September, and it never ceased. Here and there, at long intervals, a dusty road took off to disappear into the vagueness. We saw no human being, though occasionally sighted a reminder that some poor soul had tried to live here until one desperate day when he could stand it no longer and walked away, leaving his house as it stood, or leaned, complete with a rusting cultivator in the yard, and a mile or so of barbed wire between pitiful posts supported by little piles of stones.

I have never heard more melancholy a sound than the wind picking the barbed strings and moaning through the tumbleweed that marks the borders of these small empires of failure. . . . Why didn't he wait for the water? Less than fifty miles away, I knew, was the lush green brought by the big dam's first irrigating waters. Why didn't he wait? God save you, he *did* wait. He waited for water, he waited and prayed to the government for water, he prayed to the Lord for water, he even hired a Nez Perce medicine man to conjure water. For forty years he worked and waited for water to come from this vast river which flowed so near. It did not come, and the only moisture to touch his acres was snow, and the winds blew it away before it could melt.

There comes a time when a man, even a tough Spartan of the early settler breed, knows he has had enough. Most but not all of the Grand Coulee region homesteaders were born too soon. They could not wait for May 15, 1948, when at 11:10 in the morning the first water from Grand Coulee poured into the sagebrush.

At Bridgeport were all of the things that go with the big-dam projects—the monotonous though neat settlements built for the construction crews, the trailer camps, the collections of shacks and tents, the stretches of penny-catchers of all sorts, and enough empty beer cans to erect a mountainous memorial to the infinite thirst of dam builders in the desert. Chief Joseph Dam was authorized in 1946, and the schedule called for everything to be ready July 1, 1956, when it was to rank second only to Grand Coulee as a powerhouse.

From Bridgeport to Wenatchee the Columbia's banks presented an almost continuous series of orchards, including the vast apple estate of the Beebe family of Wakefield, Massachusetts, and Virginia City, Nevada, who, like other orchardists of this region, developed their own irrigating systems that were to make Wenatchee the Apple Capital of the World. No little of the water for these orchards comes not from the Columbia but from tributary streams, including its shortest, the Chelan, which flows only four miles but drops 380 feet between Lake Chelan and the Columbia.

Lake Chelan is one of the real beauties of the Columbia's system, fifty miles long, at least 1,479 feet deep, mountainlocked with vertical walls that rise 6,000 feet, and of late years bordered with orchards. Chelan town lies at the eastern end of the lake. It's an all-year-round place of mixed attitudes. It has "smart" motels and restaurants for tourists alternating with the false fronts of pioneer establishments which obviously care little whether or not anybody comes, nor trouble even to brag that temperatures here average fifteen degrees cooler in summer and fifteen degrees warmer in winter than those at Wenatche thirty-five miles away.

Twenty miles below Wenatchee, on the plateau above the east bank of the Columbia, one comes to the astonishing evidence of the effects of water on this desert country. This is the Quincy Project of Grand Coulee's irrigation. (Reported in an earlier chapter.) No man needs see more than this to be convinced. Here, rather than in the networks of transmission lines, is as near a miracle as the human eye can take in. The generation and transmission of electric power is something a modern man may accept on faith. But to see what he looked at only yesterday and knew that here neither snakes nor buzzards could live, to see it now was to know that a river indeed had come out of Eden to water the garden and bring forth every herb-bearing seed and every fruit-bearing tree. One understood, of course, the effect of water on soil; yet to see a land one knew to be as desolate as Gaza become suddenly a land of plenty comes as close to the miraculous as many of us can hope to find. One leaves this sample of Grand Coulee's reclamation enheartened, filled with hope.

Forty-five miles south of Quincy, on the west bank of the Columbia and fair in the shifting sands of Grant County, is the mystery called the Hanford Engineer

Works, source of some of the essences for the bomb of Hiroshima. One hardly knows how to go about describing what one sees there. From a distance it seems suddenly to rise up out of the desert like a mirage, an enormous mirage of almost templelike buildings, glinting silver and white in the sun, with illusive things like detached columns, and perhaps a few isolated globes, the whole mass changing its internal shapes as one watches, taking on new forms, leaving one confused and certain of nothing at all save that he is looking at a hallucination.

The mirage continues to change and evolve into different illusions as one approaches; and at last begins to take on the recognizable forms of masses of concrete structures set in a bewildering forest of transformers and their lines, not unlike a congress of power plants. Yet, even here one sees he is dealing with something other than a conventional powerhouse installation. Here and there in the sands and sagebrush are small ponds of water that will remind no one of the old swimming hole. The water came from the nearby Columbia and was used to cool some of the materials with which Hanford deals; and now that the water, too, is hot, it must cool before it is diverted back to the river. Otherwise, the Columbia below Hanford would soon become several degrees warmer and also grow "hot" in the modern manner, which means radioactive.

One may muse upon the hell-brews at this oasis in the desert and at the same time be struck with admiration for the mind that thought up the corporate style of Hanford Engineer Works, a title which few if any corporations can match in the way of euphemism.

After dark, from a distance, the place is transformed

into a carnival nightmare of white and yellow and green and red lights, astonishingly brilliant in this never-never land of space that is still enveloped with the enduring silence which blanketed it when Lewis and Clark were here and pitied the natives they found suffering from chronic and grievous eye troubles due to sun, wind, and sand. I left Hanford Engineer Works, reflecting that the two Captains would comprehend no more than I what went on there of a technical nature, a reflection which gave me little enough of comfort.

At Pasco, where the Snake comes in, both the tributary and main river have become, since 1954, a part of the lake that backs up seventy miles behind McNary Dam at Umatilla. The bothersome rapids have gone. So has all sign of old Walulla, where Dorsey Baker's famous railroad took off for Walla Walla; and nearly one hundred miles of modern railroad had to be relocated on higher ground before the gates of the new dam were closed. A few miles below where the highway leaves the river for Walla Walla city is Port Kelly, a place of no great history or importance but a spot unlikely to be forgotten.

All one saw *in* Port Kelly, to which pointed only one small sign on Highway 410, was the hulk of a grain elevator and a bright, fine and big houseboat, with a small sailing skiff moored in front. I had never heard of Port Kelly until I saw it, and have heard nothing since except to learn on inquiry that for many years it had been a station to load wheat into scows. The place appeared lifeless when we stopped. It remained so for the half hour I needed to judge the immensity of its sweep of the river.

Here on the last notable bend of the Columbia, where it starts its final surge that will take it through the mountains, I saw more of the river than I would have believed possible from one spot. Away to the north it seemed to approach over a horizon infinitely remote from Port Kelly; while to the west there was nothing but space and the river for more miles than I cared to guess. Nothing, that is, except for a tiny far spot on the naked hills of the north bank which may have been a ranch house. It was too far to be sure without a glass. I went away thinking there was no place on the whole river where one could look further and see less of civilization than at the wheat landing of Port Kelly. Neither Sam Hill's castle nor Crown Point was quite comparable.

Continuing downriver, both the highway and the Union Pacific tracks come to cross a little stream that few will notice at Heppner Junction. This is Willow Creek, a branch of which destroyed the village of Heppner and took the lives of 225 citizens, all within twenty minutes on the Sunday afternoon of June 14, 1903. It was the greatest disaster that any tributary of the Columbia has known. It was the Balm Fork of Willow Creek, normally eight feet wide and a foot deep, which did it, and it will seem incredible unless one has visited Heppner, forty-two miles from the Junction to see its geography and to learn about cloudbursts.

When signs begin to indicate to the traveler that he is approaching Biggs, let his eye sweep the bare high hills on the Washington shore and he will see Sam Hill's Castle called Maryhill. Mark it well. Its glory is that there is no utility about it. It generates no power. It waters no land.

It was built by a man with a dream as confused as it was naive and fantastic; but a man of good will. It may well be what so many visitors have called it, which is the most unusual museum in the United States. For several years the castle has looked down upon the activity of the dam builders at The Dalles, laying a barrier that will wipe out Celilo Falls and the ship canal in a lake twenty-five miles long. It will also add something to the Northwest Power Pool, according to an official announcement, which says the project will "include 14 units rated at 78,000 kilowatts each" and that its ultimate capacity will have twenty-two such units.

For the next forty-four miles below The Dalles, the Columbia is the lake behind Bonneville Dam. In the hurried present, a new highway pretty much follows the river at water level. It is much "faster" than the old, and what has been gained in speed is thought by many to more than make up for the beauty that was lost when the Columbia Gorge route was abandoned. Here and there along the new highway one will note a sign that points to "Scenic Drive." If the traveler accepts the implied if casual invitation, he will come to Crown Point, and be glad ever after. The Point stands seven hundred feet above the river, which is no great height around here, yet it is so situated as to command an unmatched perspective of river, foothills, mountains and sky all at once; and will prompt an understanding of the time, the power and the persistence which the Columbia must have expended to conquer this mountain barrier. Compared to that effort, the mere turning of a few thousand turbines is as nothing.

There are no more turbines below Bonneville. From

there to the sea the Columbia is a tidal river. Though the channel is deeper, this piece of the river must look today, except for bridges at Portland-Vancouver and Rainier-Longview, much as it did to the first explorers.

One is glad to know that in spite of adverse winds and strong incoming tides, old whitewater man Lorraine made good time here on the lower river, and arrived on November 9, 1921, at Astoria, where he pitched his tent at the foot of 19th Street in the railway yards not far from the passenger depot. He was then 150 days out of Canal Flats. Astoria was hospitable, and the morning paper "gave my journey down the Columbia an extended write-up." The write-up appears to have been correct enough, but Lorraine was offended by the headline, which said FLOATS DOWN GREAT RIVER. It was the verb that troubled him.

"I presume," Lorraine commented, "that the author of the headline thought that because the Columbia has a current, all one has to do to navigate down the stream is to sit lazily in his boat . . . and *float* to Astoria. Nothing is farther from the truth." He went into some detail to show how fatuous was the use of *that* verb to describe *his* efforts, and added that he had lost exactly thirty pounds on the voyage. But he bore no grudge, and in his book, *The Columbia Unveiled,* he added a footnote on the great fire which, less than a month after he left, destroyed much of Astoria; and closed with the hope that the city "would rise phoenix-like, better and grander than ever."

Since the time during the war of 1812 when a British ship came to take Fort Astoria, no enemy vessel has entered the Columbia. In 1898, however, when the

United States declared war on Spain, a sudden hysteria gripped citizens in Astoria and as far upstream as Portland and Vancouver. The peerless Battleship *Oregon* had been dispatched from Puget Sound to join the fighting Navy, and for seventy-one days its voyage down around the Horn, then up into the Caribbean, was wonderful; and poets, who are traditionally ready for butchery of any kind, sprang to arms:

> When your boys shall ask what guns are for,
> Then tell them the tale of the Spanish war,
> And the breathless millions that looked upon
> The matchless race of the Oregon.

But did not her departure leave the Northwest coast an inviting target for the Spanish torpedo boats? Letters to the papers demanded that the Navy send warships. "We are dealing with a treacherous and bloodthirsty foe, and we know not what he may attempt on our unprotected coast." Then, some man of telescopic vision sighted a "strange craft, undoubtedly a Spanish torpedo boat" off Pacific Beach in the Grays Harbor country. Excitement rose higher, and at last somebody in the government at Washington sent word to Governor Lord of Oregon that the Army Engineers had been ordered "to plant mines in all rivers and harbors." This probably eased the tension which ebbed again after news came that the Spanish fleet had been destroyed near Santiago.

It is apparent that the people of Astoria and Portland had little faith in the bastion which even in 1898 stood watch on the Oregon side at the mouth of the river. This was Fort Stevens, a coast artillery post that was established in 1864 in time to prevent the Confederate Navy from capturing the Oregon country. It may have some significance that in 1904, when Japan was whipping Russia, Fort Stevens was refurbished somewhat and a new battery, consisting of two 10-inch disappearing guns, was added. For the next thirty-eight years the Fort and its guns, along with two other similar posts—Fort Canby and Fort Columbia—on the Washington side of the river's mouth, grew old in the manner of American forts in times of peace.

Then, on the night of June 21, 1942, a guard walking post at Fort Stevens thought he saw a bright flash in the dark of the sea offshore. An instant later a shell exploded less than two hundred yards short of where he stood. It was 11:20 P.M. It was the first time in 130 years a fortification within continental United States had been subjected to artillery fire from a foreign enemy. Eight more shells ripped trees and crashed close to Fort Stevens in the next twenty minutes.

The gun flashes indicated the attack to come from a submarine approximately eighteen thousand yards offshore. No return fire was made from Fort Stevens's guns, the extreme range of which was only fifteen thousand yards. The entire Northwest was of course immediately alerted, yet the surprise was so complete, wrote Colonel Frederick C. Dahlquist in *The Oregonian* of Portland, that "there was disbelief that the shelling was caused by an enemy firing from the sea." No submarine or other craft was sighted. A day or two later an unofficial report said that a depth bomb dropped from a searching plane over a suspicious spot near the mouth of the river had "brought oil and debris to the surface," and many took comfort in the belief that the attacking sub had been destroyed. This was the usual wishful thinking of wartime. Seven years later, while on occupation duty in Japan, Colonel Dahlquist learned that the Japanese underwater boat had returned safely to its home base and that its captain who had shelled the Oregon fort had become the skipper of a freighter plying between Japanese ports.

There are no longer any fortifications at the mouth of the Columbia River. "Aircraft," as Colonel Dahlquist commented, have made the fixed armament of harbor defenses obsolete, and the once proud and elite coast artillery corps is more of the dead past than even horse cavalry."

The dead past that is Fort Stevens has long since been abandoned, and the craters made there by enemy shells are overgrown with weeds. There has been talk that the place may be made into Fort Stevens State Park. One can hope this will happen, and that somewhere in the park a suitable marker will remind a short-memoried people that this military establishment was unable, because of archaic equipment, to return the fire of an enemy submarine.

One may reflect, too, that up the Columbia, less than four hundred miles as an energetic gull would fly it, is a symbol of the power that has made virtually all fortifications obsolete, and hope that the busy engineers of Hanford Engineer Works will manage to keep the river at its normal temperatures according to season.

Hanford will do, along with the many dams built and building, to represent the Columbia River that is flowing in mid-century. They compose the perfect symbol of the day, the essence of modernity, the contemporary river. The river may rise in a wilderness that is yesterday, yet on its way it hurries into today and tomorrow before it is lost in the sea that knows no time. No other river in the United States is more in the true spirit of the times.

If Hanford and the dams will do more to represent the present and the future, we ought also to have something to remind us of the river's stately past. There comes to mind a historic spot where the Lewis and Clark party wintered near the Columbia's mouth. For many years the place has had a historical marker of sorts, and there has long been talk of a restoration of Fort Clatsop. That is what the two captains named their camp on Young's Bay at Astoria.

Lewis and Clark were not the first white men to see the river, and they explored less than a quarter of its length. Yet the very circumstance of their being here was of immeasurable aid in making it American; and their effort served also to remove the great River of the West from the void of rumor, guess and fantasy which had surrounded it for two centuries. After *them*, the Columbia was something the mind could deal with, and did.

If a restoration of Fort Clatsop is made, it will appear as a log stockade fifty feet square. A row of three cabins will face another row of four. Between them will be a parade ground twenty feet wide. It will have the directness and simplicity of the American frontier at its best. Nothing less will do for the river of continuous woods that had flowed through solitudes since the flight of years began.

Acknowledgments

WITHOUT THEY or I knowing it, a large number of people contributed something or other to the making of this book. I met them at odd times during the thirty-five years since I first saw the Columbia, beside which I have lived almost as long. They all gave me a piece of fact, or a legend, or even a piece of misinformation. Neither they nor I knew I was to write a book about the river; and now that I have, I regret I cannot thank or chide them by name.

There are also two score or so individuals and institutions whom I asked for help once I had decided, as the phrase has it, to write a book. In every case it was given wholeheartedly, and to them I tender my wholehearted thanks:

J. A. Abrahamson, Katherine Anderson, Bill and Elsa Carmichael, Earle Dickey, Paul Ewing, Norman Hacking, W. H. Hutchinson, Bruce Hutchison, Elizabeth Johnson, Alphonse Kemmerich, Thomas King, Mildred Kline, A. W. Lundell, Herbert Lundy, John Lunney, W. F. McCulloch, the Rev. Harry S. McDonald, Walter Mattila, Stanley Manning, Anthony Netboy, Philip H. Parrish, Louise Prichard, Leverett Richards, Frank Branch Riley, John Shave, Captain Homer Shaver, W. O. Silverthorn, James Stevens, Jessie Booth Williams; Bonneville Power Administration, British Columbia Department of Lands & Forests, Bureau of Reclamation, Canadian Pacific Railway Company, Corps of Engineers, U. S. Army, Oregon Historical Society, Portland Library Association, United States Fish and Wildlife Service.

The manuscript was made handsomely legible for editors and printers by Miss Esther L. Watson; and my daughter, Miss Sibyl M. Holbrook, helped to prepare the Index.

Portland, Oregon,   Stewart H. Holbrook
June 1, 1955.

Bibliography

BOOKS

Bonneville Power Administration, *Your Columbia River*, n.d., n.p.

Canadian Pacific Railway Company, *Facts and Figures*, Montreal, 1946.

Cobb, John N., *Pacific Coast Fisheries*,

Corps of Engineers, U. S. Army, *Water Resources Development in Washington, Oregon, Idaho*, Portland, 1953, 3 booklets.

———, *Power, Navigation and Fish Facilities on the Columbia River at Bonneville Dam*, 1948.

Craig, Joseph A., and Hacker, Robert L., *The History and Development of the Fisheries of the Columbia River*, Washington, D.C., 1940.

De Voto, Bernard, *Across the Wide Missouri*, Cambridge, Houghton, Mifflin, 1947.

———, *The Course of Empire*, Cambridge, Houghton, Mifflin, 1952.

Dictionary of American Biography, New York, Scribner, 1928-1944, 24 vols.

Freeman, Lewis R., *Down the Columbia*, New York, Dodd, Mead, 1921.

Fuller, George W., *A History of the Pacific Northwest*, New York, Knopf, 1931.

Gill, John, *Dictionary of the Chinook Jargon*, Portland, J. K. Gill, 1909.

Haig-Brown, Roderick L., *Return to the River*, New York, Morrow, 1941.

Harvey, Athelstan George, *Douglas of the Fir*, Cambridge, Harvard University Press, 1947.

Hoffman, Arnold, *Free Gold*, New York, Rinehart, 1947.

Holbrook, Stewart H., *Holy Old Mackinaw*, New York, Macmillan, 1938.

———, *Burning an Empire*, New York, Macmillan, 1943.

———, *The Story of American Railroads*, New York, Crown, 1947.

———, *Far Corner*, New York, Macmillan, 1952.

Hume, R. D., *Salmon of the Pacific Coast*, Astoria, 1893.

Irving, Washington, *Astoria: or, Anecdotes of an Enterprise Beyond the Rocky Mountains*, Chicago, Belford, Clarke, n.d.

Johnson, Kate, *Pioneer Days of Nakusp*, Nakusp, B.C., 1951.

Jones, Nard, *Evergreen Land*, New York, Dodd, Mead, 1947.

Lewis, Lloyd, *Captain Sam Grant*, Boston, Little, Brown, 1950.

Lockley, Fred, *History of the Columbia River Valley*, Indianapolis, S. J. Clarke, 1928, 3 vols.

Lorraine, M. J., *The Columbia Unveiled*, Los Angeles, Times-Mirror, 1924.

McArthur, Lewis A., *Oregon Geographic Names*, Portland, Binfords, 1944.

McClelland, John M., Jr., *Longview*, Portland, Binfords & Mort, 1931.

McKeown, Martha Ferguson, *The Trail Led North*, New York, Macmillan, 1948.

Mills, Randall V., *Stern-wheelers Up Columbia*, Palo Alto, Pacific Books, 1947.

Morgan, Murray, *The Columbia*, Seattle, Superior, 1949.

———, *The Dam*, New York, Viking, 1954.

Newell, Gordon R., *Ships of the Inland Sea*, Portland, Binfords, 1951.

Oregon Fish Commission, *The Effects on Salmon Populations of the Partial Elimination of Fixed Fishing Gear*, 1948.

————, *Research Briefs*, Vol. 1, Nos. 1 and 2, 1948.

————, *Research Briefs*, Vol. 2, No. 1, 1949.

————, *Some Factors Influencing the Trends of Salmon Populations in Oregon*, 1950.

Parrish, Philip H., *Before the Covered Wagon*, Portland, Metropolitan Press, 1931.

————, *Wagons West*, Portland, The Oregonian, 1943.

Ross, Alexander, *Adventures of the First Settlers on the Oregon or Columbia River*, London, Smith, Elder, 1849.

Scott, Harvey W., *History of the Oregon Country*, Cambridge, Riverside Press, 1924, 6 vols.

Smith, Charles W., *Pacific Northwest Americana*, revised and extended by Isabel Mayhew, Portland, Binfords, 1950.

Smyth, Fred J., *Tales of the Kootenays*, Cranbrook, B.C. Courier, 1938.

Sundborg, George, *Hail Columbia*, New York, Macmillan, 1954.

Symons, Lieut. Thomas W., *Report of an Examination of the Upper Columbia River*, Washington, US Govt., 1882.

Thompson, David, *Narrative of Explorations in Western America, 1784-1812*, Toronto, The Champlain Society, 1916.

Thwaites, Reuben Gold, *Original Journals of the Lewis and Clark Expedition, 1804-1806*, New York, Dodd, Mead, 1905.

Trail, A Half Century, Trail, B. C., 1951.

U. S. Bureau of Reclamation, *Columbia Basin Project*, Washington, 1952.

————, *Magic Water and the Columbia Basin Project*, Washington, 1953.

Union Fishermen's Co-operative Packing Co., 50th Anniversary, Astoria, 1946.

Villard, Henry, *The Early History of Transportation in Oregon*, Eugene, University of Oregon, 1944.

Washington State Dept. of Fisheries, *Marine Fishes*, Seattle, n.d.

Wheeler, A. O., *The Selkirk Range*, Ottawa, Government Printing Bureau, 1905, 2 vols

379

Wolle, Muriel Sibell, *The Bonanza Trail*, Bloomington, Indiana University Press, 1953.

Wright, J. F. C., *Slava Bohu*, New York, Rinehart, 1940.

ARTICLES IN PERIODICALS AND NEWSPAPERS

Apsler, Alfred, "The Genteel Life at Fort Vancouver," *The Oregonian*, Oct. 18, 1953.

Campbell, Burt R., "Revelstoke's Three Townsites," *Revelstoke Review*, Oct. 28, 1954.

Clark, Ella E., "The Bridge of the Gods in Fact and Fancy," *Oregon Historical Quarterly*, March 1952.

Cunningham, Glenn, "Oregon's First Salmon Canner," *Oregon Historical Quarterly*, Sept. 1953.

Dahlquist, Col. Frederick C., "Enemy Attack on the Oregon Coast," *The Oregonian*, Sept. 19, 1954.

Fitzsimmons, James, "Columbia River Chronicles," *British Columbia Historical Quarterly*, April 1937.

Galbraith, John S., "The Early History of the Puget Sound Agricultural Company," *Oregon Historical Quarterly*, Sept. 1954.

Hirsch, Dorothy D., "Study of the Foreign Wheat Trade in Oregon 1869 to 1887," *Reed College Bulletin*, Aug. 1953.

Hacking, Norman, "Steamboat Days on the Upper Columbia and Upper Kootenay," *British Columbia Historical Quarterly*, Vol. XVI, Nos. 1 and 2, January-April, 1952.

Holbrook, Stewart, editorials and signed articles in *The Oregonian*, 1928-1955.

Humphrey, Tom, "Rampant River," six articles in *Oregon Journal*, beginning Apr. 9, 1953.

Meing, Donald W., "Wheat Sacks Out to Sea," *Pacific Northwest Quarterly*, Jan. 1954.

Sage, Walter W., "David Thompson and Boat Encampment," *Revelstoke Review*, Sept. 17, 24, 1953.

Stewart, George R., "The Source of the Name 'Oregon,'" *American Speech*, Apr. 1944.

"The Columbia and Kootenay's Columbus," *Nelson* (B. C.) *Daily Times*, Nov. 2, 1954.

"B. C. Will Pay for Mistakes on the Columbia," *Rossland* (*B.C.*) *Miner*, Oct. 7, 1954.

"Big Stakes in Power Policy for Columbia," *Victoria Daily Times*, Oct. 9, 1954.

"David Thompson Monument," *Castle News*, Castlegar, B.C., Sept. 16, 1954.

"The Columbia's Salmon Industry," *The West Shore*, July 1887.

Index